MW00622516

Recipes

Compiled by

Nick Delgado

Delgado Medical

16152 Beach Boulevard, #140

Huntington Beach, CA 92647

Walter's Cookbooks - 215 5th Ave. S.E. - Waseca, MN 56093

Walter's serving Church, School, and Civic Organizations
for over 25 years.

Printed in U.S.A.

TABLE OF CONTENTS

THE SAFEST, MOST EFFICIENT WEIGHT LOSS AND HEALTH PLAN EVER

This cookbook has tasty recipes that are zero cholesterol, low fat, low salt, low sugar and ideally balanced in protein. This cookbook can help you reduce the risk of health problems like high cholesterol, hypertension, adult onset diabetes, hardening of the arteries, some types of cancer of the breast and colon, certain forms of arthritis and digestive disorders. The Delgado Program is a natural approach using nutrition and exercise, without any drugs and free of surgery.

If you want fast weight loss, then select the recipes that are highest in water content and lowest in food density, such as soups, salads, fruits and vegetable dishes. At the beginning of the ingredient list for each recipe, it will denote "fast weight loss" .... As you approach your ideal weight, you will need to start eating foods that are lower in water content and higher in food density, such as grains, pastas, rice, breads, beans and sweet potatoes.

All of the recipes in this cookbook are low in fat, sugar and salt. These foods are high in fiber, vitamins and minerals. Your whole family can benefit from following this nutritionally balanced plan.

We have purposely designed our recipes without any oils, dairy products or meat (except for the last section) for six primary reasons.

1. Meat, chicken, fish, turkey and dairy products contain cholesterol which clogs arteries. Any food that has legs, wings, tail or that could wiggle or move has cholesterol in it.

2. Dairy products are the leading cause of food allergies.

3. Meat, dairy products and oils are devoid of fiber, which leads to digestive disease.

4. Meat, dairy products and oils are more concentrated in pesticides, chemicals and hormones than any other food group.

5. Meat, dairy products and oils are higher in fats than all other foods. Excess fats are associated with obesity, cancer, high blood pressure, diabetes and arthritis.

6. Meat and dairy products are too high in protein, which is the major cause of osteoporosis and kidney damage.

The last section of this cookbook contains meat and dairy products. You may choose to avoid this section for the reasons listed above, and to feel the greatest you ever have. If you use the meat and dairy recipes, it should only be on a limited basis, and certainly not for every meal. A safe level of use would be about two or three times a week.

As you eat less fat and more natural foods, you will notice a need to eat more volume of food, along with additional in-between snacks. This is because complex carbohydrates digest at a faster rate than fatty foods. This is a good sign that you're following the plan correctly.

Delgado Medical now offers a program which combined the expertise of doctors and health educators. You may make an appointment at our medical and education center in Huntington Beach, California to take care of symptoms, risk factors, and health problems.

At your first visit, we will recommend the best treatment to achieve ultimate health. You will start to notice improvements, as you use the information provided to you at each follow-up visit to our center. The number of visits and the instructions given to you will depend on your individual health needs.

Delgado Medical now offers a set of cassette tapes, books and video tapes on health and nutrition which may be purchased by phone order or in person.

The founder and Director of Delgado Medical is Nick Delgado. A graduate of U.S.C., he worked with Nathan Pritikin in 1979-1981 as Director of the Pritikin Better Health Program. Mr. Delgado conceived this rejuvenating and amazingly successful program that has helped literally thousands of people. He is a regular host on radio shows heard every week on such stations as KKLA 99.5 FM. You can meet Nick Delgado by appointment, where you will learn revealing facts about how to improve your health.

To make an appointment to come to our clinic, just call or write us. Our office is open 9:00 A.M. until 6:00 P.M. Monday through Saturday and closed on Sunday.

Services and office visits are available to you and your family at a remarkable cash savings. (Visa, MasterCard and American Express accepted.) We accept most insurance plans for office visits and medical testing.

For more information, requests or brochure, call (714) 841-6281.

COLLEN VINCENT, "I lost 42 pounds in four months and I have maintained my new ideal weight for eight years. I lost all the excess fat from my hips and thighs. This is the only program that works for me because it is a way of eating good for life, and not a fad liquid diet. It's easy to follow the Delgado Plan for a lifetime."

JOAN POLLACK, "Most expertly presented program on health and nutrition I have ever attended. Mr. Delgado, teacher and founder of Delgado Medical, teaches and inspires one to study and practice good nutrition. His cookbook is terrific! Everyone should have one for a lifetime of reference and use."

MR. AND MRS. JOHN KENT, "John's cholesterol level is down...his blood pressure went to normal...and we both lost weight. His heart specialist is impressed - saying it's the most dramatic improvement he's seen."

BOB WEILAND, "The Delgado Plan helped me reduce my weight of 242 pounds down to 130 pounds, a loss of 112 pounds in only nine months. My cholesterol dropped from over 300 mg. to 130 mg. Your plan helped me to have the energy to complete the walk across America - 2,994 miles - on my hands (Bob is a double amputee) in 3 1/2 years, ending in a meeting with President Ronald Reagan, July 7, 1986."

WALT HERD, "I have a great feeling of excitement and accomplishment since starting the program. I started your program right after the results of my blood test came in. The results revealed a cholesterol level of 242, exactly 100 points higher than it should be for my age. This frightened me into action because my father had just had a seven-way - yes, 7-way - bypass operation and in no way was I interested in being in that position in my future. So, in earnest, I followed your program and in seven weeks my cholesterol was reduced to 144. AND I FEEL GREAT ABOUT IT!"

RICHARD DOLGENOW, "I lost 40 pounds. I have lost six inches in the waist, going from 38 to 32; dropped my cholesterol from 205 to 130. Not one day goes by without someone coming up to me, to tell me how good I look and asked me how I did it. I had stomach problems, headaches, hurt all over my body and felt very low about myself. In just a few months, many good things have happened to me. Many new friends. I feel like 18 and people say I look like 35 and I will be 50 in January. The only thing that I regret is that I do not have a before picture. I really did not believe this program would work. With all the odds, people at first poking fun at me, people pushing the wrong type of foods at me, and making me feel like a fool, I held with the program and won. Thank you."

HAROLD E. KIMZEY, "Some of the problems I was trying to control or eliminate will be familiar to many. Now in my early 60's, I was 60 to 70 pounds overweight and a borderline diabetic. I had high blood pressure, high triglycerides and suffered from irregularity of my bowels. In the short time that I've been with Delgado Medical, I've found that my blood pressure is returning to normal, my triglycerides are coming down, I am no longer diabetic, I have regular bowel movements and I've lost 20 pounds. Also, my energy level has increased and I'm aware of a keener sense of well being. With a record like that, it's difficult to say just what I like about Delgado best. Certainly their care and personal concern for my problems rate high on the list. Results of tests are explained to me and I have copies of everything to examine and compare...I am on a diet that is working and I'm NEVER hungry. The food that I eat is good (and quite normal) and I can have it in quantity. I am receiving first rate medical service at an affordable price! Who can beat that?

Please take the time to quickly glance through each of the recipes and take note of those which appeal to you. You may also use these recipes to inspire your own creations and combinations. This cookbook helps to make the Delgado Health Plan fun, easy and a worthwhile experience.

Appetizers
&
Beverages

BEAN SALSA DIP

1 (30 oz.) can Rosarita   1 (8 oz.) jar Pace Picante Sauce
  Vegetarian Refried Beans

Blend together and serve with homemade tortilla chips.

BLACK BEAN DIP

8 oz. dried black beans, cooked &   1 shallot bulb, chopped
  drained   1 clove garlic, minced
1 lg. onion, chopped   1 tsp. paprika
1 jalapeno pepper, seeded &   1 tsp. dried mustard
  sliced   3 parsley sprigs, chopped
1 sm. green pepper, chopped   Chili powder to taste
2 lg. scallions, chopped

Combine all ingredients in blender, making certain that they are evenly distributed. If mixture becomes too thick while blending, add water. Refrigerate in glass or plastic containers until ready to serve. Serves 4.

CHILI SAUCE DIP

Fast weight loss.
1 (12 oz.) bottle chili sauce   1/4 c. finely chopped celery
3 tbsp. lemon juice   1 tbsp. minced parsley
3 drops Tabasco sauce
2 tbsp. horseradish

Combine all ingredients and chill. Serve with tortilla chips or fresh raw veggies. Yield: about 1 1/2 cups.

BARBECUE SAUCE

1 c. tomato paste, low salt
3 tbsp. honey or other sweetener
1 tsp. horseradish
1 tbsp. onion powder
1 tbsp. low-sodium dijon
    mustard

1 tsp. garlic powder
Dash red cayenne pepper or
    Tabasco sauce
1/4 tsp. ground cloves
1/2 tsp. liquid smoke

Combine all ingredients in jar and mix well. Store in refrigerator.

CRANBERRY SAUCE

1 c. grape juice concentrate
1/2 c. orange juice
1/2 c. apple juice concentrate

2/3 c. dates
1 (12 oz.) pkg. cranberries, fresh
    or frozen

Combine all ingredients in blender and blend for 2 minutes at high speed. Chill and serve. Yield: about 3 cups.

CUCUMBER ONION DIP

1 sm. avocado
1 can split pea soup
2 c. cucumber, peeled & chopped
    fine
1/4 tsp. pepper
1/2 tsp. onion powder

4 tbsp. dried onion
1/2 tsp. paprika
1 tsp. Worcestershire sauce
2 tsp. lemon juice
Dash of Tabasco

Place avocado, split pea soup, 1/2 cup cucumber, pepper, onion powder, 2 tablespoons dried onion, and remaining ingredients in blender and mix until smooth. Stir in remaining cucumber and onion and chill for several hours. Serve as topping for baked potatoes, or serve with whole wheat crackers or fresh vegetables. Yield: 3 cups.

FRIED ZUCCHINI

Fast weight loss. Microwave.

1/3 c. Butter Buds
1/3 c. Italian style seasoned
   bread crumbs

1 tsp. basil
1 tsp. paprika
3 zucchini, sliced

Prepare Butter Buds. In a plastic bag, combine bread crumbs, basil and paprika. Dip zucchini in Butter Buds. Shake in crumb mixture to coat evenly. Arrange vegetables on a dish, cover with a paper towel. Microwave on full power 2 minutes. Rearrange, moving outside pieces to center of dish. Cook on full power 1 more minute. 16 servings.

GARBANZO SPREAD

1/2 c. red onion, chopped
1/2 bunch parsley, chopped
   finely
Salt to taste (opt.)
1 tsp. basil
1/2 tsp. cumin

1/4 tsp. garlic powder or 2 cloves
   garlic, fresh
3 c. cooked, mashed garbanzo
   beans
2/3 c. toasted sesame seeds (opt.)

Blend all ingredients together. Makes about 3 cups. Use as vegetable or cracker dip, sandwich spread or with falafels.

Cook 1 cup dry garbanzo beans with 4 cups water for 3 to 4 hours. Yield: 2 cups.

GARBANZO BEAN SPREAD - HUMMUS

1/2 onion, chopped
1/4 c. parsley, finely chopped
1 tbsp. basil
1 tbsp. oregano
2 tbsp. curry powder or to taste

1 sm. clove garlic, minced
Juice of 1 lemon
3 c. well-cooked garbanzo beans,
  mashed
2 tbsp. toasted sesame seeds

Saute onions in a non-stick pan until transparent. Add a small amount of stock or water if needed to keep the onions from sticking. Add all of the other ingredients except garbanzos and saute until parsley is soft. Add mixture to garbanzos and mix well. Serve cold as a sandwich spread or dip.

HUMMUS BEAN DIP - QUICK

1 (6 oz.) box Hummus dip mix
  (any brand)

Mix in a bowl with 1 full cup of water, if too thick, add a little more water until you get desired smoothness. Dip fresh raw vegetables, like carrots, celery, broccoli, etc.

GARBANZO "NUTS"

Soak dried garbanzo beans in water overnight. Drain well, then place on non-stick baking sheet in a single layer. Sprinkle on onion and garlic powder to taste. Bake in 350 degree oven for 1 1/2 hours until beans are brown and crisp. Great for snacking. Unique nutty flavor.

MOCK CAVIAR

Fast weight loss.

1 lg. eggplant
1 onion, chopped fine
1 clove garlic, minced
1/2 c. bell pepper, finely chopped

1 1/2 tbsp. lemon juice
Ground pepper
Pam non-stick spray

Slice eggplant in half and spray each half with Pam non-stick spray. Place halves cut side down on baking pan. Broil on middle rack of oven for 20 to 25 minutes. Cool slightly, then scoop out pulp and mash with fork. Saute onion and garlic in non-stick pan (use non-stick spray). Stir onion and garlic into eggplant pulp with remaining ingredients. Chill for 2 to 3 hours. Sprinkle with chopped parsley and serve with bread rounds or toast. Yield: about 2 1/2 cups.

LENTIL DIP

1/2 c. dry lentils
1/4 c. minced onions
1 clove garlic, minced
3 c. water

1 tsp. ground cumin
4 tsp. green taco sauce
1/4 c. tomato sauce

Place lentils, onion and garlic in water. Bring to a boil, then reduce heat to low. Cook until lentils are soft, about 30 minutes. Drain and save liquid for stock. Put mixture into blender or food processor. Add cumin, lemon juice, chili powder, taco and tomato sauces. Puree until smooth. Chill. Yield: 1 1/2 cups.

MARINATED MUSHROOMS I

Fast weight loss. Preparation Time: 15 minutes. Chilling Time: 2 to 3 hours.

1 lb. bite sized mushrooms
2 green peppers, cut into 3/4"
  pieces
1 sm. onion, cut into wedges &
  then separated
1 c. red wine vinegar

1 c. water
1 tbsp. honey
2 tsp. dry mustard
2 tsp. low sodium soy sauce

Prepare mushrooms by cleaning and trimming stems. Set aside with green pepper and onions in a bowl. Combine water, vinegar, honey, mustard and soy sauce in a pan. Bring to a boil. Pour over mushrooms, green peppers and onions. Cover. Marinate in refrigerator for several hours.

Before serving, thread on small bamboo skewers. Serve as an appetizer.

MARINATED MUSHROOMS II

Fast weight loss.

20 lg. mushrooms
2 tbsp. fresh chopped parsley
2 tbsp. sherry
1/2 c. defatted chicken broth

1/2 c. no oil Italian dressing
1/4 tsp. tamari
Garlic powder to taste

1. Saute mushrooms and parsley in sherry in a saute pan for a few minutes.

2. Remove from heat, transfer to a bowl, add the rest of the ingredients, and marinate for 1 hour.

Makes 4 servings. Each serving contains 40 calories. 7% fat, 121 mg sodium and 0 mg cholesterol.

MUSHROOM ANTIPASTO

1 1/4 c. tomato puree
1/2 c. water
2 tbsp. red wine vinegar
1 tsp. toasted dehydrated onion
   flakes
2 cloves garlic, minced
1/2 green pepper, seeded & diced

1/2 red pepper, seeded & diced
1/4 c. chopped fresh parsley
1 tsp. salad herbs or Italian herb
   blend
2 tbsp. apple juice concentrate
1/4 tsp. freshly ground nutmeg
1 lb. sm. fresh mushrooms,
   quartered

1. Combine tomato puree and water.
2. Then combine with all other ingredients except mushrooms and mix thoroughly. Pour over mushrooms and marinate overnight. Serve as hors d'oeuvres or antipasto.

Makes 4 servings. Each 1-cup serving contains 75 calories. 6% fat, 26 mg sodium, 0 mg cholesterol.

MUSHROOMS & SPICY CHILI

Fast weight loss.

1/2 c. vinegar
1 c. water
1 tbsp. bell pepper, diced
2 tbsp. peppercorns or cracked
   black pepper

1 tbsp. garlic, minced
2 sm. whole hot dried red chili
   peppers
1 lb sm. whole mushrooms, fresh
   or canned

Mix vinegar, bell pepper, peppercorns, garlic and chilies together in a quart jar or small saucepan.

Add mushrooms to mix and microwave for 4 minutes at 70% power or heat in small saucepan over medium heat until just below boiling.

Strain into a quart jar. Add mushrooms back to strained marinade and cool to room temperature, then refrigerate.

Marinate at least 4 to 6 hours before serving. Mushrooms are best the next day, but will keep refrigerated for up to 2 weeks.

Serving Size: 8 servings, 4 to 5 mushrooms each. Per Serving: 25 Calories. 25 mg sodium.

POTATO BALLS

Preparation Time: 10 minutes. Cooking Time: 20 minutes.

2 c. leftover mashed potatoes or   1/2 c. bread crumbs
    use Potato Buds

Form potatoes into balls about 1 1/2" in diameter. Roll in bread crumbs. Place on a non-stick baking sheet and bake at 350 degrees about 20 minutes, until browned. Turn once or twice for even browning.

POTATO POPPERS

1/4 onion, chopped   1 c. mashed potatoes
1 c. cooked brown rice   2 tbsp. tomato sauce
1 c. whole grain bread crumbs

Preheat oven to 350 degrees. Simmer onion in a small amount of water. Combine all ingredients and form into 1 1/2" balls. Place on a non-stick baking sheet and bake until slightly browned, about 15 minutes. Turn once for even browning. Makes about 12.

POTATO CHIPS (FAT FREE)

Fast weight loss.

3 med. baking potatoes or sweet potatoes

Salt-free vegetable or Italian seasoning, ground pepper or dried herbs (opt.)

1. Preheat oven to 375 degrees. Line a baking sheet with cooking parchment or one side of a brown paper bag. Scrub or peel potatoes.
2. In a food processor, using the fine slicing blade (1 mm), slice potatoes. Or, slice potatoes paper thin by hand.
3. Place potato slices in a single layer on the paper and sprinkle with seasonings, if using. Bake for 7 minutes, then turn the chips and bake for another 7 to 10 minutes, or until golden brown and crisp. Check often and remove any chips that brown too quickly.
4. Let chips cool on the baking sheet, then store in a paper bag. makes 2 servings, approximately 100 chips.

SEASON "SALT"

2 tsp. sesame seeds
1/2 tsp. paprika
3/4 tsp. red dried bell peppers
1/4 tsp. thyme
1 can Schilling vegetable flakes

1 1/4 tsp. cornstarch
1/2 tsp. celery powder
1 tsp. onion powder
1 tsp. garlic powder

Grind all ingredients that are not fine in food processor and blend with remaining ingredients. Vary ingredients according to taste.

LOW-SODIUM CATSUP

1 c. tomato paste, low salt
3 tbsp. lemon juice
2 tbsp. honey or other sweetener
1 tsp. horseradish
1 tbsp. low sodium Dijon
  mustard
1 tbsp. onion powder
1 tsp. garlic powder
Dash red cayenne pepper or
  Tabasco sauce
1/4 tsp. ground cloves

Combine all ingredients, store in refrigerator.

FRIES, CAJUN STYLE

Fast weight loss.
No stick cooking spray
4 baking potatoes
1 lemon
2 tsp. cajun seasoning

Serves 4. Preheat the oven to 425 degrees. Spray a cookie sheet with no stick cooking spray. Cut the unpeeled potatoes into thin, long strips. Place in a bowl of ice water with the juice of 1 lemon to prevent potatoes from browning.

Drain the potatoes. Distribute evenly over the cookie sheet and sprinkle with cajun seasoning. Bake for 20 to 25 minutes, turning potatoes several times. Potatoes will be cooked and lightly browned. Serve immediately. Each Serving: 0 mg cholesterol, 125 calories.

HOME FRIES

Fast weight loss. Microwave.

3 potatoes, peeled, cut in cubes or slices
1 pkg. Butter Buds, prepared
1/4 c. chopped onion

1/2 tsp. browning sauce
1/2 tsp. garlic powder
1/4 tsp. dill weed
1/4 tsp. thyme
1/2 tsp. paprika

In a 1 1/2 quart casserole dish, combine all ingredients. Make sure potatoes are evenly coated. Microwave on full power 9 minutes or until potatoes are fork tender. 4 servings.

SESAME KOMBU

Soak in water to cover for 15 minutes 20" piece of kombu or wakame. Wipe kombu off with paper towel and cut in small squares.

Bring 1/2 cup water to a boil. Drop in 6 to 8 scallions, sliced in 1/4" rounds and cook for 1 minute. Drain, rinse with cold water and squeeze out excess liquid.

Mix together in a bowl:

2 tbsp. light miso
2 tbsp. tahini

1/3 c. water

Add scallions and kombu to miso mixture. Serve as a side dish at room temperature or chilled. Yield: about 1 cup. Per 2 tablespoon serving: 40 Calories; 1 gm Protein; 3 gm Carbohydrates; 5 gm Fat.

VEGETABLE HUMMUS POCKET SANDWICHES

1/2 c. finely chopped green
  onions
1/2 c. finely chopped green bell
  pepper
3 tbsp. fresh parsley
1 tbsp. sesame seeds
1/2 tsp. whole oregano
1/2 tsp. mint flakes
1/2 tsp. garlic powder

1/8 tsp. red pepper
1 (15 oz.) can garbanzo beans,
  rinsed & drained
4 (6") whole wheat pita bread
  rounds, cut in half crosswise
1 med. tomato, cut into 8 (1/4")
  slices
2 c. alfalfa sprouts

Combine first eight ingredients in a 1 quart casserole. Cover with a heavy duty plastic wrap and turn back one corner to vent. Microwave on high for 3 minutes. Place bell pepper mixture and garbanzo beans in blender or food processor for 1 minute or until smooth. Spoon about 1/4 cup bean mixture (hummus) into each pita bread half. Cut tomato slices in half, open sandwiches and place two tomato slices and 1/4 cup alfalfa sprouts into sandwich half. Serve immediately. Serves 8.

ZUCCHINI PIZZA HORS D'OEUVRES

4 zucchini, cut into 1/4" thick
  slices
1 c. pizza sauce
1/2 c. olives, chopped

1/3 c. green onions, sliced
1 1/2 c. mushrooms

Arrange sliced zucchini on baking sheets. Top with 1 to 2 teaspoons pizza sauce, a few olive pieces and green onions and a sprinkling of mushrooms. Broil about 6" from heat until lightly browned (4 to 6 minutes). Serve hot. 5 dozen hors d'oeuvres.

BANANAS IN COCONUT MILK
KLUAY BUAT CHEE

This dish is not widely know to foreigners, even those in Thailand. Among the Thai it is seldom served to guests. Siamese Buddhist nuns dress in white, from whence comes the Thai name for the dish, Kluay Buat Chee; exactly translated: Nun Bananas.

5 ripe bananas, peeled &
    quartered
1 1/2 tsp. perfumed thick
    coconut milk*
1/2 tsp. salt

2 tbsp. apple juice concentrate
2 tbsp. roasted mung beans,
    crushed

In a 2 quart coated saucepan, place all the ingredients except the mung beans. Bring to a boil, then simmer for 2 minutes. Pour into a serving dish and sprinkle with mung beans. Serve warm or chilled. 4 to 5 servings.

*Add 2 to 3 drops jasmine essence (Yod Nam Malee).

SMOOTHIES

2 bananas
1/2 c. apple juice

1/2 c. frozen fruit (raspberries,
    strawberries, blueberries,
    etc.)

OR:
2 frozen bananas
1/2 c. frozen & crushed pineapple

1/2 c. apple juice

Blend until smooth. To freeze bananas, peel, wrap in plastic wrap and place in freezer for 6 hours.

TROPICAL SMOOTHIE

Fast weight loss.

2 c. unsweetened pineapple juice
2 bananas

1/2 c. oat bran
8 ice cubes

Place all ingredients in blender and blend for about 1 minute at high speed. Serves 4.

FRUIT SHAKE

2 peeled oranges
2 peeled bananas
2 c. crushed ice

1 1/2 c. apple juice
Dash of cinnamon

Blend in blender. (Add ice gradually.) Sprinkle cinnamon on top.

STRAWBERRY SHAKE

4 c. orange juice
2 c. frozen strawberries

1/2 tsp. almond extract

Place all ingredients in blender and serve cold. Serves 4.

CRANBERRY DELIGHT

1 c. cranberry juice, chilled
1 tbsp. lemon juice

1 egg white
1/2 c. crushed ice

Blend all ingredients until foamy. Serve immediately. Serves 2.

ORANGE DELIGHT

1 c. orange juice
1 banana
1 c. apple juice

1 tsp. honey (opt.)
Shake of cinnamon
1 c. crushed ice

Blend at high speed until frothy. Serves 2 to 3.

CRANBERRY TEA PUNCH

Fast weight loss.

5 herbal tea bags or 5 tsp. loose
   tea
1/4 tsp. ground cinnamon
1/4 tsp. ground nutmeg
2 1/2 c. boiling water

2 c. cranberry juice
1 1/2 c. water
1/2 c. orange juice
1/3 c. lemon juice

Steep tea and spices in hot water in covered teapot for 5 minutes.
Remove tea bags and strain. Cool mixture; when cooled add remaining
ingredients. Chill and pour over ice cubes. Serves 6 to 8.

CRANBERRY SPRITZER

Fast weight loss.

3 c. cranberry juice, chilled
1 c. unsweetened pineapple juice,
   chilled
1/2 c. lemon juice, chilled or
   orange juice, chilled

1 (33 oz.) bottle club soda,
   chilled
Lime slices (opt.)

Combine juices in pitcher as above. Repeat process as above for each
serving. Garnish with lime slices if desired. Serves 6 to 8.

PEACHY SPRITZER

2 (21 oz.) cans peach nectar,
    chilled
1 c. unsweetened orange juice,
    chilled
1/2 c. lemon juice, chilled

Crushed ice
1 (33 oz.) bottle club soda,
    chilled
Orange slices (opt.)

    Combine juices together in a large pitcher stirring well. Pour 1/2 cup mixture over crushed ice in a tall glass; add 1/2 cup club soda. Repeat for each serving; garnish with orange slices if desired. Serves 6 to 8.

LEMON COOLER

4 c. apple juice
1/2 c. lemon juice

2 tbsp. frozen pineapple juice
    concentrate, thawed
Lemon wedges for garnish

    Place all ingredients in blender and process for 2 minutes. Serve ice cold and garnish with lemon wedges. Serves 4.

CARROT-APPLE JUICE

2 oz. fresh apple juice
2 oz. fresh carrot juice

1 sm. apple, coarsely chopped
3 ice cubes

    Combine in blender and liquify. Serves one.

PINEAPPLE-CUCUMBER JUICE

    Fast weight loss.
3 oz. cucumber, peeled
1 oz. fresh pineapple
2 parsley sprigs

1/2 fresh apple, coarsely chopped
3 ice cubes

    Combine in blender and liquify. Serves one.

SPIKED TOMATO JUICE

Fast weight loss.

4 c. tomato juice

4 long stems or green onions

Trim and wash stems. Sip juice through stem.

CRANBERRY GLOG

1 (40 oz.) bottle cranberry-apple
  juice
1/2 c. raisins
1/4 c. cranberries

4 orange slices, each studded
  with 2 whole cloves
1/2 tsp. or 1 stick cinnamon
1/2 tsp. cardamom (opt.)

Combine all ingredients in a medium saucepan. Bring to a boil, then simmer for 30 minutes. Let stand 1 hour. Serve hot in mugs. Serves 6.

HARVEST PUNCH

1 gallon apple cider
4-8 whole cloves
4 tsp. allspice
6 cinnamon sticks

1 c. orange juice
Dash of honey (opt.)
Juice of 1 lemon

Bring all ingredients to a slow boil and simmer about 10 minutes. Strain and serve hot. Serves 20.

HOT CAROB THIRST QUENCHER

1/2 c. cold water
1/2 c. rice milk
1/3 c. carob powder

2 tsp. dry Postum
2 c. boiling water

Place the cold water, rice milk, carob powder and Postum in a blender. Blend until the dry ingredients look wet. Add the boiling water and blend at high speed for about 30 seconds or until mixture becomes frothy and all the ingredients are well blended. Serve immediately. Makes 2 servings.

HOT FRUIT TEA PUNCH

8 c. boiling water
4 cinnamon sticks, broken
1 tbsp. whole cloves
A few dashes nutmeg
4 herbal teabags

Juice of 2 lemons
1 lg. can unsweetened pineapple
juice
1 (6 1/4 oz.) can frozen grapefruit
juice or orange juice or 1 (48
oz.) can apple juice

Bring water to a boil in a large stainless steel or enamel saucepan. Add spices and tea bags. Remove tea bags after 3 minutes of steeping; let remainder of spices simmer about 20 minutes. Add lemon juice, pineapple juice and one other juice. (If frozen juice is used, prepare according to directions.) Bring to a boil; leave on lowest heat to keep warm. For a larger crowd add another can of pineapple juice. Serves 30.

HOT SPICED CIDER

1 (32 oz.) bottle apple cider
4 sticks cinnamon

1 strip lemon peel
4 whole cloves

With sharp knife, peel a strip of lemon peeling from ripe lemon. In saucepan, slowly heat all ingredients. Simmer at least 10 minutes. Serve with stick of cinnamon in each mug. Serves 4 (8 oz.).

HOT SPICED CIDER II

1 qt. apple cider
1/2 tsp. whole cloves

1/2 tsp. allspice
2 sticks cinnamon

Combine all ingredients in 2 quart casserole. Heat in microwave oven on full power for 9 minutes. Then simmer on low for 4 minutes. Remove spices and serve.

SNAPPLE

4 c. fresh apple cider or juice
1/4 c. cinnamon sticks
1 tbsp. whole cloves

1/8 tsp. ginger
1/8 tsp. allspice
1 whole vanilla bean or dash of
vanilla extract

Place all but 1/4 cup of cider in a saucepan. Wrap cinnamon sticks in a clean piece of cheesecloth and place in saucepan. Mix powdered spices in blender with remaining 1/4 cup of cider and add to pan. Finally, add whole vanilla bean or dash of vanilla to mixture. Heat over low flame until warm. Remove cheesecloth mixture and vanilla bean and serve warm. Variation: Add dash of orange or lemon extract in place of or in addition to vanilla. Serves 4.

WHITE LIGHTNING

3 c. white grape juice
1 c. grapefruit juice

1 (40 oz.) bottle cranberry juice
1 lemon, sliced

Combine juices and lemon in a large saucepan. Bring to a boil. Cover and simmer for 10 minutes. Remove lemon slices and serve hot in mugs. Serves 16.

EXTRA RECIPES

Breakfast

BREAKFAST POTATOES

15 sm. red potatoes, cubed
1 med. onion, chopped
1 red bell pepper, chopped
1/2 green bell pepper, chopped
1 tsp. garlic powder

1 tsp. onion powder
1/4 tsp. black pepper
1/2 tsp. oregano
1/2-1 c. water
1 packet Butter Buds mixed with
water

Place 1/2 cup water and Butter Buds in non-stick skillet and heat. Add potatoes and cook for about 5 minutes. Add remaining ingredients and simmer until tender.

BREAKFAST SAUSAGE

1 lg. jar Seitans wheat meat
1 packet Butter Buds
1/4 tsp. cumin
1/4 tsp. marjoram
1/4 tsp. oregano
1/4 tsp. cayenne pepper

1/2 tsp. basil
1/2 tsp. thyme
1/2 tsp. sage
1/2 tsp. garlic powder
1 tbsp. oat bran

Sprinkle wheat meat with spices and oat bran and refrigerate for several hours. Bake in 400 degree oven until done or cook in non-stick pan. Serves 8.

OMELETTE

1 sm. tomato, diced
1/2 yellow onion, chopped
1 zucchini, sliced & quartered
3 oz. fresh mushrooms, sliced
1/4 c. green bell pepper, chopped

2 tbsp. chili salsa
6 egg whites, beaten
4 pieces whole wheat toast
Dash pepper to taste

In a non-stick skillet, saute first five ingredients (use non-stick spray). Add salsa and pepper. While mixture simmers, pour egg whites into pan, stirring while it cooks to keep from sticking. Cook until egg whites are set. Spoon over toast. Serves 2 to 3.

OMELET WITH STRAWBERRIES

Microwave.

4 egg whites
3 tbsp. water
1/2 c. strawberries

1/4 tsp. cream of tartar
Pam spray

Beat egg whites, water and cream of tartar until egg whites are stiff. Spray browning skillet with Pam spray. Pour omelet mixture into skillet. Cook on medium high for 3 1/2 minutes or until knife inserted in center comes out clean. Spread half of the strawberries on omelet. Fold omelet over and spread remaining strawberries over top before serving.

VEGETARIAN OMELET

12 egg whites
1/2 c. salsa
1 c. cauliflower, sliced
1/2 lb. Italian green beans
1 pkg. frozen, chopped spinach,
    thawed
8 oz. tofu

1 tbsp. Butter buds
1/2 tsp. basil
1/2 tsp. oregano
1/2 tsp. Veg-It seasoning
1 onion, chopped
2 cloves garlic, minced
1/4 lb. mushrooms

Steam fresh beans and cauliflower over boiling water until crisp tender (4 to 5 minutes). Drain tofu and cut into 3/4" cubes. Heat Butter Buds in a frying pan over medium heat. Add onion, garlic and mushrooms and cook until onion is soft. Add beans, cauliflower, spinach, basil, oregano and Veg-It seasoning. Cook until heated through. Add egg whites. Add tofu. Cook until eggs are set. Pour salsa on top.

CREPES

1 c. whole wheat flour
1 1/2 c. apple juice

4 egg whites, stiffly beaten
1 tbsp. apple juice concentrate

Blend egg whites with apple juice. Then add apple juice concentrate and blend in the flour. Pour 1/3 cup batter into heated Silverstone (non-stick pan). (Be sure to spray pan with Pam and wipe with damp paper to remove excess.) Brown crepe on both sides to golden. NOTE: Crepes may be served as breakfast pancakes alone or with fruit or other toppings.

YEAST CREPES

Served plain, these are little eggless omelets. Try rolled around ratatouille or filled with mushrooms.

2 c. whole wheat pastry flour
1/3 c. nutritional yeast flakes
(saccharomyces cerevisiae)

1/2 tsp. baking powder
1 tsp. salt
3 c. soy milk or water

Combine all ingredients in blender or beat well by hand. Batter can rest for 30 minutes in the refrigerator. Heat a 9" skillet and put a few drops of oil on the bottom. Rotate pan to coat bottom. Pour 1/4 cup of batter into pan and immediately tilt and rotate pan so batter forms an even layer over the whole bottom. Cook over medium high heat until the top starts to dry up and edges loosen. Slide pancake turner under the crepe, flip over and cook the other side.

Nutritional yeast tastes cheesy in spreads, sauces, salad dressings, crackers, breading meal and on vegetables and popcorn. Added to soups, gravies and gluten, it has a good, nutty flavor. You can add it to your baby's food, too. Store in a cool, dark place.

Do not use brewer's yeast or torula yeast in this recipe. Use only Saccharomyces cerevisiae (a rich source of Vitamin B12 and B-complex.) It comes in golden or bright yellow flakes or powder. If you use any other kind, this recipe will not taste the same.

FRENCH TOAST

4 slices whole grain bread
1 c. apple juice
1 tbsp. tapioca granules
1/2 tsp. cinnamon

1/2 tsp. vanilla
1 tbsp. date pieces
1 ripe banana

Put all ingredients except bread into blender in order given. Process 3 minutes. In a bowl, dip bread into mixture and bake on a non-stick griddle (use non-stick spray). Cook until browned. Serve with homemade fruit spread. Serves 4.

FRENCH RAISIN TOAST

2 slices whole wheat raisin bread
2 egg whites
1 tsp. vanilla extract

1/2 tsp. cinnamon
1/2 c. apple juice or rice milk
2 tbsp. apple juice concentrate

In shallow bowl, beat egg whites together with other ingredients. Dip both sides of bread in batter until soaked with mixture. Spray griddle with non-stick spray, brown on both sides. Serve with fruit topping or apple butter.

HUEVOS RANCHEROS

1 steamed corn tortilla
1 egg white, poached

1/4 c. green chilies
1/4 c. salsa

Top steamed tortilla with poached egg white, chilies and salsa. Makes 1 serving. Each serving contains 93 calories.
Variation: You may also add 1/2 cup cooked beans (vegetarian refried) or no oil.
6% fat, 156 mg sodium, 0 mg cholesterol.

APPLE-SPICED OATMEAL

1/2 c. old fashion rolled oats
1 1/2 c. water
2 tbsp. apple juice concentrate

2 tbsp. raisins
1/2 tsp. cinnamon

Bring water to a boil. Stir in oats and other ingredients. Simmer, stirring occasionally, for 15 to 20 minutes, or until oats are cooked and mixture has thickened. Serves 1.

CORNMEAL HOT CEREAL

1 c. whole grain cornmeal
1 1/2 c. water
1 c. unfiltered apple juice

1/2 tsp. cinnamon
1/4 c. raisins or currants

In a saucepan, add all ingredients and stir constantly over medium heat until it thickens. Remove from heat and serve. Serves 2 to 4.

OAT BRAN CEREAL

Weight loss.
2/3 c. oat bran
1 c. water
1 c. unfiltered apple juice

1/2 tsp. cinnamon
1/4 c. raisins or currants (opt.)

In a saucepan add all ingredients, stirring constantly to blend. Cook 2 minutes approximately over medium heat until desired thickness. Serves 2.

GRANOLA I

5 c. uncooked rolled oats
4 c. Grape-Nuts cereal (not the
  flakes) or Nutty Rice
1 c. brown rice flour
3 tsp. cinnamon
6 lg. apples, peeled & grated

7 tbsp. frozen concentrated apple
  juice
1/2 tsp. coconut extract
2 1/2 tsp. vanilla extract
1/2 tsp. almond extract

Combine all ingredients in a large bowl. Spread mixture on a flat non-stick pan or cookie sheet. Bake at 275 degrees for about 45 minutes (until mixture is dry and rather crumbly).

Microwave: Combine all ingredients in a bowl as above. Place bowl in microwave and cook on high for 10 minutes. Makes 20 servings.

GRANOLA II

3 1/2 c. old fashioned rolled oats
1 c. chopped walnuts
1 c. shredded coconut
1 c. chopped almonds
1/2 c. sesame seeds

1 tsp. cinnamon
1/2 tsp. ground cloves
1/4 c. honey
2 tbsp. grated orange peel
1/2 c. dried apricots
1/2 c. raisins

Combine all ingredients. Spread mixture in two large baking pans. Bake, uncovered at 200 degrees for 55 minutes. Cool completely, then stir in 1/2 cup raisins and 1/2 cup chopped dried apricots. Cover and store at room temperature. (For Quick Granola try Muesli.) Makes 8 cups.

TROPICAL MUESLI

4 c. rolled oats
1 1/3 c. flaked coconut
4 oz. banana chips

3/4 c. Brazil nut pieces
4 oz. candied pineapple
1 c. bran

Mix all ingredients together, making sure they are evenly distributed. Store in a large screw-top jar. Yield: about 6 cups.

BANANA PANCAKES

1 c. whole wheat pastry flour
2 tsp. baking powder
1 1/2 c. nut milk, rice milk or
   fruit juice

2 tbsp. unsweetened applesauce
1 med. banana, firm but ripe,
   finely chopped

Mix flour and baking powder together. Mix liquid with applesauce. Add to dry ingredients and stir until just moistened. Fold in banana. Spoon batter onto a non-stick griddle. Turn when bubbles appear.

BANANA BUCKWHEAT PANCAKES

1/2 c. Fearn buckwheat pancake
   mix
1/2 c. wheat & soya pancake mix
1/2 c. oatbran

1 tbsp. cinnamon
1 egg white
1 1/4 - 1 1/2 c. water
1 banana, mashed
1/4 c. raisins

Mix dry ingredients together. Add egg white and mix. Add water a little at a time until there is a thick creamy texture. Stir in banana and add raisins. Cook on non-stick pan. Flip pancakes when bubbles begin to pop. Makes about 9 medium sized pancakes.

BUCKWHEAT PANCAKES

1 c. Aunt Jemima buckwheat
   pancake mix

1 c. *Amazake rice milk or soy
   milk
4 egg whites

Spray a nonstick skillet with non-stick coating. Place on a medium heat to warm pan. Mix all ingredients. Pour batter onto hot pan. Turn when tops are covered with bubbles. Turn only once. Serve with fresh fruit spreads, apple butter or fresh fruit slices.

OATMEAL PANCAKES

2 c. old fashioned rolled oats
2 c. water
1/2 c. whole wheat pastry flour

2 stiffly beaten egg whites
1 tsp. vanilla
8 tbsp. apple juice concentrate

Chop rolled oats coarsely using low speed on blender. A food processor is even better if you have one. Mix rolled oats and water, let stand for 5 minutes. Stir in flour, add remaining ingredients. Fold in stiffly beaten egg whites. Bake on a non-stick skillet, using high heat at first and turning down heat as bubbles appear. Makes 15 (4") pancakes.

WHOLE WHEAT PANCAKES

3/4 c. whole wheat flour
1 tsp. baking powder
1/3 c. ground toasted almonds
2 tbsp. coarsely chopped toasted
   almonds

1/2 c. rice milk, soy milk or nut
   milk
2 tbsp. Butter Buds
2 tbsp. honey
2 egg whites
Pinch of cream of tartar

Sift flour and baking powder into medium bowl. Add ground and chopped almonds. Lightly whisk rice milk, Butter Buds and honey in another bowl. Add to dry ingredients and mix just until moistened. Beat whites with cream of tartar in large bowl until stiff but not dry. Gently fold whites into batter. Let stand 10 minutes. Heat non-stick griddle or skillet over medium heat. Ladle batter onto griddle. Cook until bubbles begin to appear. Turn and cook other side. 12 pancakes.

ZUCCHINI PANCAKES

3 c. shredded zucchini
1/3 c. minced onion
6 egg whites
3/4 c. whole wheat flour

3/4 tsp. baking powder
1/4 tsp. pepper
1/2 tsp. oregano leaves
Grated Parmesan cheese (opt.)

Blend all ingredients (except Parmesan cheese). In a non-stick skillet, spoon about 3 tablespoons of the zucchini mixture for each pancake. Cook 4 pancakes at a time, turning once, until golden brown on each side. Sprinkle with Parmesan cheese. 4 servings.

WAFFLES

3 c. water
2 c. rolled oats
1 c. barley flour

1/2 c. whole wheat pastry flour
1 tbsp. unsulphured molasses or
    malt syrup

Combine all ingredients in blender and blend until smooth. Let batter "rest" for 15 minutes. Ladle onto preheated waffle iron. Use about one cup of batter for a 4 section waffle. Lightly spray with a non-stick spray to prevent sticking. Makes about 4 large waffles.

APPLESAUCE

1 c. water
1 lemon, juiced
2 pippin apples

1 Delicious apple
1/2 tsp. cinnamon
2 tsp. cornstarch

Put 3/4 cup water into a heavy saucepan. Add lemon juice. Heat water to gently simmer. Wash and slice apples. Place in hot water. Add cinnamon. Cook for 8 to 10 minutes until apples are barely soft. Turn off heat. Mix cornstarch with 1/4 cup water. Add to apple mixture stirring constantly. Remove from heat when apple mixture thickens. May be used to spoon over pancakes.

EASY BLUEBERRY SAUCE

This sauce is a perfect replacement for the butter and maple syrup that usually top pancakes. It is also delicious on cake (instead of fat-dense frosting) or with muffins or cornbread.

2 c. apple or mixed berry juice
1 (10 oz.) jar blueberry preserves
2-3 tsp. kudzu or arrowroot
1/2 c. cold water
Pinch sea salt

Pinch cinnamon or nutmeg
1 tsp. vanilla
1 pt. blueberries (fresh or frozen)
1-2 tsp. lemon juice (opt.)

Pour juice into a saucepan and slowly bring to a boil. Add blueberry preserves and continue to simmer. Dissolve kudzu or arrowroot in cold water and add to simmering sauce. Stir until the sauce thickens and becomes clear and shiny. Stir in salt, cinnamon or nutmeg and vanilla. Add blueberries and lemon juice if desired. Stir. Lower flame and keep warm until ready to serve. Serves 8.

Helpful Hint: Extra sauce can be stored in the refrigerator for several days.

Per Serving: 57 calories; 0.3 g protein; 0.3 g fat; 14 g carbohydrates; 9 cholesterol; 0 mg sodium.

FRUIT SYRUPS

2 pkgs. frozen fruit
1/2 c. apple juice concentrate

1 c. apple juice
2 tbsp. cornstarch

Mix frozen fruit with unsweetened apple juice and apple juice concentrate. Add cornstarch, mix until blended and heat to thicken. Especially delicious with strawberries or blueberries. Other variations include peaches, apples, cherries, apricots, strawberry-banana, grape and pineapple. Delicious over pancakes or as a spread on toast.

ORANGE APPLE MARMALADE

2 c. very thinly sliced oranges
with peeling
3 c. dried Golden Delicious
apples, ground

1 c. orange juice concentrate
2 1/2 c. apple juice concentrate
3 c. water

Put all ingredients in large pot. Cook slowly about one hour or until oranges are tender. Vary orange and apple juice to taste.

BLUEBERRY JAM

2 c. blueberries

24 pitted dates (1/3 lb.)

Blenderize blueberries. Add dates, a few at a time. Blenderize until smooth. Put in jars. May be kept up to 3 days if refrigerated. Other jams can be made, substituting other fruit for the blueberries: strawberries, peaches, apples, etc. Makes 1 lb. or 1 1/2 cups.

PEACH JAM

2 tbsp. frozen orange juice
concentrate

2 1/2 c. mashed sweet peaches
3 tsp. pectin

Mix juice concentrate with peaches, stir in pectin and let stand 30 minutes. Stir 3 times vigorously. Serve fresh or may be frozen to retain fresh taste.

PEACH OR APRICOT JAM

3 c. diced fresh peaches or
   apricots
1 1/2 tsp. fresh lemon juice

1 1/2 tsp. unflavored gelatin
2 tbsp. apple juice concentrate

Place peaches or apricots in saucepan. Cover and cook over very low heat without water for about 10 minutes. Remove lid and bring the juice to the boiling point. Boil for one minute and remove from heat. Soften gelatin in lemon juice for 5 minutes. Pour some of the hot juice from the fruit into the gelatin mixture and stir until the gelatin is completely dissolved. Stir the dissolved gelatin into the fruit. Add 2 tablespoons apple juice concentrate. Allow to cool to room temperature and store in the refrigerator. 35 calories in 1 level tablespoon.

APRICOT BREAKFAST BARS

1/2 c. apple juice
1 banana
1 egg white
1/2 tsp. lemon extract
1/2 tsp. cinnamon

1/2 c. oat bran
1/2 c. pitted dates
4 fresh apricots, pitted
1 tsp. vanilla extract

Combine first six ingredients in blender. Pour into a non-stick 10" x 1 1/2" baking dish (use non-stick spray). Bake at 350 degrees for 30 minutes. While mixture is baking, blend dates, apricots and vanilla in blender. You may have to stop blender and press mix away from blades as mixture is sticky. Top bars with this apricot mixture after 30 minutes and bake 10 minutes and bake 10 minutes more at 400 degrees. Serves 4.

BARLEY BREAKFAST PUDDING

1 c. cooked barley
1/4 c. unfiltered apple juice
1/2 c. diced apples
1/8 tsp. nutmeg

1/4 tsp. cinnamon
1/2 tsp. vanilla
3 tbsp. raisins
1 tbsp. chopped walnuts

Mix all ingredients together and bake in a non-stick pan (use Pam) for 30 minutes at 350 degrees. Serves 2.

BREAKFAST CHERRY COBBLER

3 c. frozen cherries
  (unsweetened)
3/4 c. Old Fashioned Oats
1/2 c. Grape Nuts, Nutty Rice or
  Nuggets
1/2 tsp. cinnamon

1/2 c. chopped walnuts or pecans
6 oz. cherry cider or apple cider
1/2 tsp. pure vanilla extract

In an 8"x 10" glass baking dish, sprayed with non-stick, spread cherries on bottom, evenly. Sprinkle each dry ingredients evenly over cherries to form a topping. Combine cherry cider and vanilla together and pour evenly over top. Bake at 350 degrees for 20 to 30 minutes. Delicious.

CINNAMON PRUNE STICKS

1 box Sunsweet pitted prunes

1 c. spicy apple cider
2 cinnamon sticks

In a medium saucepan, empty the box of prunes, add cider and cinnamon sticks. Simmer on low for 30 minutes. Enjoy these spiced prunes hot or cold; 3 or 4 daily is recommended. Makes 8 to 10 servings.

EXTRA RECIPES

Bread, Muffins & Desserts

BANANA BREAD I

1 1/2 c. whole wheat flour
1/4 c. wheat germ or oat bran
1 tsp. cinnamon
2 tsp. baking powder
1/2 tsp. baking soda

1/2 c. chopped nuts
1/4 c. Butter Buds
1/2 c. honey
3/4 tsp. vanilla
1 c. mashed banana
2 egg whites

Preheat oven to 350 degrees. Combine dry ingredients, including nuts. Combine wet ingredients and stir into dry mixture until thoroughly blended. This will make a thick batter. Spread in a floured 8 1/2" x 4" loaf pan. Bake for 45 to 50 minutes, or until a toothpick inserted comes out clean. After cooling for 10 minutes in the pan, transfer to a cooling rack. Allow banana bread to cool completely before cutting.

NOTE: To save time, obtain a bread maker by Dax or Panasonic or similar unit that mixes dough and cooks bread to completion.

NOTE: For any bread recipe that calls for oil, just replace oil with the equivalent volume of applesauce, water or rice milk (amazake).

BANANA BREAD II

1 pkg. Fearn Banana Cake Mix
  (available in health food
  stores)
1 pkg. Butter Buds
1/2 c. honey

2 mashed bananas
2 egg whites
1/3 c. rice milk
1 c. walnuts, chopped

Preheat oven to 350 degrees. Mix Butter Buds and honey. Add bananas and egg whites and mix again. Add contents of cake mix and rice milk alternately, ending with mix. Add nuts and stir until uniform. Turn into a 1 pound loaf pan. Bake for 60 minutes. (After 30 minutes, loosely place a sheet of foil over top of bread to prevent crust from browning excessively.)

CARROT BREAD

1 c. whole wheat pastry flour
1 c. oat bran
2 tsp. baking powder
1 tsp. baking soda
1 tsp. cinnamon
1/4 tsp. nutmeg

4 egg whites
1 pkg. Butter buds, made into
  liquid
1/3 - 1/2 c. pineapple concentrate
1/2 - 1 c. raisins
2 c. grated carrots

Combine all ingredients and mix well. Bake in non-stick loaf pan at 325 degrees for 45 minutes.

GARLIC BREAD

Whole wheat bread without
  sugar or milk

Butter Buds
Fresh or powdered garlic

Mix 1 packet of Butter Buds in 1/2 cup hot water. Let sit in refrigerator for 5 to 10 minutes. Brush on bread and sprinkle with garlic. Broil in oven.

PUMPKIN BREAD

1/3 c. prepared Butter Buds
1/2 c. orange juice concentrate
4 egg whites
1 c. mashed pumpkin (canned)

1 tsp. baking soda
1 tsp. cinnamon
1/2 tsp. nutmeg
1/8 tsp. ginger
1 3/4 c. whole wheat flour

In a blender, process Butter Buds, juice concentrate and egg whites. While blending, add pumpkin, soda, cinnamon, nutmeg and ginger. Gradually add flour until you get a doughy consistency. Bake in a non-stick loaf pan (use non-stick spray) in a preheated 350 degree oven for 45 to 60 minutes. Toothpick should come out clean when done. Makes 1 loaf.

SOUR DOUGH BREAD

STEP A:
1 c. Sour Dough Starter
1 c. warm water

1 1/2 c. whole wheat flour,
    spooned into cup & mixed
    with 3 tsp. baking powder

STEP B:
1 c. whole wheat flour

In a large bowl, mix ingredients for Step A.

Blend 1/2 minute on low speed, then 3 minutes at medium speed, scraping the bowl all the time. Gradually stir in ingredients for Step B. Dough should remain soft and slightly sticky. Turn dough onto well floured board and sprinkle with flour so it doesn't stick to hands. Knead about 250 turns, adding flour as required. Shape for placing in loaf pan. Place in 9"x 5"x 3" loaf pan that has had cornmeal sprinkled on the bottom. Let rise in a warm place until doubled in size, about 1 hour. Gently slash top of dough with razor blade or sharp knife.

Bake in preheated oven on lowest rack position. See instructions below for oven temperature and baking time. Cool about 5 minutes on cake rack until bread shrinks from sides of pan. Remove from pan and cool on rack.

Bake at 400 degrees for approximately 35 minutes.

Extra Quick Version: After placing dough in baking pan, bake immediately at 400 degrees approximately 45 minutes.

SPROUTED WHEAT BREAD

2 c. wheat or rye berries   1 1/2 c. water

Soak the berries in the water for 12 hours in a 2 quart jar. Pour off the excess water after soaking. Drink the water or feed it to your plants. This sprouting wheat does not need to be rinsed in the winter, but rinse it once or twice a day in the summer to keep it moist. However, do not rinse it on the day of use. This will prevent the wheat from becoming too moist.

After wheat has sprouted to the length of the wheat berry itself (about 2 days), grind in meat grinder.* Form into a 2 1/2" high by 8" long loaf by patting with Pam sprayed hands in a 9" Pam sprayed pie pan. Bake at 250 degrees for 2 hours.

*If dough seems too moist, add freshly ground whole wheat flour to desired texture. For a fruit bread, stir in the following after the wheat sprouts are ground: 1/2 cup chopped almonds, dates, raisins, currants, dried apricots, figs, prunes, etc.

SWEET CORNBREAD

1 1/2 c. yellow whole grain cornmeal	1 c. rice milk
1/2 c. millet (opt.)	1 egg white
1 tsp. baking soda	3/4 c. unsweetened applesauce
	3 tbsp. unfiltered apple juice

In a large bowl combine all ingredients and mix well. Pour into glass baking dish sprayed with non-stick spray. Bake at 400 degrees for 20 to 25 minutes. Serves 6.

TEXAS CORNBREAD

1 pkg. Old Mill Cornbread Mix (or other whole grain mix)	1/4 c. corn kernels
1/4 c. diced green chilies	1 tsp. cumin
	1 tsp. chili powder

Follow directions for cornbread, omitting egg yolk (add 2 tablespoons water if dry). Mix in remaining ingredients. Bake in non-stick, sprayed bakeware. Serves 6.

ZUCCHINI BREAD

3 c. whole wheat flour
3 c. grated zucchini
1 1/4 c. oat bran
4 1/2 tsp. baking powder
1 tsp. nutmeg

2 tsp. cinnamon
1 c. chopped nuts
4 egg whites
1 3/4 c. applesauce
2 tsp. vanilla extract

Preheat oven to 350 degrees. Mix together the flour, oat bran, baking powder, nutmeg, cinnamon and nuts. In another bowl, mix the egg whites, applesauce and vanilla extract. Stir in the grated zucchini. Add the flour mixture to the zucchini mixture, gradually stirring until blended. Turn the batter into 2 (8 1/2″ x 4 1/2″) loaf pans and bake 1 hour.

APPLE CORN MUFFINS

3/4 c. whole grain flour
2/3 c. whole grain cornmeal
1 tsp. Rumford baking powder

1 apple, finely grated
2 stiffly beaten egg whites
1/2 c. unfiltered apple juice
1/4 c. pureed dates or date
    powder

Blend all ingredients together; mix well. Pour into non-stick muffin pan 2/3 full and bake in preheated oven for 15 to 20 minutes or until done. Makes 8 muffins.

BISCUITS

1 c. whole wheat pastry flour

1 pkg. Butter Buds
1/2 c. water

Mix thoroughly. With wet hands form into small biscuits. Bake on non-stick cookie sheet at 400 degrees for 6 minutes.

BRAN MUFFINS

2 egg whites, beaten
1 c. apple juice concentrate
1/2 c. unbleached flour
1/2 c. whole wheat flour
1 c. oat bran
3 tsp. cinnamon
1 1/2 tsp. baking powder

1 tsp. ground cloves
Grated orange rind
1/2 c. unsweetened pineapple
1/4 c. chopped pecans or walnuts
1/4 c. raisins

Mix all dry ingredients. Add raisins, nuts and spices; mix well. Add orange rind, apple juice and egg whites. Bake at 400 degrees for about 25 minutes. Makes 12 muffins.

BURGER BUNS

In a large bowl, combine and let foam:
1/4 c. warm water
1 tbsp. yeast

1 tsp. barley malt syrup or honey

Stir in, using your hands as dough gets stiff:
3 - 3 1/2 c. whole wheat flour
1 c. water

2 - 2 1/2 tbsp. toasted sesame
seeds
1/2 tsp. sea salt

Knead for about 10 minutes on lightly floured surface. Spray a clean bowl with Pam, turn dough around to coat, cover bowl with a warm, damp towel and let rise until double in a warm draft-free place.

Toast in a 350 degree oven in a flat pan for 10 minutes:
2 tbsp. toasted sesame seeds

Press dough down, divide into 8 balls. Flatten into 1/2" thick rounds, pressing top of dough into the seeds. Place seed side up on a lightly oiled baking sheet. Lay a piece of waxed paper loosely over the top of the rolls, let them rise double. Heat oven to 375 degrees and bake buns 16 to 18 minutes. Remove to rack to cool.

Per bun: Calories 175; Protein 6 gm; Carbohydrates 33 gm; Fat 3 gm.

FRUIT AND NUT BRAN MUFFINS

2 tbsp. Butter Buds
3 tbsp. apple juice concentrate
2 egg whites
3/4 c. rice milk

1 c. bran
1 c. whole wheat flour
2 tsp. baking powder
1 c. chopped cashews
3/4 c. raisins

Preheat oven to 425 degrees. In a large bowl, mix Butter Buds and apple juice concentrate and egg whites. Add rice milk and bran. Stir. Add flour and baking powder; stir. Quickly fold in nuts and raisins. Fill muffin pans sprayed with Pam 2/3 full. Bake 20 minutes. 12 muffins.

OAT BRAN MUFFINS

2 egg whites
1 c. apple juice concentrate
1 c. whole grain pancake mix
1 c. Mother's Oat Bran by Quaker

2 tsp. cinnamon
1/2 c. unsweetened crushed
   pineapple
1/4 c. chopped pecans or almonds

Beat the egg whites in a bowl with a mixer. Mix in the apple juice concentrate. In a separate bowl, mix the pancake mix, oat bran and cinnamon. Mix dry and liquid ingredients together until well blended. Do not beat. Add the crushed pineapple and pecans. Divide into 12 equal sized muffins. Bake in a non stick muffin pan at 400 degrees for 15 minutes.

NOTE: Paper muffin cups do not work well with this recipe. Teflon muffin tins improve the texture greatly.

OAT BRAN PINEAPPLE MUFFINS

2 1/2 c. oat bran
2-3 tbsp. honey
1 tbsp. baking powder
1/2 c. rice milk

2 egg whites, beaten
1 lg. can crushed pineapple, with
   juice
1/4 c. raisins (opt.)

Mix dry ingredients. Add liquid and mix well. Bake at 425 degrees for 17 to 20 minutes. Makes 16 muffins.

PRUNE MUFFINS

1 c. concentrated apple juice
1 egg white
1 tsp. cinnamon
1 c. pitted prunes

1 c. grated zucchini
1 c. oatmeal
3/4 c. oat bran
1/4 c. whole wheat flour

In blender, combine first four ingredients. In a bowl, combine rest of ingredients with blender mixture. Pour into non-stick muffin pans (use non-stick spray) and bake at 350 degrees for 30 minutes. Makes 12 muffins.

WHOLE WHEAT PUMPKIN MUFFINS

Microwave.

3/4 c. canned pumpkin
4 egg whites
1/2 c. honey
1/2 c. apple juice concentrate
1 1/2 c. whole wheat flour

1 tsp. pumpkin pie spice
3/4 tsp. baking powder
1/2 tsp. baking soda
1/2 c. walnuts, chopped
1/2 c. raisins

Combine pumpkin, egg whites, honey and apple juice concentrate. Add to combined dry ingredients in large mixing bowl. Mix until just blended. Stir in nuts and raisins. Spoon 2 tablespoons of batter into plastic muffin tray lined with paper liners. Bake on full power for 1 minute.

In a large bowl, combine all ingredients and mix well. Pour into muffin tins sprayed with non-stick. Bake at 425 degrees for 15 to 20 minutes. Very good and very healthy.

APPLESAUCE OATMEAL COOKIES

1/2 c. unsweetened applesauce
1 c. unfiltered apple juice
1 egg white
1 tsp. vanilla extract
3 c. old fashioned oats

1/2 c. whole wheat flour
1/2 c. oat bran
1/2 tsp. baking soda
1/3 c. chopped nuts and/or
   raisins

Combine all ingredients in a mixing bowl and blend well. Drop by rounded teaspoons onto cookie sheets sprayed with non-stick. Bake at 350 degrees for 12 to 15 minutes. Serves 24.

APPLE SPICE COOKIES

3 egg whites
2 c. unsweetened applesauce
1 c. frozen apple juice concentrate
1 c. frozen orange juice
   concentrate

4 c. whole wheat flour
1 tsp. nutmeg
1 1/2 tsp. cinnamon
1/2 c. Grape Nuts cereal
1 c. raisins

Beat egg whites until foamy. Add applesauce and juices to egg whites. Combine dry ingredients. Drop onto non-stick baking sheet by teaspoon. Bake at 400 degrees 8 to 10 minutes. Makes 4 to 5 dozen.

BANANA COOKIES

1 c. banana puree (2 med.
   bananas)
1/2 c. date pieces

1/4 c. chopped almonds
1 tsp. vanilla
1 1/2 c. uncooked oatmeal

Pour banana puree into a bowl and add remaining ingredients. Mix well; drop by tablespoons onto a non-stick cookie sheet (use non-stick spray). Bake at 375 degrees for 20 minutes. Makes 2 dozen.

BANANA RAISIN COOKIES

1 1/4 c. rolled oats
1 c. whole wheat flour
1 tsp. cinnamon
1/2 c. apple juice

2 ripe bananas, mashed
3/4 c. raisins
1 tsp. vanilla

Preheat oven to 350 degrees. Combine all dry ingredients in a large bowl. Add remaining ingredients and mix well. Batter should be a little stiff. Drop by teaspoon onto non-stick cookie sheet and flatten slightly. Bake for 15 minutes. Makes 15 to 18 cookies.

CAROB BROWNIES

2 egg whites
1 tbsp. honey
1 1/2 tsp. vanilla extract
1 c. grated zucchini
3 tbsp. carob powder

1/2 c. oat bran
1/2 c. apple juice
1 c. whole wheat flour
1/2 c. chopped dates

Beat egg whites, honey and vanilla for 1 minute. Slowly while beating, add remaining ingredients. Bake in a non-stick 9" square pan (use non-stick spray) for 30 minutes at 350 degrees. Serves 8 to 10.

HARVEST APPLE COOKIES

1 1/4 c. whole wheat flour
1/2 tsp. non-aluminum baking
   powder
1/2 tsp. cinnamon
1/2 c. prepared Butter Buds
1/4 c. unsweetened applesauce

1/2 c. unfiltered apple juice
1/2 c. chopped dates or date
   nuggets
1 c. apple, chopped & peeled
1/2 c. old fashioned rolled oats
1/4 c. oat bran

Preheat oven to 350 degrees. Combine dry ingredients; mix wet ingredients into dry. Mix batter until smooth. Drop by teaspoons onto non-stick cookie sheet sprayed with Pam. Bake 15 to 20 minutes until lightly browned. Makes 24.

OATMEAL COOKIES

1 env. (1/2 c.) prepared Butter
  Buds
1 c. unfiltered apple juice
1 egg white
1 tsp. pure vanilla extract
3 c. old fashion oats

1 c. whole grain flour (whole
  wheat or any whole grain)
1/2 tsp. soda
1/3 c. chopped nuts and/or
  raisins (opt.)

Combine all ingredients in a mixing bowl and mix well. Drop rounded teaspoons onto sprayed (non-stick spray) cookie sheets. Bake 350 degrees for 12 to 15 minutes. Voila; a natural delicious cookie with no cholesterol and no sugar.

RAISIN CHEWS

Preheat oven to 350 degrees. Combine in a mixing bowl:

3 egg whites, beaten slightly
12 oz. frozen apple juice
  concentrate
1/4 tsp. cloves
3 tsp. ground coriander
1 c. "Nutty Rice" cereal or
  equivalent
2 c. raisins

1 tsp. allspice
3 tsp. anise
1/2 tsp. vanilla
2 c. whole wheat flour
1/2 c. oat bran

If mixture is too wet to form drop cookies, add 1 to 2 cups oatmeal as needed. Drop by spoonfuls onto ungreased cookie sheet. Bake at 350 degrees for 5 to 10 minutes or until cookies start to spring back when you touch them. Makes about 50 cookies, 61 calories each.

SOFT PUMPKIN COOKIES

1 3/4 c. whole wheat flour
1/4 c. oat bran
1 tbsp. non-aluminum baking
  powder
1 tsp. cinnamon
1/2 tsp. nutmeg
2/3 c. chopped nuts (opt.)

2/3 c. sunflower seeds, raw (opt.)
1/2 c. raisins
1/2 c. unfiltered apple juice
1/2 c. unsweetened applesauce
1 1/2 c. mashed pumpkin

Preheat oven to 350 degrees. Combine ingredients in order given, mixing wet ingredients well. Stir batter until well blended. Drop by tablespoon onto non-stick cookie sheets sprayed with Pam. Bake 10 to 12 minutes until firm and lightly browned. Makes 2 dozen.

WHOLE WHEAT COOKIES

1 1/2 c. whole wheat flour
1/2 c. apple juice concentrate
1 pkg. Butter Buds
2 tbsp. orange juice
1/2 tsp. vanilla extract

1/2 tsp. baking soda
1/2 tsp. cinnamon
2 egg whites, lightly beaten
1 c. walnut pieces
1 c. golden raisins

Preheat oven to 375 degrees. Mix Butter Buds and apple juice concentrate until smooth. Beat in orange juice and vanilla. Combine flour, baking soda and cinnamon, and add to the creamed mixture alternately with the beaten egg whites. Stir in nuts and raisins. Drop by rounded teaspoonfuls onto an ungreased baking sheet. Bake for 10 to 12 minutes until golden. Transfer to a rack and cool. Makes 2 dozen 2" cookies.

APPLE SPICE CAKE

4 c. finely diced apples (5-6 apples)
1/2 c. frozen apple juice concentrate
1/2 c. water
1/2 c. raisins
1 1/4 c. rice flour
1 1/4 c. whole wheat pastry flour

2 tsp. baking powder
2 tsp. baking soda
2 1/2 tsp. cinnamon
1/4 tsp. nutmeg
1/4 tsp. allspice
4 egg whites
1 tsp. vanilla extract
1 c. Grape Nuts cereal

Combine the diced apples, apple juice, water and raisins in a bowl. Cover with plastic wrap and store in refrigerator for 4 to 6 hours. Sift both flours, baking powder, baking soda, cinnamon, nutmeg and allspice into a large bowl. Beat the egg whites until soft peaks form and then fold into the flour mixture. Add the apple raisin mixture (including the juice). Add vanilla extract and the Grape Nuts; stir well. Pour into a non-stick bundt pan. Bake at 325 degrees for 1 1/2 hours. Turn the cake out of the pan onto a large sheet of aluminum foil. Wrap the cake completely in foil and let sit for several hours. Makes 12 servings.

BLUEBERRY CAKE

6 c. apple juice
1 tsp. lemon rind
1 tsp. vanilla

2 c. couscous (precooked semolina wheat product)
1 pt. blueberries

Bring first three ingredients to a boil in a medium pan. Add couscous, reduce heat and stir until almost thick, about 5 minutes. Add the blueberries to the hot mixture (berries will burst, leaving streaks and cake will be very colorful). Remove from heat.

Rinse a 9"x9" square glass baking dish with cold water. Pour mixture into pan and chill in refrigerator until set, about 45 to 60 minutes. Remove from refrigerator, place a serving platter over baking dish, and turn upside down. Cut into squares. Can be garnished with chopped nuts or Whipped Tofu Cream. Serves 10 to 15.

CARROT CAKE

2 c. shredded raw carrots
1 c. raisins
1 1/2 c. apple juice concentrate
1/3 c. Butter Buds
2 c. whole wheat flour

1 1/2 tsp. baking soda
1/2 tsp. ground cloves
1/2 tsp. ground allspice
1 tsp. nutmeg
1 tsp. cinnamon
1 c. chopped walnuts

Place carrots, raisins, apple juice concentrate and Butter Buds in a 3 quart pan and bring to a simmer over medium heat. Simmer 5 minutes, remove from heat and let cool.

In a bowl, sift together flour, baking soda, cloves, allspice, nutmeg and cinnamon. Stir into carrot mixture, until flour is moist. Add vanilla and walnuts. Spoon into a 9" square baking pan, sprayed with Pam.

Bake in a 350 degree oven for 35 minutes. 12 servings.

Carrot Cake Frosting: In a saucepan, cook and stir 1 cup apple juice with 3 tablespoons tapioca until thickened. When cooked, add 1 teaspoon vanilla. Spread frosting on cake and serve.

CRUNCHY CARROT CAKE

3 egg whites, whipped
1 c. grated carrots
1 (20 oz.) can crushed pineapple
   in its own juice
1 tsp. baking soda
1 tsp. cinnamon

1 c. unfiltered apple juice
1 c. oat bran
1 c. whole grain pastry flour
1/2 c. raisins
1/2 c. chopped walnuts

Combine dry ingredients together. Combine dry ingredients together. Blend together; mix well. Pour into non-stick baking dish. Bake at 350 degrees for 45 minutes. Serves 15.

COFFEE CAKE

1 c. raisins
4 1/2 c. whole wheat pastry flour
2 tbsp. baking powder
1 1/2 tbsp. carob powder
2 tsp. cinnamon
1/2 tsp. cardamom
1/2 tsp. nutmeg

10 oz. frozen apple juice
   concentrate
3/4 c. water
3 tbsp. dry sherry (opt.)
3 tbsp. mineral water
1 tbsp. vanilla
2 lg. bananas, mashed
4 egg whites

Cover raisins with hot water to soak. In a large bowl sift together the flour, baking powder, carob powder and spices. Mix together the remaining ingredients except the egg whites. Stir this mixture into the dry ingredients. Beat the egg whites until stiff peaks form, and fold them into the batter. Add the drained raisins and stir well. Pour the batter into a large non-stick baking pan. Sprinkle streusel topping evenly over the cake. Bake in a preheated 350 degree oven for 50 to 60 minutes. Cool cake completely. Store covered.

COFFEE CAKE TOPPING:
1 c. Grape Nuts cereal
2 tbsp. frozen apple juice
   concentrate
1 tsp. vanilla extract

1/2 tsp. cinnamon
1/4 tsp. nutmeg
1/2 tsp. cardamom

Process Grape Nuts in the blender just long enough to reduce the coarseness of the cereal. Add the other topping ingredients and sprinkle on the cake.

DATE CAKE

3 egg whites
1/3 c. apple juice
1 tsp. baking soda
1/2 c. grated carrots
1 c. grated zucchini
1 tsp. cinnamon

1 c. water
1 c. oat bran
1 c. whole grain pastry flour
1 c. date pieces

Combine together in order given, blending with hand mixer. Pour into cake pan sprayed with non-stick. Bake in preheated oven at 350 degrees for 30 minutes.

DATE FROSTING

1 c. apple juice
1/2 c. date pieces

1 tsp. vanilla
3 tbsp. tapioca granules

Place all ingredients in blender and process for 2 minutes. Cook in saucepan 5 minutes over low heat, stirring constantly. Cool down to a warm temperature and frost cake. Can be served or at room temperature. Serves 15.

LEMON APPLESAUCE CAKE

1 c. Stone Buhr 7 Grain Cereal,
  uncooked
1 c. unsweetened applesauce
1 c. whole wheat flour
1/2 c. oat bran
1 tbsp. baking powder
1 tsp. cinnamon

1 tsp. lemon rind, grated
1/2 c. unfiltered apple juice
1 env. prepared Butter Buds
2 egg whites
1/2 c. raisins
1/2 c. chopped nuts

One hour before starting, combine cereal and applesauce. Mix, cover and set aside at least one hour or overnight. Preheat oven to 350 degrees. In a medium bowl combine apple juice, Butter Buds, egg whites, raisins and nuts; mix well. Add in dry ingredients and applesauce mixture mixing well. Pour into 8" or 9" cake pan sprayed with non-stick. Bake at 350 degrees for 30 minutes. Cool before slicing. Serves 14.

PINEAPPLE UPSIDE-DOWN CAKE

TOPPING:

6 slices canned unsweetened
   pineapple rings

Pecan or walnut halves
2 tbsp. Butter Buds
1/4 c. honey

CAKE:

4 egg whites
2 tbsp. pineapple juice
1/2 c. whole wheat flour

1/2 tsp. baking powder
1/2 c. honey

Preheat oven to 350 degrees. Line a 9" layer cake or square pan with wax paper.

For Topping: Melt Butter Buds, combine with honey and spread over the paper. Arrange pieces of pineapple artistically in the pan. Place nuts in the open spaces.

To make the cake, mix honey and juice. Sift flour and baking powder over the juice mixture and fold to completely blend. Beat egg whites stiff and fold into flour batter. Spread batter over pineapple in baking pan. Bake for 30 minutes until golden. Cool for 10 to 15 minutes in the pan, invert and peel off paper. Cool completely. Don't worry if the cake sinks a little.

PUMPKIN SPICE CAKE

3 c. pumpkin
1 c. unfiltered apple juice
1/2 c. raisins
2 c. whole grain pastry flour
1 tsp. baking soda
1 tsp. baking powder

2 tsp. cinnamon
1/4 tsp. nutmeg
1/4 tsp. allspice
4 egg whites, whipped
1 tsp. pure vanilla extract
1 c. Grape Nuts
1/4 c. honey or applesauce

Combine dry ingredients together. Combine wet ingredients together then blend both, mixing well. Pour into non-stick baking dish. Bake at 350 degrees for about 45 minutes. Serves 15.

WHOLE WHEAT FRUITCAKE

2 c. coarsely chopped dried figs
2 c. chopped dried apricots
1/2 c. chopped candied lemon
   peel
1 1/2 c. golden raisins
1 1/2 c. chopped dates
2 c. chopped pecans
2/3 c .green candied cherries,
   halved
2/3 c. red candied cherries,
   halved
1 1/2 c. whole wheat flour
1 1/2 c. brown rice flour

1 tsp.b baking powder
3/4 tsp. nutmeg
1/2 tsp. cinnamon
1/2 tsp. ground cloves
1/2 tsp. ground cardamom
2 pkgs. Butter Buds
12 egg whites
1 1/2 c. apple juice concentrate
1 c. red wine
1/2 tsp. baking soda
2 tbsp. water
Brandy

In a large bowl combine the figs, apricots, lemon peel, raisins, dates, pecans and cherries. In another bowl sift together the flours, baking powder, spices and Butter Buds. Add the flour mixture to the fruit and toss them together until all the bits of fruit are separated and coated. Beat the egg whites with the apple juice concentrate. Stir in the wine. Dissolve the baking soda in the water and stir it in too. Combine the egg mixture with the flour and fruit mixture, and thoroughly stir them together.

Pour into 6 medium-small (7 1/2" x 3 1/2") loaf pans. Bake the cakes in a preheated oven at 275 degrees for 2 hours. Allow the cakes to cool and remove them from the pans. Wrap each cake in several layers of cheesecloth and soak the cloth with as much brandy as it will absorb. Wrap the cake again, in foil or plastic wrap, to retain the moisture. To allow the fruit cakes to develop their full flavor, store them in a cool place for 4 weeks. Makes 6 medium sized fruitcakes.

CRUNCHY CARROT CAKE

3 egg whites, whipped
1 c. grated carrots
1 (20 oz.) can crushed pineapple
in own juice
1 tsp. baking soda
1 tsp. cinnamon

1 c. unfiltered apple juice
1 c. oat bran
1 c. whole grain pastry flour
1/2 c. raisins
1/2 c. chopped walnuts

Combine dry ingredients together. Combine wet ingredients together. Blend together, mixing well. Pour into non-stick baking dish. Bake at 350 degrees for approximately 45 minutes.

FROSTING: In a saucepan, cook and stir 1 cup apple juice with 3 tablespoons tapioca until thickened. When cool add 1 teaspoon vanilla. Spread frosting on top of cake, cut and serve.

DATE CAKE

3 egg whites
1/3 c. honey or apple juice
1 tsp. baking soda
1/2 c. grated carrots (2 sm. carrots)
1 c. grated zucchini (1 sm.)

1 tsp. cinnamon
1 c. water
1 c. oat bran
1 c. whole grain pastry flour
1 c. date pieces

Combine together in order given, blend with hand mixer. Pour into cake pan sprayed with non-stick. Bake in preheated 350 degree oven for 30 minutes.

DATE FROSTING:
1 c. apple juice
1/2 c. date pieces

1 tsp. vanilla
3 tbsp. tapioca granules

Blend in blender 2 minutes. Cook in saucepan 5 minutes over low heat, stirring constantly. Cool down to warm and frost cake. This oustandingly delicious cake can be served warm or room temperature. Serves 15.

LEMON APPLESAUCE CAKE

1 c. Stone Buhr 7 Grain Cereal
   (uncooked)
1 c. unsweetened applesauce
1 c. whole wheat flour
1/2 c. oat bran
1 tbsp. baking powder

1 tsp. cinnamon
1 tsp. lemon rind, grated
1/2 c. unfiltered apple juice
1 env. prepared Butter Buds
2 egg whites
1/2 each raisins & chopped nuts

One hour before starting, combine cereal and applesauce. Mix, cover and set aside at least 1 hour or overnight. Preheat oven to 350 degrees.

In medium bowl, combine dry ingredients. In large bowl, combine apple juice, Butter Buds, egg whites, raisins and nuts; mix well. Add in dry ingredients and applesauce mixture, mixing well. Pour into 8" or 9" cake pan sprayed with non-stick. Bake at 350 degrees for 30 minutes. Cool before slicing.

APRICOT PIE

For oat nut crust, whiz in blender until a coarse meal:
1 1/2 c. rolled oats

Mix in a bowl with:

1/2 c. walnuts, chopped fine   **1/4 c. apple juice**
1/4 c. water

Let stand 30 minutes. Oil a 9″ pie pan and press mixture firmly into bottom and sides, using the back of a large spoon. Bake at 350 degrees for 30 minutes until edges begin to brown.

For filling, snip into small pieces with scissors dipped in cold water:
1 c. dried apricots

Place apricots in saucepan, add:
1 1/2 c. apple juice

Bring to a boil, reduce heat and simmer 15 minutes until fruit is soft. Sprinkle on top to dissolve:
2 tbsp. kanten flakes

Stir in and cook over medium heat, stirring 3 minutes. Set off heat to cool. When it begins to set, pour into baked pie shell. Chill. This dessert can be made the day before. Yield: 8 servings.

Per Serving: 227 Calories; 6 gm Protein; 38 gm Carbohydrates; 6 gm Fat.

BANANA PECAN PIE

CRUST:
1 1/2 c. Grape Nuts   1 tsp. cinnamon
1 1/3 c. apple juice concentrate

Mix above ingredients into 9″ pie pan. Press to form shell. Bake at 350 degrees for 10 minutes.

FILLING:
1 pkg. Hain Natural Banana   1 1/2 c. water
   Pudding Mix or Banana   2 ripe bananas, sliced
   Tapioca Mix   Pecans
1/2 c. apple juice concentrate

Empty contents of package into 1 quart saucepan and add liquids. Slowly bring to boil, stirring frequently. (Filling will not thicken until cooled.) Add bananas. Pour into pie shell. Top with a few pecans and chill.

BANANA CREAM PIE

In blender add:
1/2 c. tightly packed cooked   1/3 c. apple juice concentrate
   brown rice

Blend until thick and smooth. Add:
2 1/4 c. water   1/4 c. sugar or honey (occasional
1 tsp. Butter Buds   use)
1 tbsp. cornstarch   4 tbsp. flour

Continue to blend until thoroughly mixed. Pour contents of blender into saucepan. Bring to a boil, stirring constantly. Remove from heat and allow to cool 15 minutes. Slice 2 large ripe bananas and stir into mixture. Pour into a prebaked crust. (Use one of our crust recipes.) Refrigerate for at least 2 hours. When ready to serve, top with a few banana slices and pecan halves. Makes 1 large 11″ pie.

CRUMB TOPPED FRUIT PIE

CRUST:
1 1/3 c. fine whole wheat bread
  crumbs mixed with 1/3 c. bran
1 tbsp. each pectin & arrowroot

1 tbsp. vanilla extract
t1 tsp. coriander
1/2 tsp. lemon extract

FILLING:
3 c. sliced fruit or berries of
  choice

1/3 c. frozen apple juice
  concentrate

TOPPING:
1 c. fine whole wheat bread
  crumbs

1 tbsp. cinnamon
1 tsp. vanilla extract

To Make Crust: Place ingredients in a bowl, mixing well. Using a rubber spatula, press the mixture into the non-stick pie pan firmly (bottom and sides) to form an even crust. Bake the crust at 350 degrees for 15 minutes until lightly browned. Remove from oven and allow to cool.

To Make Filling: Place filling ingredients in a saucepan. Bring to a boil; then lower the heat and simmer for a few minutes, stirring frequently until the mixture is thickened. Pour the fruit filling into the prepared crust.

Combine the topping ingredients, mixing well. Sprinkle the topping over the filling, lightly pressing it in the fruit with a spatula. Bake at 375 degrees for 15 minutes. Let pie cool; then slice to serve. Serves 6 to 8.

FRUIT PIE

1 1/2 c. Grape Nuts or Nuggets
1/3 c. apple juice concentrate
1 tsp. cinnamon
1 (8 oz.) can pineapple chunks
(juice pack)

1 3/4 c. unsweetened pineapple
juice
1 env. unflavored gelatin
2 sm. bananas
2 c. strawberries, sliced
2 kiwi fruit, peeled & sliced

Mix Grape Nuts, apple juice concentrate and cinnamon together. Press into 9" pie pan. Bake at 350 degrees for 10 minutes.

In a small saucepan stir together pineapple liquid and gelatin. Let stand 5 minutes. Cook and stir over low heat until gelatin dissolves. Cover and chill to the consistency of unbeaten egg whites.

Slice bananas. Arrange over cooled crust, then top with 2/3 cup of glaze. Arrange strawberry slices over glaze. Stir together pineapple pieces and remaining glaze, then spoon over strawberries. Chill for 2 to 4 hours. Just before serving, then spoon over strawberries.

The kiwi fruit contains enzymes that breaks down the gelatin, so be sure to put it on at the last minute.

FRENCH APPLE PIE

CRUST:

2 c. Grape Nuts or Nutty Rice
Cinnamon

1/3 c. apple juice concentrate
Additional water

Mix ingredients into a large pie pan and press to form shell. Sprinkle with cinnamon.

FILLING:

4 med. Granny Smith apples

Cinnamon
2 tsp. lemon juice

Arrange sliced apples in shell. Sprinkle with lemon juice and cinnamon. Cover with foil and bake for 45 minutes at 350 degrees.

GLAZE:

1/2 c. apple juice concentrate

1 tbsp. cornstarch
1/2 c. water

Combine cornstarch and liquids in saucepan. Cook and stir until mixture thickens and becomes clear. Pour or spoon over pie. Chill.

MOCK CHOCOLATE PUDDING PIE

14 Medjool dates, remove pits
1 very ripe sm. banana
3/4 c. apple juice concentrate
3 c. water
4 tbsp. carob powder
1 tsp. Postum

1 tsp. cinnamon
1 tsp. vanilla extract
1/2 tsp. almond extract (opt.)
1 1/2 tsp. arrowroot or
    cornstarch
1 1/2 env. unflavored gelatin
1 c. water

In blender and in stages for easier liquifying, add dates, banana, apple juice, water; blend well. Add the next six ingredients and continue to blend thoroughly.

In large saucepan, dissolve gelatin in water following directions. Add contents of blender to pan and cook 15 minutes mixing periodically. Let cool 15 minutes. Pour over baked crust. Refrigerate until firm, approximately 8 hours. Top with sliced bananas and chopped walnuts, if desired. Makes one large pie and one small pie.

Pour into a glass a small amount of mixture from blender, tastes like a malt!

PUMPKIN PIE I

CRUST:

1 1/2 c. Nuggets or Grape Nuts
    cereal

1/3 c. apple juice concentrate
1 tsp. cinnamon

Mix above ingredients in a 9″ pie pan. Press to form shell.

FILLING:

3/4 c. apple juice concentrate
1/4 c. honey
1 tbsp. molasses
1/2 tsp. cinnamon
3/4 tsp. ginger
1/4 tsp. nutmeg

1/4 tsp. ground cloves
2 c. pureed cooked pumpkin
6 egg whites
3 tbsp. sweet dark rum
3 tbsp. crystallized ginger,
    chopped

In a bowl combine the apple juice concentrate, honey, molasses, spices and pureed pumpkin. In another bowl beat the eggs with the rum. Combine the two mixtures and blend thoroughly. Sprinkle the crystallized ginger over the bottom of the pie crust. Carefully ladle the filling over the ginger. Bake the pies in the preheated 400 degree oven for 35 to 40 minutes or until a knife inserted comes out clean.

PUMPKIN PIE II

CRUST:
1 1/2 c. Grape Nuts cereal
1 tsp. cinnamon

1/2 c. apple juice concentrate

FILLING:
1 can canned pumpkin
1/2 c. water
1/2 tsp. cinnamon
1/4 tsp. ginger

2 1/2 tsp. vanilla extract
1 env. unflavored gelatin
1/2 c. apple juice concentrate
2 egg whites

Combine crust ingredients and press into standard pie plate. Combine filling ingredients (except for gelatin, apple juice and egg whites). Sprinkle gelatin over apple juice concentrate and let stand for 2 minutes. Heat gently until dissolved and stir into pumpkin filling mixture. Chill for 30 minutes. Beat egg whites stiffly and fold into pumpkin mixture. Mound into pie pan and chill until firm.

SUMMER FRUIT PIE

CRUST:
1 1/2 c. Grape Nuts cereal or
   Nutty Rice cereal

1/3 c. apple juice concentrate
1 tsp. cinnamon

Mix above ingredients in a 9″ pie pan. Press to form shell. Bake in 350 degree oven for 10 minutes.

FILLING:
1 (8 oz.) can pineapple slices
   (juice pack)
Unsweetened pineapple juice

1 env. unflavored gelatin
2 sm. bananas
2 c. sliced strawberries
2 kiwi fruit, peeled & sliced

For glaze, drain pineapple slices, reserving juice. Cut pineapple into small pieces and set aside. Add enough unsweetened pineapple juice to the reserved juice to make 1 3/4 cups total liquid.

In a small saucepan stir together pineapple liquid and gelatin. Let stand 5 minutes. Cook and stir over low heat until gelatin dissolves. Cover and chill to the consistency of unbeaten egg whites (partially set).

Slice bananas. Arrange evenly over cooled crust, then top with 2/3 cup of the glaze. Arrange strawberry slices over glaze. Stir together pineapple pieces and remaining glaze, then spoon over strawberries. Chill for 2 to 4 hours or until set. Just before serving, arrange kiwi fruit on pie. Makes 8 servings.

SWEET POTATO PIE

3-4 sweet potatoes, baked
1 (16 oz.) can crushed pineapple
   in own juice
1/3 c. unsweetened coconut,
   shredded

1/4 c. chopped nuts (pecans,
   walnuts or almonds)
1/3 c. Nutty Rice or Nuggets
   cereal
1 tsp. pure vanilla extract
1/2 tsp. pumpkin pie spice

Spray a glass pie pan with non-stick spray. Peel sweet potatoes, dice and mash in a large mixing bowl. Add can of pineapple with juice, vanilla extract and pumpkin pie spice. Beat thoroughly with mixer, whipping until smooth. Pour into the pie pan or any glass baking dish and top with coconut, chopped and Nutty Rice cereal. Bake at 350 degrees for 25 minutes. Voila; a natural delicious dessert with fiber and no sugar. Enjoy.

PEARADISE PIE

3 1/2 c. flaked whole grain cereal
1/4 c. toasted wheat bran
1/4 c. Butter Buds
1 (12 oz.) can pear nectar
1 tbsp. cornstarch
1 tsp. vanilla

2 tbsp. lemon juice
1 tbsp. water
2 sm. bananas
2 c. fresh strawberries, sliced
1/2 of a sm. cantaloupe, seeded,
   sliced & peeled
Whole strawberries (opt.)

For crust, crush cereal into fine crumbs. Measure 1 1/4 cups crumbs; combine with wheat bran and Butter Buds. Press onto bottom and up sides of a 9" pie plate to form a firm, even crust. Bake in a 375 degree oven for 4 to 6 minutes. Cool on a wire rack.

Meanwhile, for glaze, combine nectar and cornstarch. Cook and stir over medium heat until thickened and bubbly. Cook and stir 2 minutes longer. Stir in vanilla; set aside.

To assemble pie, in small bowl, combine lemon juice and water. Dip in banana and pear slices, being careful not to mash the bananas. In crust, layer 1/4 cup of the glaze, the banana slices, another 1/4 cup of the glaze, the sliced strawberries and another 1/4 cup of the glaze. Arrange pear and cantaloupe slices atop. Top with remaining glaze. Chill 2 to 4 hours. Makes 8 servings.

APRICOT COBBLER

2 3/4 c. mashed fresh apricots,
   pitted but not peeled (20-25
   sm. apricots)
1 c. apple juice
1 c. pitted dates

1 tsp. cinnamon
1/3 c. oatmeal
1/3 c. dates
1/2 tsp. cinnamon

     Spread apricots evenly in the bottom of a 6"x10" baking dish. Pour apple juice in a blender and add dates. Puree; then add 1 teaspoon cinnamon. Pour over apricots. Make topping by grinding oatmeal, dates and 1/2 teaspoon cinnamon in blender.

CHERRY COBBLER

CRUST:
1 1/2 c. Grape-Nuts
1/3 c. apple juice concentrate

1 tsp. cinnamon

     Mix above ingredients into 9" pie pan. Press to form shell.

FILLING:
3 c. frozen cherries
3 tsp. cornstarch

2 tsp. water
1 c. walnuts, chopped

     Place cherries, water and cornstarch in a saucepan. Mix well to dilute cornstarch. Bring to a boil, reduce flame to low and simmer for 3 to 5 minutes. Stir to prevent lumping and sticking. Remove from flame and allow to cool. Add walnuts. Pour over crust in pie pan. Bake at 375 degrees for about 15 minutes. Serves 6.

PEACH COBBLER

1 c. pineapple juice
1/2 c. pitted dates
1 tsp. vanilla
1 tsp. cinnamon
1 tsp. tapioca

3 c. mashed fresh peaches
1 tbsp. almonds
1/2 c. pitted dates
1/3 c. oatmeal

Blend first five ingredients. In a non-stick baking dish layer peaches; pour juice mixture over. Grind remaining ingredients as topping and spoon over top. Bake at 350 degrees for 45 minutes. Serves 6 to 8.

APPLE CRISP

5 lg. pippin apples
Juice of 1/2 lemon
1 tbsp. cinnamon

2 tbsp. whole wheat pastry flour
3/4 c. dark raisins

TOPPING:
1 1/2 c. rolled oats or cereal
    flakes
3/4 c. whole wheat pastry flour

3/4 c. honey or apple juice
    concentrate
1 tbsp. cinnamon

Core and slice apples in thin pieces. Place in a 9"x13" baking dish. Sprinkle with lemon juice, cinnamon and flour. Mix well, making sure the apples are evenly coated. Sprinkle raisins over apples. In a separate bowl, combine oats, 3/4 cup flour and cinnamon. Mix in honey. Drop topping evenly over the apple mixture. Cover with foil and bake at 350 degrees for 25 minutes. Uncover and bake 15 minutes more, or until browned.

In glass baking dish; sprayed with non-stick, spread fruit evenly, then sprinkle and continue layering all ingredients in order. Blend apple juice and vanilla together and pour evenly over all. Bake at 350 degrees for 20 minutes.

BLUEBERRY-APPLE CRISP

1 c. Grape Nuts or Nuggets
1 c. toasted oat cereal

1/4 c. Butter Buds
1/4-1/3 c. apple juice concentrate

FILLING:

3 apples, cored & sliced (or 1 can
  water packed apples)
1 c. blueberries

1/2 c. apple juice concentrate
1/4 c. cornstarch

Combine crust ingredients and set aside. Combine filling ingredients in a bowl. Pour filling ingredients in baking pan, sprinkle with crust ingredients. Bake at 350 degrees for 30 minutes or until bubbly.

PEACH OR PEAR CRISP

1 lg. can peaches or pears totally
  drained in colander
1/2 c. raisins
1/4 - 1/2 c. chopped walnuts or
  pecans
1/4 c. unsweetened coconut,
  shredded (opt.)

1/2 tsp. cinnamon
1/2 c. cold fashioned oats
1/2 c. Grape Nuts or Perky's
  Nutty Rice cereal
6 oz. apple juice
1/2 tsp. vanilla extract

In glass baking dish, sprayed with non-stick, spread fruit evenly, then sprinkle and continue layering all ingredients in order. Blend apple juice and vanilla together and pour evenly over all. Bake at 350 degrees for 20 minutes.

CHOCOLATE BANANA BROWNIES

No stick cooking spray
4 tbsp. cocoa powder
3/4 c. water
1 very ripe banana
1 c. white sugar or pitted dates or
   apple juice concentrate

2 lg. egg whites
1 tsp. vanilla extract
1 tsp. baking powder
1/4 tsp. salt
1 c. all purpose flour or whole
   wheat flour
1/2 c. oat bran (for best results
   use an oat bran that is
   coarsely milled)

Preheat the oven to 350 degrees. Spray an 8" round or square cake pan with no stick cooking spray.

Place the cocoa, 1/4 cup water, and the banana, into a large blender cup or into the bowl of a food processor that has been fitted with a steel blade. Blend until it is smooth. Add the sugar, egg whites, vanilla extract, baking powder and salt and blend until the mixture is smooth. Add the flour, oat bran and 1/2 cup water a little at a time and blend again until smooth.

Pour the chocolate mixture into the prepared pan. Bake at 350 degrees for 20 to 25 minutes. Wait until the brownies have cooled to cut into servings. Store brownies in the refrigerator. Each Brownie: 0 mg Cholesterol; 123 calories.

LEMON CUSTARD

2 c. pear or apple juice
2 c. natural lemonade
2 bars agar-agar (or 3 tbsp. agar flakes)
Pinch sea salt
1 tsp. vanilla

1 c. lemon non-dairy frozen dessert
1 pt. berries (raspberries, strawberries or blueberries) (opt.)

Combine juice and lemonade in a saucepan. Rinse agar bars, tear into 1" pieces and add to saucepan (or measure flakes and sprinkle on juice). Stir until agar softens. Bring mixture to a light boil, lower heat and simmer for 10 minutes, until agar dissolves. Add salt and vanilla. Add frozen dessert, stir to dissolve and pour into shallow, heat proof dish. Place dish in refrigerator for 30 minutes, until custard is set. Serve as is or with berries. Serves 6.

Variation: For extra creaminess, place chilled custard in a blender and whip for 30 seconds immediately before serving.

Per Serving: 138 calories; 1 g protein; 2 g fat; 32 g carbohydrates; 0 cholesterol; 9 mg sodium.

PINEAPPLE BARS

CRUST:
1/2 c. almonds, ground fine 1/4 c. water
1/4 c. whole wheat flour 1 c. granola crumbs

Mix together with a fork in bottom of 9"x13" pan. Press against bottom. Bake 5 to 10 minutes at 350 degrees.

FILLING:
1 1/2 c. apple juice 2 tbsp. cornstarch
1 c. dates 1 tsp. vanilla
2 1/2 c. crushed pineapple Coconut for topping

Blend water and dates in blender until smooth. Mix together with other ingredients, pour over crust and sprinkle with coconut, then bake at 350 degrees for 15 minutes or until coconut is light brown. Cool well before cutting into desired squares.

ORANGE PILLOWS, TART

Preheat oven to 375 degrees. Beat together until smooth:
5 peeled, baked potatoes (about 2 12 oz. frozen orange juice
   1/2 c.) concentrate
3 bananas 1 tsp. almond extract

Beat 6 egg whites into stiff peaks. Fold into above mixture. Drop by heaping spoonfuls onto ungreased cookie sheet. Bake 15 minutes. Remove from oven and let sit 5 minutes before removing from cookie sheet. Makes 90 pillows, 17 calories each. For variety, replace orange juice concentrate with apple juice concentrate and the almond extract with vanilla extract to make apple pillows, sweet.

SWEET QUINOA PUDDING

2 c. cooked quinoa*
1 c. apple juice concentrate
1/2 c. raisins
1 c. chopped water chestnuts

1 1/2 tsp. vanilla extract
Grated zest of 1 lemon
Pinch of ground cinnamon
1 kiwi fruit for garnish

1. In a medium saucepan combine quinoa, apple juice concentrate, raisins, water chestnuts, vanilla, lemon zest and cinnamon. Cover pan and bring to a boil, then reduce heat and simmer for 15 minutes.

2. Slice kiwi fruit. Divide pudding among 5 dessert dishes and top with kiwi fruit slices. Makes 5 servings.

*Quinoa (pronounced Keen-wa) has the texture of whole cereal grains but, like buckwheat, is actually the fruit of an annual herb. It's available in most large health food stores and in some supermarkets.

To prepare 2 cups of cooked quinoa: Thoroughly rinse 1/2 cup quinoa and drain. Combine quinoa with 1/2 cup water in a saucepan and bring to a boil. Cover pan, reduce heat to medium-low, and simmer for 10 to 15 minutes, or until water is completely absorbed and grain is translucent.

SWEET POTATO APPLE CASSEROLE

1 1/4 lbs. sweet potatoes
1 lb. apples
1 c. apple juice

2 tbsp. cornstarch
4 tbsp. water
Cinnamon

Cook (either bake or steam) sweet potatoes until tender. Peel and slice. Layer in a non-stick casserole. Core and slice apples. Lay apple slices on top of sweet potatoes. Heat apple juice to boiling point. Combine cornstarch and water and add to juice, cooking until sauce is clear and thickened. Spoon sauce over apples, sprinkle with cinnamon. Bake at 350 degrees for 30 to 45 minutes. Serves 6.

SWEET POTATOES WITH ORANGE

4 lg. sweet potatoes
1/2 c. orange juice
2 crushed pineapple

Grated zest of 1/2 orange
Pinch of grated nutmeg
Pinch of white pepper

1. Place potatoes in a large pot of water, bring to a boil and cook for 30 to 40 minutes, or until tender. Set aside to cool slightly.

2. When potatoes are cool enough to handle, peel them, place in a bowl, and mash with the orange juice, crushed pineapple, orange zest, nutmeg and pepper.

3. Return mashed potatoes to the pot and reheat over medium heat. If not serving immediately, cover bowl and refrigerate mashed potatoes until one hour before serving. Transfer to an ovenproof dish, cover and reheat in a 350 degree oven for 25 minutes, or until hot. Makes 5 servings.

YAM SOUFFLE

2 c. cooked, mashed yams
4-5 egg whites

1 tbsp. cinnamon
1 tbsp. grated orange peel

Beat the egg whites to soft peak stage. Fold egg whites, cinnamon and orange peel into the yams. Divide into four individual souffle dishes and bake at 350 degrees for 25 minutes. Serve immediately. Serves 4.

GLAZED YAMS

1 lb. yams
1/3 c. unsweetened pineapple
   juice

1/4 c. fresh orange juice
1 tsp. cornstarch

1. Bring a large saucepan of water to a boil. Add yams, and cook for about 15 minutes, or until barely tender. Drain and set aside to cool slightly.

2. When yams are cool enough to handle, peel and cut into 3/4" slices. Place in a single layer in a baking dish.

3. Preheat oven to 350 degrees. In a small bowl, combine pineapple and orange juices with cornstarch and stir until cornstarch is dissolved. Pour the mixture over yams and bake for 45 minutes. Makes 8 servings.

TAHINI CUSTARD

3 apples
1/2 c. raisins
2 c. apple juice
2-3 tbsp. Erewhon Sesame
    Tahini

Pinch of Instead of Salt
5 tbsp. Erewhon Agar Flakes
2 c. spring water

Wash, core and slice apples. Place in a pot with the liquids, tahini, salt, and agar. Mix well. Bring to a boil, reduce heat to low and simmer 2 to 3 minutes. Chill in a shallow bowl until almost hardened. Place cooled mixture in a blender and blend until smooth and creamy. Place custard back in serving bowl and chill once more before serving.

CHAROSES

Jewish Passover Ceremonial Food.

Made from apples, raisins and sweet wine to resemble the mortar used in laying the bricks for the pyramids. It also symbolizes the sweetness of freedom.

6 med. apples, chopped very fine
1/2 c. raisins

1/2 tsp. cinnamon
1/4 c. sweet wine
1/2 c. chopped nuts

Mix and serve.

BANANA-PINEAPPLE ICE CREAM

Fast weight loss.

4 lg. bananas, cut into chunks
4 oz. crushed pineapple, frozen &
   unsweetened (or any fruit you
   desire)

1 tsp. vanilla

Cut bananas into slices, Lay on cookie sheet and freeze. Pour pineapple into a bowl and freeze. Place the frozen fruit and vanilla in a blender. Blend, stopping the motor to stir frequently until the mixture is smooth. Serve at once. Serves 2.

CHOCOLATE BANANA ICE CREAM

1 c. apple juice concentrate
1 c. apple juice
3 tbsp. brown rice flour
1/2 c. carob powder

2 tbsp. tahini
2 tbsp. maple syrup
4 ripe bananas

Combine juice and concentrate in a saucepan. Blend in rice flour and carob powder. Bring to a boil, stirring constantly. Pour into blender or food processor and blend with remaining ingredients. Chill well and freeze. Remove from freezer and blend in food processor until smooth. Serves 8.

PUMPKIN ICE CREAM

1 pkg. unflavored gelatin
1/4 c. hot water
1 c. frozen orange juice
   concentrate
1 lb. can pumpkin

1/2 tsp. nutmeg
1/2 tsp. ginger
1/2 tsp. cinnamon
1/2 c. rice, nut or soy milk

Dissolve gelatin in hot water. Place orange juice, pumpkin and spices in blender, then add rice milk. Put in shallow freezer trays and freeze. Stir often to break up ice crystals. Serves 4 to 6.

ROCKY BANANA CREAM

10 med. ripe bananas   2 c. chopped, dried apricots

Blend bananas in blender until smooth. Fold in apricots. Turn mixture into a freezer container. Stir once when semi frozen, then freeze overnight to harden. Serve with slices of fresh fruit. Fresh strawberries, blueberries or raspberries can be substituted for apricots. Serves 6.

STRAWBERRY JUICE

1 c. apple juice   2 tbsp. tahini
1 c. frozen apple juice concentrate   2 tbsp. honey
2 tbsp. arrowroot   2 c. fresh strawberries
                                        2 tsp. vanilla

Combine juice and juice concentrate in a saucepan. Blend in arrowroot. Cook until thickened, stirring constantly. Place in blender or food processor and blend with remaining ingredients. Pour mixture into a shallow metal tray and freeze for 1 to 2 hours, until edges are firm but center is still slushy. Stir well and return to freezer until firm. Process in food processor or beat with an electric mixer until smooth. Serves 8.

APRICOT SORBET

1 lb. California fresh apricots   2 tsp. finely chopped, candied
  (about 2 1/2 c.), peeled &   ginger (opt.)
  sliced   1 c. water
2 tbsp. fresh lemon juice   1/2 c. apple juice concentrate
2 tbsp. rum or orange juice

Plunge whole apricots into a pan of boiling water, about 30 to 60 seconds. Remove to ice water. Peel and puree apricots. Stir in lemon juice. Add rum and ginger, as desired; set aside. Cook water and sugar over low heat, stirring occasionally. When sugar dissolves, bring to full boil over medium high heat; simmer about 5 minutes. Remove syrup from stove; chill. Combine syrup and apricot mixture. Freeze in ice cream maker according to manufacturer's instructions. Best served fresh. Makes 1 quart (8 servings).

STRAWBERRY SORBET

4 c. ripe strawberries, washed &
   hulled, plus 8 whole
   strawberries for garnish

1 c. apple juice concentrate
Juice of 2 oranges
1 tbsp. lemon juice

1. Place 4 cups of strawberries in a food processor or blender and process until pureed.

2. Transfer puree to a large bowl, add apple juice concentrate; orange and lemon juices and mix well.

3. Freeze and serve according to instructions in Raspberry Sorbet recipe.

4. Scoop sorbet into dessert dishes and garnish each serving with a whole strawberry. Makes 8 servings.

WATERMELON SORBET

Fast weight loss.

1 sm. watermelon
3 egg whites

Finely chopped mint

Scoop out watermelon, puree in blender and pour in ice cream trays and freeze. Remove from freezer and scoop out mixture and fold through egg whites until well combined. Refreeze until ready to serve. Remove from freezer to soften slightly before serving. Garnish with fresh mint. Serves 6.

PINEAPPLE BANANA SHERBET

1/2 c. orange juice
2 tbsp. fresh mint, plus
   additional for garnish
1 lg. ripe pineapple, peeled, cored
   & coarsely chopped

1 tbsp. fresh lime juice
2 tbsp. honey
1 lg. ripe banana

Blend orange juice and mint together in a blender until mint is very finely chopped or liquified. Blend in remaining ingredients except garnish, and puree until smooth. Pour into ice trays or a baking dish and freeze until just beginning to set. Remove from freezer and beat with an electric mixer or whisk to break up ice crystals. Place in freezer again and repeat once more when just beginning to set. Pack into a container and freeze. If frozen solid, let soften in refrigerator one hour before serving. Serve garnished with fresh mint. Serves 4.

PINEAPPLE SHERBET

Fast weight loss.
1 pineapple, sweet & ripe
1 pt. fresh strawberries, sliced

Fresh mint sprigs

Blend pineapple until smooth in blender. Pour into a freezer container and freeze semi-hard. Then stir well and fold in sliced strawberries. Freeze overnight. When serving, garnish with fresh mint. Serves 4.

BLUEBERRY HONEYDEW ICE

Fast weight loss.

4 c. honeydew melon   2 c. frozen blueberries

Combine the ingredients in blender and puree until smooth. Pour into a bowl or shallow pan. Place in freezer. Stir or beat the mixture every 15 minutes to break up ice crystals. Ready to serve in about 2 hours. Serves 8.

For a variation, blend 4 cups honeydew melon or cantaloupe with 2 cups orange juice, juice of 1 lemon, 2 cups crushed ice. Garnish with mint leaves.

PINEAPPLE-COCONUT TOFU DESSERT

1 c. tofu, whipped in blender   4 tbsp. frozen apple juice
1 c. diced fresh pineapple   concentrate
1 c. grated fresh coconut   1 tsp. vanilla

Combine all ingredients. Chill. Spoon into dessert dishes and garnish with kiwi fruit slices and fresh strawberries. Serves 4.

APRICOT MOUSSE

1 1/2 c. dried apricots   1 1/2 c. agar agar
Generous squeeze lemon juice   2 tbsp. undiluted soy milk or rice
1 1/3 c. orange juice   milk

Wash the apricots then cover them with boiling water and leave to soak overnight. Add lemon juice and cook the apricots gently 10 to 20 minutes or until tender. Set aside to cool; drain well then mash or puree. Put the orange juice in a saucepan and bring gently to a boil. Whisk in the agar agar and continue heating and whisking a few minutes. Combine the apricot puree with the orange juice, mixing well. Stir in enough soy milk to give the mixture a creamy color. Divide among 4 glasses and leave to cool then chill well before serving. Top with chopped nuts if desired. Serves 4.

BANANA MOUSSE

6 very ripe bananas
1 1/2 c. unsweetened applesauce

2 tbsp. carob powder
1/4 tsp. vanilla extract

Blend the applesauce and the bananas in a food processor using the steel blade. (Cut the bananas into quarters and add them to the blending applesauce one piece at a time.) Add carob powder and vanilla extract. Continue to blend until the mixture is smooth and all of the bananas have been blended with no chunks remaining. Spoon into individual dessert cups. Refrigerate for 30 minutes before serving. Serves 4.

FROZEN CHERRY MOUSSE

1 container Amazake rice milk
   (plain or almond)
1/2 c. frozen cherries
1/2 pkg. gelatin, softened in hot
   water

1 tbsp. apple juice concentrate
1 egg white
1/2 tsp. almond extract

Pour rice milk in a bowl and place in freezer. In food processor or blender, whip egg white with sweetener. Add frozen rice milk, cherries, gelatin and almond extract. Whip 1 minute. Transfer to serving dish. Freeze 1 hour before serving.

BROWN RICE PUDDING

1 c. cooked brown rice
2 egg whites
2 c. rice or nut milk

1/2 tsp. vanilla extract
1/2 c. raisins
1/2 tsp. cinnamon

In blender, mix milk, vanilla, egg whites and cinnamon. Spray 8"x10" glass baking dish with non stick spray. In a separate bowl, mix together brown rice, raisins and the blender mixture. Pour entire recipe into the baking dish; sprinkle with additional cinnamon and bake at 350 degrees for 35 to 40 minutes. Serve warm or cold.

DATE NUT BREAD PUDDING

1 1/3 c. fresh whole grain bread
   crumbs
1/4 c. wheat germ
1 c. chopped dates

1/4 c. chopped almonds &
   sunflower seeds
2/3 c. orange juice

Combine all dry ingredients. Add juice until mixture is moist but not soggy. Line a 9" pie pan with waxed paper and press mixture into pan. Cover loosely with wax paper, foil or plastic wrap and chill for several hours. To serve, lift wax paper with pudding from pan and slice into very thin wedges. This dessert is very rich so serve small portions.

RICE PUDDING

2/3 c. hot rice
1/4 c. cashews
2 tsp. vanilla

1/2 tsp. salt
3-4 soft dates
3 c. hot water

Just stir all together and eat. Delicious.

APPLESAUCE SOUFFLE

1 1/4 c. unsweetened applesauce
1/2 tsp. cinnamon

2 tsp. raisins
3 egg whites

Preheat oven to 350 degrees. Blend applesauce and cinnamon. Spoon 1 tablespoon of applesauce into bottom of each of 4 (6 ounce) cups. Top with raisins. Beat egg whites until stiff but not dry. Fold half into remaining applesauce and blend well. Fold remaining whites into applesauce very gently. Spoon into cups and sprinkle tops with cinnamon. Bake about 15 to 20 minutes, until puffed and brown. Serve immediately. Serves 4.

BAKED APPLE

1/2 c. cranberry juice
1/2 c. red wine
1 baking apple

1 tsp. apple juice concentrate
Pinch cinnamon
1 tbsp. raisins

Core apple and stand it bottom down in a baking dish. Sprinkle with sweetener and cinnamon, making sure some gets inside the apple. Stuff raisins into the center of the apple. Pour juice and wine into baking dish around apple. Bake, uncovered at 350 degrees for 20 to 25 minutes or until skin splits and the apple is tender.

BAKED BANANAS NEW ORLEANS

2 bananas, peeled
1 tsp. Butter Buds
3 tbsp. apple juice concentrate
1/2 c. orange juice
1 tsp. cinnamon

1/2 tsp. nutmeg or mace
3 tbsp. Grand Marnier or other
    orange liqueur (opt.)
3 tbsp. rum, dark preferred

Place bananas in small baking dish (cut in half if desired). Dot with Butter Buds and sprinkle with apple juice concentrate, cinnamon and nutmeg or mace. Pour orange juice over all. Bake lightly covered 15 minutes at 375 degrees or microwave approximately 4 minutes.

To serve, place bananas in dessert dishes. In medium ladle or dish, pour the liqueur and rum. Heat slowly over flame (while stove burner will do, a candle is more dramatic). Tip ladle slightly into fire or light with a match. Pour flaming liquid over the individual dishes. Serves 2.

FLAMING PINEAPPLE

Easy weight loss. Microwave.

1 pineapple, halved lengthwise
1 c. strawberries, sliced

1 c. melon balls
1/2 c. blueberries
1/4 c. light rum

Remove fruit in chunks from each pineapple half, leaving a 1/2" thick shell. Cut pineapple in cubes. In a large bowl, combine pineapple, strawberries, melon balls and blueberries. Fill pineapple halves with fruit mixture. Cover with wax paper. Microwave on full power for 4 minutes. In a 1 cup glass measure, microwave rum on full power for 25 seconds. Pour over fruit mixture, carefully ignite. Makes 10 servings.

BANANA AMBROSIA

1 lg. ripe yellow banana
1/4 c. pineapple or orange juice
1 lg. ripe papaya
1/4 c. vanilla rice dream or
 strawberry sorbet

1/2 tsp. vanilla extract
1/2 tsp. coconut extract
Pinch of powdered ginger
1 tbsp. sesame seeds or sesame
 tahini

Peel and mash banana with fork. Place in bowl and add juice. Cut papaya in half, scoop out and discard seeds. Scoop out papaya meat with spoon and add with rice dream or sorbet to bowl. Mix in seasonings. Stir until well mixed.

FRUIT AMBROSIA

Fast weight loss.

2 oranges, sectioned & cut
2 c. fresh pineapple, diced
2 bananas, sliced
2 nectarines, sliced

2 baskets fresh strawberries
1/2 c. shredded coconut
1/4 c. lemon juice

Peel the fruit, cut it up and toss very lightly in a bowl. Add the coconut and the lemon juice. Cover and chill. 8 servings.

FRUIT COMPOTE

2 tbsp. water
1 tbsp. honey
1 1/2 tbsp. lime juice
1 tsp. grated lime rind

1 c. cantaloupe balls
1/2 c. seedless green grapes, halved
1 kiwi fruit, peeled & coarsely chopped
Fresh mint

Combine honey and water in a small non-aluminum saucepan. Simmer over low heat until honey dissolves, stirring occasionally. Remove from heat and let cool. Add lime juice and rind. Combine fruit in a medium bowl; add lime syrup, tossing gently. Cover and chill 2 hours. Garnish with mint. Serves 2.

FRUIT KABOBS

Fast weight loss.
2 Spanish blood oranges, sm. navel oranges or mandarins
12 kumquats or seedless grapes
2 thick slices fresh pineapple

1 lg. ripe kiwi fruit
12 strawberries or pitted cherries
Watermelon, honeydew or cantaloupe, cut into 12 (1") cubes

Cut fruit into bite sized slices, cubes or wedges. Spear fruit on thin skewers. Stand spears in bowl or bucket of crushed ice or use a hollowed-out pineapple or watermelon filled with ice, to support the skewers. 12 servings, 1 skewer each. 40 calories per serving. 2 mg sodium.

GLAZED PEARS

4-6 ripe pears, cut in half
1 c. apple juice
1 tbsp. Erewhon Kuzu

Pinch of Instead of Salt
1/2 tsp. grated fresh ginger

Place pears in a baking dish facing up. Pour juice over the pears, cover the baking dish and cook in a 350 to 400 degree oven until soft. When done, drain the liquid from the pears into a small pot, add the kuzu dissolved in a little cold water and stir thoroughly. After 30 minutes add the salt and the ginger to the pot. Stir occasionally and cook until the mixture thickens and becomes transparent, usually only several minutes. Pour topping over the pears and bake for 15 minutes more until glazed. Be careful pears don't burn.

SUMMER FRUIT PARFAITS

1/2 c. sorbet or rice dream
2 peaches, sliced
1 tbsp. lemon juice

2 c. seedless grapes
1/2 c. blueberries

Toss peaches with lemon juice. In 4 wine glasses layer grapes, peaches and blueberries. Drizzle with sorbet or frozen rice dream. Serves 4.

WHIPPED CREAM SUBSTITUTE

1 c. cashews
2 c. water
2 tsp. cornstarch

1 tsp. vanilla
1 tbsp. honey
1 tsp. apple juice concentrate

Put cashews, water and cornstarch in a blender. Blend about 1 minute, until smooth. Place in saucepan, add the rest of the ingredients. Cook over medium heat until thickened, stirring constantly. Use as a topping on desserts.

WHIPPED TOFU CREAM

1 (8 oz.) container soft tofu,
   drained
1/4 c. maple syrup

2 tsp. vanilla extract
1 tsp. lemon rind
1 tsp. lemon juice

Place all ingredients in blender and whip for 5 minutes. Stir 4 or 5 times, then whip again for 5 minutes until creamy. Serves 4 to 6.

MONKEYS IN A BLANKET

1 slice whole grain bread
1/2 banana

1/2 tbsp. Butter Buds
Cinnamon
Honey

Preheat oven to 400 degrees. Roll bread flat with a rolling pin and trim crust. Spread with a thin layer of honey. Place banana on half of bread and wrap jelly roll fashion. Prepare Butter Buds. Allow 1 tablespoon for each whole banana. Roll bread-covered banana in Butter Buds, sprinkle with cinnamon and bake for 15 minutes until crust is crisp and banana is hot and creamy.

PEACH FROST

3 c. fresh peaches

3 c. fresh orange juice

Blend peaches, then blend with orange juice. Pour mixture in shallow freezer trays. Freeze until solid. Cut frozen mixture into strips and put through food grinder and blender. Serves 6.

VANILLA FRUIT CREAM

1 c. millet   2 c. water

Bring water to a boil, add millet and cook for 30 to 40 minutes.

1 c. raw cashew pieces, washed   1 tsp. salt
1 c. water   1/4 c. honey
                                                    4 tbsp. vanilla

Blend cashews in water until smooth. Blend in other ingredients and add millet until smooth. Refrigerate unused portions. Goes great on fruit or bread. Recipe by Country Life Restaurant.

CHERRY SOUP

2 pkgs. frozen and pitted sweet   8 tbsp. apple juice concentrate
   dark cherries   1/4 c. white wine
5 c. water

Place the cherries in a large pot along with the apple juice concentrate and water. Bring to a boil and simmer for about 15 to 20 minutes. Remove cherry (save the water) and puree them. Return pureed cherries to water and add the white wine. Serves 6.

EXTRA RECIPES

Main Dishes: Italian

EGGPLANT ITALIAN

1 eggplant, sliced 1/2" - 1" thick
(do not peel)
1 jar Johnson's Spaghetti Sauce
(no oil)

Mushrooms
1 tsp. garlic powder
Italian bread crumbs

Place some of the eggplant in the bottom of baking dish. Cover with some of the spaghetti sauce and sprinkle some of the garlic powder and mushrooms over sauce. Continue this layering process until pan is full. Sprinkle a coating of Italian bread crumbs on top. Bake in oven at 350 degrees for about 1 hour or until eggplant is tender.

FETTUCCINE WITH TOMATOES & WILD MUSHROOMS

1/2 c. Butter Buds
1/4 c. minced shallots
6 oz. fresh mushrooms, chopped
6 tomatoes, sliced

White pepper to taste
1 lb. whole wheat fettuccine
2-3 green onions, sliced

Place Butter Buds in skillet, add shallots and stir 1 minute over medium heat. Add mushrooms and tomatoes and stir 3 minutes. Season with pepper.

Cook fettuccine in a large pot of boiling water until just tender. Drain well. Transfer to a large bowl. Add mushrooms and tomatoes. Garnish with green onion and serve.

HOMEMADE MARINARA SAUCE

Fast weight loss.

5 tomatoes, chopped
2 (15 oz.) cans tomato sauce
1 can tomato paste
1 onion, chopped
3 cloves garlic, minced
1 sm. bell pepper, diced
12 mushrooms, sliced
2 carrots, sliced

2 sm. zucchini, sliced
1 tbsp. soy sauce
1/4 c. red cooking wine
2 bay leaves
1 tsp. black pepper
1/2 tbsp. basil
1/2 tbsp. oregano
1/4 tsp. sage

Add all the ingredients together (except for the dry herbs) into a large pot on the stove. Simmer for about 2 hours. Add the dry herbs and simmer for another 1 to 2 hours. Use sauce on spaghetti, in lasagna and with any other Italian dishes.

BAKED VEGETABLE ITALIANO

Fast weight loss.

1 lg. eggplant, peeled & diced
1 (9 oz.) pkg. French cut green
  beans
1 (16 oz.) can tomatoes, mashed

1 zucchini, sliced into rounds
1 clove garlic, minced
2 tsp. oregano

Combine vegetables in casserole dish. Stir in seasonings. Bake at 375 degrees for 30 to 40 minutes. Serves 6.

ITALIAN EGGPLANT CASSEROLE

4 oz. whole wheat spaghetti, broken into 2" pieces
1 lg. eggplant, peeled & cut into 1/2" cubes (6 c.)
1 med. onion, chopped
1 med. carrot, chopped
1 sm. zucchini, chopped

1 (4 1/2 oz.) can sodium reduced tomatoes
1 (6 oz.) can sodium reduced tomato paste
2 cloves garlic, minced
1 1/2 tsp. dried oregano, crushed
1 tsp. dried basil, crushed
1/2 tsp. pepper

Cook spaghetti according to directions; drain. Meanwhile, in a steamer basket place eggplant, onion, carrot and zucchini. In a Dutch oven place filled basket over, but not touching boiling water. Cover, reduce heat. Steam for 5 to 7 minutes or until vegetables are crisp-tender; remove from Dutch oven.

In a large mixing bowl, stir together steamed vegetables, undrained tomatoes, paste, garlic, basil, oregano and pepper. Spread 2 cups tomato mixture on the bottom of a 12" x 7 1/2" x 2" baking dish. Top with cooked spaghetti; sprinkle with Parmesan cheese if desired. Spoon remaining tomato mixture over top; sprinkle with a dash more Parmesan. Bake, uncovered in a 350 degree oven for 30 to 35 minutes or until bubbly. Serves 6.

ITALIANO ZUCCHINI

Fast weight loss.
1/2 c. onions, chopped
1/2 c. green bell peppers, chopped
3 celery stalks, chopped
1 clove garlic, minced
5 tomatoes, chopped

1 lg. zucchini, sliced into spears
1 tsp. Italian seasoning
Parsley sprigs
Non-stick spray for sauteing.

Place onions, peppers and celery in a pan (spray with non-stick) with garlic and saute. Add remaining ingredients and cook, covered until zucchini is done. Remove cover and evaporate tomato water. Serve with sprigs of parsley. Serves 4.

ITALIAN POTATO CASSEROLE

Fast weight loss.

5 lg. potatoes
1 lg. onion, sliced
4 c. fresh green beans
1 (28 oz.) can pureed tomatoes

2 cloves garlic, pressed
2 tsp. Italian seasoning
Freshly ground pepper

Chop potatoes into large chunks and place in large casserole dish with onion and green beans. Mix pureed tomatoes with garlic and seasoning; pour over vegetables. Add ground pepper if desired. Bake at 350 degrees for approximately 1 1/2 hours. Check potatoes with a fork for softness. Makes 4 to 6 servings.

LASAGNA

SAUCE:

1/2 med. onion, chopped
1 stalk celery, chopped
1 carrot, grated
1/2 green pepper, chopped
1/2 c. fresh mushrooms, chopped
2 tbsp. fresh parsley

1/2 tsp. basil
1 tsp. oregano
1/2 tsp. thyme
1/2 tsp. marjoram
1/2 tsp. onion powder
1 (28 oz.) can crushed tomatoes
    with added puree (Progresso)

Saute onion in 1/2 cup water. Add celery, carrots, green peppers, mushrooms and cook 5 minutes. Add herbs and onion powder. Then add the tomatoes. Simmer 10 to 15 minutes.

LASAGNA

Whole wheat or whole grain
   lasagna noodles (9-10, 12″
   strips), cooked
1 zucchini, med. sized, sliced thin

1/2 sm. eggplant, peeled & cut in
   half or quarters & sliced thin
1/2 - 3/4 c. frozen green peas

Spread a little sauce on the bottom of a shallow rectangular baking dish, 8″ x 11 1/2″. Cover with a third of the noodles. Spread one half of the zucchini, eggplant and peas over the noodles. Then spread with some (1/3) sauce. Repeat these layers. Cover with remaining noodles and sauce. Cover and bake for 45 minutes at 350 degrees. Remove the cover and bake for 10 to 15 minutes.

SPINACH LASAGNA

8 oz. uncooked lasagna noodles
1 eggplant, thinly sliced into
   rounds
1 c. spaghetti sauce (no oil)

1 lg. bunch fresh spinach, stems
   removed
1 tsp. oregano
1 1/2 c. fresh mushrooms, sliced
1 onion, chopped

Cook noodles, then remove from water immediately from water and separate. Spray 9"x14" baking dish with non-stick. Layer first with noodles, then layer of eggplant. Spread this 4 tablespoons of sauce. Then layer again with noodles and then layer with spinach. Sprinkle with oregano. Layer again with noodles, top with remaining sauce, mushrooms and onion. Sprinkle with Parmesan, if desired. Cover with foil and bake at 350 degrees for 45 minutes. Cut into squares, after allowing to cool. To serve, layer 2 squares together for thickness. Serves 4.

LENTIL SPROUT LASAGNA

1 (8 oz.) pkg. whole wheat
   lasagna
1 lg. eggplant, peeled, sliced thin

1 recipe Lentil Sprout Filling
1 (32 oz.) jar spaghetti sauce
   (meatless, sugarless)

Place sliced eggplant under broiler a few minutes, turning once. In baking dish alternate layers, beginning with whole wheat lasagna noodles, then eggplant, Lentil Sprout Filling and spaghetti sauce. Repeat once more. Heat in low heat oven (250 to 300 degrees) for 30 to 35 minutes or until warm. Makes large 9"x13" casserole.

LENTIL SPROUT FILLING:

3 c. lentil sprouts (1/2 c. dry
   lentils, sprouted for 3 days)

1 c. spaghetti sauce (meatless,
   sugarless, such as Ragu
   Natural or other brands found
   in health food stores)

Place lentil sprouts and spaghetti sauce in food processor with grinding blades. Mix lightly to resemble a meat filling.

PASTA

4 oz. Vegeroni
2 c. broccoli flowerets
1/2 c. spaghetti sauce (no oil)

1 tsp. sesame seed
1/8 tsp. garlic powder
1/8 tsp. pepper

In a large saucepan, cook broccoli and pasta in boiling water for 6 minutes or until tender; drain. Add the rest of the ingredients and serve. 4 servings.

PASTA LA MER

2 c. cooked whole wheat or
    vegetable shell macaroni
1 c. cooked wheat meat*
1/4 c. chopped celery
1/4 c. chopped green onions

1/4 c. frozen green peas (or fresh)
1/4 c. diced green bell or red bell
    pepper
1 tbsp. vinegar
1 tsp. low sodium Dijon mustard
Juice from 1 lemon
1 c. bean sprouts

Seitan Wheat Meat* is available ready made at certain health food stores. Toss all ingredients together in bowl. Chill before serving. Serves 4.

PASTA PRIMAVERA

1/2 c. peas
1/2 c. diced carrots
1/2 c. diced zucchini
1 lg. onion, diced (1 c.)
1 c. broccoli flowerettes, in sm.
   pieces

6 c. water (to boil pasta)
1/4 lb. spinach pasta shells (2 c.
   cooked)
1 c. chicken stock
2 tsp. cornstarch

Steam the vegetables until crisp-tender and set aside. Bring the water to a boil. Add the pasta, return to a boil and cook 8 to 10 minutes or until it has a slight resiliency (al dente). While the pasta is cooking, combine the chicken stock and cornstarch and stir until the cornstarch is completely dissolved. Bring to a boil. Reduce the heat and simmer, stirring constantly, until thickened; set aside. Drain the pasta thoroughly and put it in a large bowl. Pour the thickened chicken stock over the pasta and toss thoroughly. Add the steamed vegetables and again toss thoroughly. Divide into 4 servings (1 3/4 cups each).

PASTA WITH SAUCE

4 med. size zucchini
1/3 c. low sodium chicken stock, defatted
1 tbsp. low sodium soy sauce
1/2 med. size onion, thinly sliced
1 lg. red bell pepper, seeded & thinly sliced
1 (28 oz.) can unsalted peeled plum tomatoes, drained, seeded & coarsely chopped
1 tbsp. chopped fresh rosemary or 1 1/2 tsp. dried rosemary
2 tbsp. balsamic vinegar, or mild red wine vinegar
8 oz. whole wheat pasta, such as fusilli or rotelle

1. Cut each zucchini crosswise into 4 equal pieces, then cut each piece lengthwise into 6 to 8 wedges; set aside.

2. Bring a large pot of water to a boil.

3. For the sauce, heat 3 tablespoons stock and the soy sauce in a large non-stick skillet over medium heat. Add onion. Reduce heat to medium low, cover pan and cook for 3 minutes, or until onion is limp and slightly caramelized.

4. Add bell pepper and cook, covered for 2 minutes.

5. Add zucchini and remaining stock and cook, covered for 56 minutes more.

6. Meanwhile, in a large pot bring 2 cups water to a boil and add pasta. Bring back to a boil, turn heat off, cover pot with a lid and let sit for 20 minutes until al dente. While pasta is cooking, add tomatoes and rosemary to sauce and cook, uncovered, over low heat for 2 minutes. Stir in vinegar and cook for 2 minutes more.

7. Drain pasta and transfer to a large serving dish. Pour sauce over pasta and serve immediately. Makes 8 servings.

WHOLE WHEAT CRUST PIZZA

1 pkg. active dry yeast
1 1/2 c. warm water
2 tsp. dry basil
2 tsp. oregano
1/4 c. oat bran
1 1/2 c. whole wheat flour
1 1/2 c. all purpose flour
All purpose flour for kneading
1 lg. red onion
1 (15 oz.) can tomato sauce
1 (6 oz.) can tomato paste
1/2 c. red wine
2 zucchini, thinly sliced

1/2 green or red bell pepper, seeded & thinly sliced
4 green onions, including tops, thinly sliced
1 can sliced ripe olives
1 (14 oz.) can artichoke hearts, drained & quartered
1 c. diced Lifetime cheese (opt.)
4 tbsp. grated Parmesan cheese

In a large bowl dissolve yeast in water. Add 1 teaspoon basil and 1 teaspoon oregano, oat bran and all purpose flour. Beat until smooth, about 5 minutes, using an electric mixer. Using a wooden spoon, beat in whole wheat flour until dough holds together. Turn onto a lightly floured board and knead until dough is smooth and elastic, about 5 minutes. Turn over in a greased bowl, cover and let rise in a warm place until dough has doubled in size (about 45 minutes). Meanwhile, prepare tomato sauce.

TOMATO SAUCE: In a frying pan, saute the onion. Stir in tomato sauce, tomato paste, red wine, 1 teaspoon oregano and 1 teaspoon basil. Simmer, uncovered for 10 minutes.

Punch down dough and divide in half. Roll out each half to form a 14" circle, then transfer each circle onto a greased 14" pizza pan. One at a time, bake on next to bottom rack of a 450 degree oven for about 7 minutes, or until bottom of crust just starts to brown. During baking, watch carefully and prick any bubbles that form. Remove from oven and set aside.

To assemble pizza, spread tomato sauce over crust. Arrange zucchini, bell pepper, green onions, olives and artichoke quarters over sauce. Sprinkle Liteline cheese and Parmesan cheese over the top (optional).

Bake in a 450 degree oven for 12 to 15 minutes or until cheese melts. Cut hot pizzas in wedges to serve. Makes 2 pizzas; each serves 6.

PITA & VEGETABLE PIZZAS

Vegetable cooking spray (Pam)
1/2 c. chopped onion
1 clove garlic, minced
4 c. seeded & chopped tomatoes
  (about 3 lbs. whole tomatoes)
3 tbsp. red wine vinegar
2 tbsp. minced fresh basil leaves

2 tsp. dried whole oregano
1/4 tsp. pepper
3 (6") whole wheat pita bread
  rounds
3 oz. fresh mushrooms, thinly
  sliced
1 sm. zucchini, thinly sliced
1 med. yellow or green bell
  pepper, finely chopped

Coat a large, heavy pan with cooking spray. Saute onion and garlic until tender. Stir in tomatoes, vinegar, basil, oregano and pepper. Bring to a boil, reduce heat and simmer, uncovered 20 minutes or until sauce is reduced. Set aside. Cut slit around edge of each bread round; carefully split apart. Place split rounds on baking sheet; toast at 450 degrees for 5 minutes or until dry and beginning to brown. Spread 1/4 cup tomato sauce mixture evenly over each toasted round. Divide vegetables into 6 equal portions; arrange on top of toasted rounds. Bake at 450 degrees for about 10 minutes until vegetables are tender. Serves 6.

SPAGHETTI SQUASH

Fast weight loss.

1/2 spaghetti squash	1/4 tsp. pepper
1 c. grated zucchini	1/8 tsp. basil leaves
1 c. Ragu Garden Style spaghetti sauce with extra tomatoes & garlic or spaghetti sauce (no oil, no meat)	Dash of garlic powder

To Prepare: Cut squash in half lengthwise and clean out seeds.

Boiled: Place squash cut side down in a pot with 2″ of water. Cover and boil for 20 minutes.

In Microwave: Place squash cut side up in a dish with 1/4 cup water. Cover with clear wrap and cook 7 to 8 minutes. Run fork over inside of cooked squash to get spaghetti-like strands.

Scoop out spaghetti from 1/2 cooked squash. Add the other ingredients. Mix well and spoon back into empty squash. Sprinkle on 2 tablespoons grated Parmesan cheese and bake at 350 degrees for 20 minutes.

This exciting squash will separate into spaghetti-like lengths and have the texture of firm, cooked spaghetti. It has only 66 calories in an 8 ounce serving.

SPAGHETTI

6 oz. dry whole wheat spaghetti

SAUCE:

4 oz. tofu or seitans wheat meat	1 clove garlic, pressed
2 c. tomato sauce	1/2 tsp. basil
1/2 lb. mushrooms, thinly sliced	2 tbsp. chopped parsley
1/2 c. celery, thinly sliced	1 tbsp. chopped chives

Place tofu or wheat meat in a medium size saucepan. Using a fork, mash tofu into small chunks resembling cottage cheese. Add tomato sauce, mushrooms, celery, garlic and basil. Heat and stir until sauce is hot and mushrooms are cooked, about 5 to 10 minutes. Remove from heat and stir in parsley and chives. Keep warm.

To cook spaghetti boil water, add spaghetti, bring back to a boil, turn off heat, cover pan with lid and let sit for 20 minutes. Drain thoroughly and return to saucepan. Pour tomato sauce over and mix gently to coat spaghetti. Garnish with parsley sprigs.

SPAGHETTI SAUCE, TOMATO-LESS

Fast weight loss.

1/2 c. beets
4 stalks celery, sliced
4 carrots, sliced

1 green pepper, diced
1 c. warm water

Dice beets. Chop the best greens. Steam the beets, celery, carrots, green pepper, the best greens and warm water for 20 minutes or until tender.

Heat a pan, saute:

3 cloves garlic, minced
2 lg. onions, chopped

1/4 c. water
Pam spray

Add to vegetables and mash or puree in blender. Dissolve:

3 tbsp. dark miso

1/2 c. warm water

Add to vegetables with:

1/2 c. warm water
2 tbsp. tamari
2 tbsp. mirin*

1 tsp. oregano
1 tsp. basil
Pinch of cayenne

Simmer sauce 5 minutes. Serve over whole wheat spaghetti or buckwheat noodles. Per Serving: 130 calories; 4 gm protein; 14 gm carbohydrates; 2 gm fat.

*Mirin is a sauce found in the macrobiotic section of a health food store.

Main Dishes:
Mexican

BURRITOS

Whole wheat Chapati
Vegetarian refried beans
Sliced black olives

Chopped tomatoes, carrots,
celery, green onions, avocado,
lettuce, sprouts, etc.

Heat refried beans in 350 degree oven for 20 minutes. Spread onto chapati and sprinkle in vegetables. Yum. Favorite kids' treat.

BAKED BURRITOS WITH SPICY SAUCE

SAUCE:
1 onion, chopped
2 cloves garlic, pressed
1/2 c. water
1/3 c. chopped canned green
    chilies
2 tbsp. chili powder

1 tsp. cumin
1/2 tsp. ground coriander
1/2 tsp. cayenne
1 (8 oz.) can tomato sauce
1 (6 oz.) can tomato paste
3 1/2 c. water

FILLING:
1 onion, chopped
1 green pepper, chopped
3/4 lb. mushrooms, chopped
1/2 c. water
1 1/2 c. corn kernels

3 1/2 c. chopped zucchini
2 tsp. chili powder
1 tsp. ground cumin
12-15 whole wheat tortillas

To Make Sauce: Saute onion and garlic in 1/2 cup water for 5 minutes. Add green chilies and spices. Stir and saute a few more minutes. Add remaining ingredients. Mix well and simmer for 15 minutes; set aside.

To Make Filling: Saute onion, green peppers and mushrooms in water for 5 minutes. Add corn, zucchini and spices. Saute 10 minutes more; set aside.

To Assemble Burritos: Spread 1 cup of sauce on bottom of a baking dish. Place 1/3 to 1/2 cup filling down the center of each tortilla. Roll up tortillas and place seam side down in baking dish. Pour remaining sauce over burritos. Cover and bake at 350 degrees for 30 minutes. Serves 8 to 10.

BEAN DIP

1 (1 lb.) can kidney beans, well drained
1 (4 oz.) can diced green chilies, drained
2-3 tbsp. lime or lemon juice
1 lg. tomato, coarsely chopped

1/8 tsp. crushed red chili or 1/2 tsp. hot pepper sauce
2 tsp. Worcestershire sauce
2 cloves garlic
4 green onion tops. thinly sliced
12 corn or whole wheat tortillas

Drain beans thoroughly. Put all ingredients except green onions in a blender or food processor. Blend for 1 to 2 minutes, until smooth. Turn mixture into serving bowl and sprinkle with green onions. Serve immediately or chill. Makes 1 1/2 cups. 6 servings, 1/4 cup each. 48 calories per serving, 104 mg sodium.

TOASTED TORTILLA CHIPS: Use 12 corn tortillas or whole wheat flour tortillas (chapatis).

Preheat oven to 400 degrees. Cut each tortilla into 6 pie-shaped wedges. Spread half of the tortilla chips on a baking sheet. Bake in the preheated oven for 10 minutes. Remove from the oven, turn each tortilla chip over and return them to the oven for 3 more minutes. Remove from the baking sheet and let cool. Repeat with remaining tortilla chips.

GUACAMOLE

Fat free ole'.
1 can Anderson's Split Pea Soup
1 lg. tomato, chopped
1/4 med. onion, minced

1/4 tsp. garlic powder
1 tbsp. salsa
1/2 c. shredded lettuce
1/4 c. shredded cabbage

Blend all ingredients. Excellent on veggie tacos, tostadas, or dip with chips.

CORN TORTILLAS

2 c. masa harina   1 1/4 c. warm water

Mix masa flour with enough warm water to make dough hold together well. Using your hands, shape dough into a smooth ball. Divide dough into 12 equal pieces, then roll each into a ball.

Use two cloths which have been dipped in water and wrung dry. Flatten a ball of dough slightly and place between the cloths. Roll with rolling pin until cake is about 6" in diameter. Carefully pull back cloths, trim tortilla to a round shape and sandwich it between two squares of waxed paper.

Peel off top piece of waxed paper carefully. Turn over tortilla, paper side up, onto a preheated, ungreased medium-hot griddle, or into a heavy frying pan over medium heat. As tortilla becomes warm, you will be able to peel off remaining paper.

Bake for about 1 1/2 to 2 minutes, turning frequently, until tortilla looks dry. Makes 1 dozen.

CHILES RELLENOS

1 (7 oz.) can California green   8 egg whites
  chilies   Butter Buds
1 sliced zucchini   Sliced green onion tops
1/2 c. whole wheat flour

Drain canned chiles and cut a slit down side of each, gently remove seeds and pith. Stuff each chile with a slice of zucchini, about 1/2" wide, 1/2" thick and 1" shorter than the chile. Slightly lap cut edges to hold filling inside. Roll each chile in flour to coat all over; gently shake off excess.

Beat egg whites until they form soft peaks. Prepare one package Butter Buds and place in frying pan or omelet pan. Over medium heat, take about 1/2 cup of egg whites and place in frying pan. Quickly lay a stuffed chile in center of mound and spoon about 1/3 cup egg whites over top to encase chile. Cook for 2 to 3 minutes, gently turn and cook for 2 to 3 minutes longer. If you like, top with hot salsa and green onion tops. Serve immediately. Makes 3 to 4 servings.

CHILI BEANS I

If you are in a hurry, try this recipe. It is easy, delicious and an excellent source of soluble fiber. Serves 4.

1 (14 oz.) can kidney beans
2 c. salsa, Pace picante mild or
   your favorite

1 c. frozen corn

Blend all ingredients in a medium-sized saucepan. Heat to a boil, reduce heat, cover and cook for 6 to 10 minutes, until corn kernels are heated through. Each Serving: 0 mg cholesterol and 169 calories.

CHILI BEANS II

1 (29 oz.) can pinto beans
1 (27 oz.) can kidney beans
1 (15 oz.) can black eyed peas
1 (20 oz.) can tomato sauce
3 lg. tomatoes, chopped
1 onion, chopped

3 cloves garlic
1 med. green pepper
1 1/2 tbsp. chili powder
1 1/2 tbsp. cumin
1 1/2 tbsp. oregano
1 1/2 tbsp. paprika
1 tbsp. soy sauce

Add all ingredients together in large pot. Simmer for about 1 hour or until all ingredients are soft.

CHILI RANCH STYLE

8 oz. dry pinto beans
2 cloves garlic, minced
2 onions, chopped
4 oz. can green chilies, drained &
   chopped

2 jalapeno peppers, diced
28 oz. can tomatoes with liquid
1 tsp. oregano
Dash of Tabasco

Soak beans overnight. Cook about 1 hour until tender. Cook onions and garlic in small amount of water until tender. Add to beans with remaining ingredients and bring to a boil. Simmer one hour or until sauce reduces. Serves 4.

CHILI BEAN STUFFED PEPPERS

4 green bell peppers
2 c. cooked kidney beans
3 c. cooked brown rice
1 c. corn

2 tsp. chili powder
2 tbsp. chili salsa
1 c. tomato sauce

Wash peppers and cut off tops. Remove and discard seeds and pulp. Place in pot with cold water to cover, then bring to a boil, reduce heat and simmer for 5 minutes. Drain; the mix together remaining ingredients. Fill peppers with mixture, place into small baking dish and top with a mixture of salsa and tomato sauce. Cover and bake at 350 degrees for 45 minutes. Uncover and bake another 15 minutes more. Serves 4.

CHILI PIE

FILLING:

2 (15 oz.) cans kidney beans,
    drained
1 onion, chopped fine
1 green bell pepper, chopped fine
6 oz. tomato paste
1/4 c. water

1/2 c. red wine vinegar
2 tsp. chili powder
1 tbsp. low sodium soy sauce
1 c. canned corn, drained

Saute onions and pepper in small amount of water; add remaining ingredients and heat through.

CRUST:

3/4 c. cornmeal
1/4 c. whole wheat flour

1/2 c. water
1 egg white

Let water and egg white sit until they are at room temperature, then mix together. Preheat oven to 375 degrees; combine egg white and water with dry ingredients. Form a ball with dough and place into pie pan sprayed with non-stick spray. Flatten dough with fingers and form into shape of pie crust. Add filling and bake for 35 to 40 minutes or until crust is light brown. Serves 6 to 8.

ENCHILADAS

Leftover or available beans, vegetables, sprouts, potatoes
6 corn tortillas or desired quantity

Las Palmas green enchilada sauce (lg. can) or favorite sauce

Wrap corn tortillas in napkin and place in microwave for 2 minutes or until soft.

One by one fill tortillas with desired filling and form enchilada, place each one in a Pyrex baking dish. (Enchilada can be large or small depending on filling.) Pour desired sauce over enchiladas and return to microwave for heating or heat in oven at 250 degrees for 30 minutes.

ENCHILADA PIE

1 (16 oz.) pkg. dried pinto beans
1 (16 oz.) pkg. dried lentils
2 pkgs. corn tortillas
3 (10 oz.) cans Rosarita enchilada sauce
1 (29 oz.) can tomato sauce

1 (29 oz.) can tomato puree
4 tbsp. onion flakes
1/2 tsp. cayenne pepper
1 sm. can Ortega green chilies (mild)

Soak pinto beans overnight. Cook several hours until tender. Add lentils the last 3/4 hour of cooking. Layer all ingredients in a large baking pan; start with sauce and end with sauce. Bake at 350 degrees for 1 1/2 hours.

ENCHILADA BEAN CASSEROLE

6 c. enchilada sauce (see recipe
  below) or use Rosarita
  Enchilada Sauce
12 corn tortillas
4 c. cooked & mashed pinto beans
  or Rosarita Vegetarian Refried
  beans

3 c. brown rice
1 1/2 c. chopped green onions
3/4 c. chopped black olives

Spread 2 cups of sauce over the bottom of an oblong baking dish. Set aside. Place 1/2 cup beans and some rice, onions and olive sin the center of each tortilla. Repeat until all ingredients are used. Roll up tortillas and place seam side down in baking dish. Pour remaining sauce over the rolled tortillas. Cover and bake at 350 degrees for 30 minutes. Serves 6 to 8.

ENCHILADA SAUCE:

3 c. tomato sauce
3 c. water
1/2 tsp. garlic powder

1/2 tsp. onion powder
3 tbsp. chili powder
5 tbsp. cornstarch

Combine all ingredients in a saucepan. Cook, stirring constantly until mixture boils and thickens. Makes 6 cups.

MEXICAN PASTA BAKE

1 med. onion, chopped
1 clove garlic, chopped
1/4 tsp. cayenne
1 tbsp. chili powder
1 qt. undrained canned tomatoes
1 tsp. oregano
1/2 tsp. cumin

1 c. uncooked whole wheat elbow
 macaroni
1 1/2 c. corn kernels
3 c. cooked pinto beans
1/3 c. sliced olives
1 c. (5) broken corn tortillas
1 c. sliced Lifetime cheese

Saute onion and garlic for 3 minutes to soften. Add cayenne and chili powder and cook briefly. Add tomatoes, oregano and cumin and bring to a boil. Add pasta and corn and simmer, uncovered, for 15 minutes until pasta is just tender. Stir in beans and olives. Preheat oven to 325 degrees. Transfer bean mixture to a shallow 2 quart casserole. Bake for 10 minutes to melt cheese. If casserole is assembled in advance of baking and chilled, increase baking time to approximately 20 minutes, or until heated through. Serves 6.

PEPPERS AND CORN

Fast weight loss.

2 c. canned corn
1 can green chilies, chopped
2 green peppers, chopped

2 onions, chopped
4 lg. tomatoes, chopped
1/8 tsp. cayenne pepper

Combine all ingredients in a non-stick skillet adding 1/4 cup water to saute until vegetables are tender. Serve over brown rice. Serves 6.

POLENTA PIE

CRUST:
1 c. cornmeal
1/2 tsp. sage
1/4 tsp. cumin

1/2 tsp. chili powder
4 c. cold water

FILLING:
1 onion, chopped
1 clove garlic, pressed
1/2 lb. mushrooms, sliced
1 eggplant, diced
2 c. tomato sauce

6 oz. tomato paste
1 bay leaf
1/2 tsp. basil
1 tsp. oregano

Combine cornmeal, sage, cumin and chili powder in a saucepan. Stir in the cold water. Cook, stirring constantly until very thick. Pour into a non-stick oblong baking dish. Bake at 425 degrees for 30 minutes. Remove from oven and let cool for 30 minutes. In the meantime, saute onion, garlic, mushrooms and eggplant in 1/2 cup water for 10 minutes. Add remaining ingredients and simmer 20 minutes. Spoon this mixture over the cornmeal crust. Bake at 350 degrees for 30 minutes. Serves 3 to 4.

SPANISH RICE

1/2 c. celery, chopped
1 med. onion, thinly sliced
1/2 med. green pepper, chopped
1 c. brown rice, uncooked
2 tbsp. Ortega Taco Sauce (mild)
   or Pace Picante (mild)

3 (8 oz.) cans tomato sauce
3/4 c. hot water
1 tbsp. garlic powder
Dash of oregano and paprika

Heat water in skillet. Add the onions, green peppers, celery and rice. Stir over high heat until lightly browned. Add the tomato sauce and the remaining ingredients. Bring to a boil. Cover tightly and simmer 25 minutes.

SPANISH RICE & VEGETABLES

2 heads cauliflower, separated
  into flowerettes
2 lg. bell peppers, diced
4 lg. stalks celery, diced
3 tbsp. (or to taste) chili powder

4 tbsp. onion flakes
1 (46 oz.) can tomato juice
1 clove minced garlic
Salt to taste

Place all ingredients in a large pot. Bring to a boil. Simmer over low heat until cauliflower becomes tender. Mash with a potato masher until the cauliflower breaks into small rice-like pieces. Continue to simmer until mixture is the consistency of Spanish rice.

TAMALE PIE

CORNMEAL CRUST:
2 1/2 c. cold water
1/2 tsp. chili powder

1 1/4 c. yellow cornmeal

Combine all ingredients in a saucepan over medium heat. Cook until quite thick and stiff, about 10 minutes, stirring frequently. Set aside 3/4 cup. Line sides and bottom of 1 1/2 quart casserole with the rest of the mixture.

TAMALE PIE FILLING:
1 3/4 c. Dennison's chili beans
1/2 c. chopped green pepper

1/2 c. drained, sliced ripe olives
(2 1/4 oz. can)

Combine all ingredients in a saucepan over medium heat. Heat until hot. Pour into casserole. Top with rounded tablespoons of remaining crust. Bake in a moderate oven, 350 degrees, for about 25 minuets.

TAMALES PRONTO

2 c. masa harina
1 1/4 c. chicken broth
2 c. cooked corn
1/2 c. pitted olives, chopped

1/2 c. canned green chili salsa
1 med. onion, chopped
Foil

Cut 30 pieces of foil, each 6" square. Stir together masa flour and chicken broth to make a thick paste. Place about 1 1/2 tablespoons of the paste on each foil square and spread in center of foil in a 3" square.

Mix together corn, olives, onion and salsa. Place about 1 1/2 tablespoons of filling down center of each masa square. Fold foil edges together so masa edges meet, then seal all sides.

Arrange tamales in a kettle with a rack placed on the bottom, so that the tamales are not in the water. Add about 1" of water, cover and and steam about 45 minutes. About 6 servings.

TOFU TACOS

1 onion, diced
1 green bell pepper, diced
1 tsp. paprika
Water for sauteeing
1 lb. firm tofu, cut into chunks or
    seitans wheat meat

2 tbsp. flour
2 tbsp. tomato puree
Dash of Tabasco
6 taco shells

In a large frying pan, saute onion, bell pepper and paprika in a small amount of water for 3 to 5 minutes. Crumble tofu into small pieces and add to pan, saute for several minutes. Add two tablespoons of water, tomato puree. Cook until mixture is heated thoroughly. Remove from heat. Stuff taco shells with mixer. Serves 6.

BEAN TACO

2 wheat flour or corn tortillas
Vegetarian refried beans, heated
Salsa

Sliced black olives
Sliced green onions
Chopped tomatoes

Lightly brown tortillas in a 400 degree oven on both sides. Top tortillas with remaining ingredients in the order listed (tomatoes may either be added after or baked with other ingredients).

SOFT VEGGIE TACOS

An easy to fix lunch for little ones at home. Yield: 10 tacos. Have ready:

2 c. cooked brown rice
2 c. chopped Bibb or Boston
  lettuce
10 tortillas (yellow or blue corn)

1 sm. can black olives, chopped
1 chopped tomato
1 cucumber, thinly sliced

ADDITIONAL OPTIONS:

1/2 c. grated jicama
1/2 c. grated zucchini

1/4 c. grated carrots
1/2 c. sprouted sunflower seeds

Sprinkle rice with a dash of tamari, mix with chopped olives. Warm tortillas in microwave or on stove one at a time and fill with a few slices of cucumber, some rice, lettuce, veggies, tomatoes and top with taco sauce. Per Taco: 119 Calories, 3 gm Carbohydrates; 3 gm Fat.

TOSTADAS

12 corn tortillas
2 c. pinto beans (or Del Monte
 burrito filling or Rosarita
 Vegetarian beans)

1/4 head lettuce, shredded
2 tomatoes, diced
1/2 onion
Salsa, your favorite
garlic powder, as desired

Soak pinto beans overnight in water, then cook several hours; add water as needed. Cook beans about 4 hours until tender. Add garlic powder. Mash or blend the beans. Place corn tortillas on cookie sheet and bake at 400 degrees until hard and crispy, about 10 minutes. Spread beans on top of tortillas, then add lettuce, tomatoes, onions and salsa.

SALSA

Fast weight loss. Yield; 2 cups.

4 fresh, red ripe medium sized
 tomatoes
1/4 c. diced onion
1/4 c. fresh lemon juice

3 whole mild green chilies, diced
 or fresh green chili pepper
 (jalapeno or serrano) to your
 taste
1 clove garlic, minced
2 tbsp. fresh cilantro, minced

With food processor, cut tomatoes in 4 parts and place in processor with remaining ingredients. Chop, using an on-off motion (pulse) until desired consistency. By hand, mince all ingredients and combine in a bowl. Chill 1 hour before serving. Makes 2 cups.

SALSA FRESCA

Fast weight loss.

4 med. tomatoes, minced
1/2 sm. onion, minced
8 sprigs cilantro, minced

2 serrano or jalapeno peppers,
  diced
1/3 c. red wine vinegar
1/2 c. water

Mix all ingredients and serve or chill first and serve. Best when served very fresh, but will keep for 2 days in refrigerator. Yield: 2 cups.

SANTA FE SALSA

Fast weight loss.

1 c. finely chopped tomato
1/2 c. finely chopped purple
  onion
1 (4 oz.) can chopped green
  chilies, drained

1 lg. clove garlic, minced
1/8 tsp. Mrs. Dash Extra Spicy
  Seasoning

Mix all ingredients and serve. Yield: about 2 cups.

SALSA VERDE GREEN I

Fast weight loss

1/2 lb. fresh tomatillos (Mexican
  green tomato)
4-6 cloves garlic
1 c. fresh cilantro leaves

1 tbsp. fresh green chile or
  pickled jalapeno pepper

Remove brown husks from tomatillos. Wash thoroughly and cut into chunks. Place all ingredients in a blender or food processor and chop finely but do not liquify. Makes 1 cup. Serving Size: 1 tablespoon. 7 calories, 3 mg sodium.

SALSA VERDE GREEN II

Fast weight loss.

1 lb. tomatillos	2 tsp. minced jalapeno
1 chopped onion	1 c. chicken stock
1 chopped green onion	Salt & pepper to taste

Saute onion in large skillet until soft. Cook tomatillos in boiling salted water for 2 to 3 minutes, then puree in blender. Add green onions to skillet just before regular onions are ready. Combine all ingredients in a saucepan and simmer for 20 minutes. Serve at room temperature.

EXTRA RECIPES

Main Dishes: Oriental

CHINESE BROCCOLI, CAULIFLOWER & ALMONDS

4 tbsp. dry sherry
2 tbsp. soy sauce
2 cloves garlic, minced
3 c. broccoli, cut into bite sized
  pieces

3 c. cauliflower, cut into bite-
  sized pieces
1/2 c. chopped almonds

Saute garlic in a large skillet or wok, using water in place of oil. Add the sherry and soy sauce. Turn the heat to moderate and add the broccoli and cauliflower. Stir quickly to coat the veggies with the liquid. Stir-fry just until the pieces are well distributed. Serve as soon as possible.   4 servings. Top with almonds.

CHINESE EGGPLANT

Fast weight loss. Serves 6.

4 med. long eggplants
4 cloves garlic, crushed
1 thumb-size piece gingerroot
2 stalks green onions

3 tbsp. low sodium soy sauce
1/4 tsp. crushed red chili pepper
  (opt.)

Cut eggplant into 1/4″ x 1″ pieces. Cook in a small amount of boiling water until almost done, 5 to 8 minutes. Drain.

CHINESE FRIED RICE WITHOUT OIL

1/2 c. chicken broth
3 tbsp. sesame seeds
1 c. thinly sliced carrots
1 onion, sliced
2 cloves garlic, minced
1 green pepper, cut into strips

1 c. zucchini, sliced
1 c. mushrooms, sliced
2 c. bean sprouts
1 c. cooked brown rice
1 tsp. ginger
1/4 c. soy sauce
3 tbsp. cilantro, chopped

Heat chicken broth in wok. Add carrots and stir-fry for 1 minute over high heat. Mix in onion, garlic and green pepper and stir-fry for 1 more minute. Add zucchini and mushrooms and stir-fry until all vegetables are tender-crisp (about 2 more minutes). Mix in bean sprouts and rice and cook until heated through.

In a small bowl mix ginger with soy, blend into rice mixture. Serve immediately, sprinkled with cilantro and sesame seeds. 4 servings.

CHINESE SPICY VEGETABLES

Fast weight loss. 4 servings.

VEGETABLES:
1 onion, cut in half & sliced
1 c. celery, sliced
1 1/2 c. chopped broccoli
1/2 c. Chinese peas

1/2 lb. mushrooms, thinly sliced
2 c. chopped Chinese cabbage
1 c. bean sprouts

SAUCE:
4 tbsp. low sodium soy sauce
2 tbsp. cider vinegar
2 cloves garlic, crushed
3 tbsp. chopped fresh coriander

1 1/2 tbsp. cornstarch or
   arrowroot
1/4 tsp. grated fresh gingerroot
1/4 tsp. crushed red pepper

Mix sauce ingredients together. Set aside. Saute onions and celery in a small amount of water for 5 minutes. Add broccoli and Chinese cabbage, cook and stir for 5 more minutes. Add mushrooms. Cook and stir until soft, 5 minutes. Add bean sprouts. Stir in sauce. Heat through. Use to fill pita bread.

CHOP SUEY

Microwave.

2 c. wheat meat
1 c. chopped onion
1 tsp. instant beef bouillon
1 c. boiling water
2 tbsp. cornstarch
1/4 c. soy sauce
1/4 tsp. ginger

1 (4 oz.) can sliced mushrooms
1 (8 oz.) can bamboo shoots
1 (8 oz.) can water chestnuts
1 (16 oz.) can bean sprouts

Place wheat meat and onion in 2 quart casserole. Cook on Full power for 3 minutes; drain.

Combine bouillon and boiling water. Gradually stir into cornstarch. Add soy sauce and ginger. Pour over wheat meat. Cook on Full power for 6 minutes. Add remaining ingredients. Cook on Full power for 3 minutes. Serve over rice.

RAW CHOP SUEY

2 med. heads bok choy
2 lg. heads napa
2 c. broccoli florets
1/4 c. minced parsley
1/4 c. chopped watercress
4 tbsp. lime juice
3 tbsp. soy sauce or tamari
3 sheets nori, crumbled
3 c. red bell pepper strips

4 stalks celery, trimmed &
   chopped
1 c. sliced mushrooms (opt.)
1 1/2 c. mung bean sprouts
Cherry tomatoes for garnish

Cut off and discard the base ends of each head of bok choy and napa. Shred bok choy and napa in a food processor, using the medium shredding disk; place in large bowl. Add broccoli, parsley and watercress; set aside.

Puree lime juice, soy sauce or tamari, and nori in a food processor, using the metal "S" blade. Add to bok choy mixture. Stir in remaining ingredients except cherry tomatoes and mix well. Place in a serving bowl and top with a circle of cherry tomatoes. Serves 4.

Per Serving: 217 calories; 20 g protein; 2 g fat; 37 g carbohydrates; 0 cholesterol; 87 mg sodium.

CHOW MEIN

3 onions, chopped
1 c. sliced mushrooms
3 c. cooked celery
2 c. chicken broth
2 tsp. soy sauce

2 tsp. cornstarch
Water
1 c. mung bean sprouts
4 c. cooked brown rice

Put a little water in a skillet and saute the onions until cooked. Add the mushrooms and celery and cook a little more. Stir in the broth and soy sauce and bring to a boil. Mix the arrowroot with a little water until smooth and pour into the onion mixture. Add the sprouts. Serve over brown rice. 4 servings.

ORIENTAL NOODLES

1 pkg. brown rice ramen	1 red or green bell pepper, sliced
1 lb. broccoli	1/4 lb. mushrooms, sliced
1 clove garlic, minced	1 lb. tofu, drained & cut into
1 onion, chopped	cubes
2 stalks celery, chopped	3/4 c. chicken broth
2 carrots, sliced	

Cut off broccoli flowerets, peel off and discard tough outside layer of stalks, then cut stalks into 1/4" thick slices. Slice large broccoli flowerets in half or thirds lengthwise. Cook noodles, according to package directions; drain well.

Place other ingredients in work. Stir-fry on high heat for 5 to 6 minutes, until veggies are crisp-tender. Serve over noodles. 4 servings.

ORIENTAL RICE

2 tsp. minced ginger	1 c. diced bell pepper
2 lg. cloves garlic, minced	1 c. diced carrots
1/2 c. defatted chicken stock	1 1/4 c. sliced water chestnuts
3 tbsp. reduced sodium soy sauce	4 c. cooked brown rice
3 c. sliced mushrooms	1 c. chopped green onions
2 c. sliced bok choy	1 1/2 tsp. sesame seeds, toasted

1. Saute ginger and garlic in 1/4 cup chicken stock and soy sauce.

2. Add mushrooms, bok choy, bell pepper, carrots, water chestnuts and rice. Cook until vegetables are tender, adding more chicken stock as needed.

3. Add green onion and sesame seeds. Makes 10 servings. Each 1 cup serving contains 120 calories, 7% fat, 173 mg sodium and 0 mg cholesterol.

ORIENTAL STIR-FRY WITH BROWN RICE

1 (6 oz.) pkg. frozen Chinese pea
   pods
1 (16 oz.) pkg. frozen vegetables
   orient

1 (14 oz.) pkg. fresh chop suey
   mix
Parsley Patch oriental blend (no
   salt, no MSG, no sugar)

Spray a non stick pan, stir-fry the above ingredients in a large skillet over medium heat until lightly brown. Add about 1 cup cooked brown rice, stir in and blend well. Sprinkle with Oriental Blend seasoning to taste.

VEGETABLES ORIENTAL

Fast weight loss.

2 c. sliced celery
1 c. onion, sliced
1 c. sliced mushrooms
1 lb. broccoli, sliced
1/2 c. sliced water chestnuts

Water for sauteing
1 c. water
1 1/2 tsp. low-sodium soy sauce
3 tbsp. cornstarch dissolved in 3
   tbsp. water

Stir-fry vegetables in a small amount of water for about 5 minutes. Add 1 cup water and soy sauce, bring to a boil. Add cornstarch to vegetable mixture and combine thoroughly. Cook until sauce thickens. Serves 8.

MEE KROB

1 lb. rice vermicelli
1 lg. onion, finely chopped
4 cloves garlic, finely chopped
6 dried Chinese mushrooms,
    soaked & finely sliced
2 sm. fresh chilies, seeded &
    sliced

3 tbsp. soy sauce
Juice of 2 limes
2 tbsp. rice vinegar
5 tbsp. apple juice concentrate
4 egg whites
Handful of bean sprouts
6 green onions, finely chopped
4 tbsp. fresh coriander, chopped

Boil the noodles in water until tender. Saute the onions and garlic in a little water. Add the mushrooms and chilies. Reduce heat. In a separate bowl mix the egg whites, soy sauce, lime juice, vinegar and apple juice concentrate. Add this to mixture and simmer until it becomes thicker. Add the bean sprouts, noodles, green onion and coriander. Heat the combination through.

NAM PRIK (THAI)

Choose an assortment of vegetables, i.e. carrot sticks, cucumber rounds, green pepper strips, whole green onions - and arrange on a tray around the chili sauce.

1/2 c. shredded green apple
2 tbsp. chopped canned green
    chilies
2 tsp. apple juice concentrate

1/2 tsp. anchovy paste
1 tsp. grated lime peel
2 tbsp. lime juice
2 tbsp. green onion

Combine all ingredients in a small dish. 1/2 cup servings.

SWEET AND HOT CHILI SAUCE - SAUS PRIK

Yield: 3 1/2 cups, approximately.

Saus Prik is my attempt to re-create the marvelous, hot sauce served in so many Thai restaurants. Similar sauces may be purchased bottled and labeled "All Purpose Sauce". They are also sweet-hot and garlicky but lack the personality of homemade. It is interesting to experiment and find you own application. This recipe yields 3 1/2 cups and will noticeably become more spicy with age.

1 1/2 c. seedless golden raisins
5 tbsp. white vinegar
3 tsp. red chili flakes
8 cloves garlic
1 tsp. Instead of Salt

2 fresh red chili peppers, seeded
   & sliced
1 c. whole canned tomatoes, with
   juice
12 oz. Red Plum jam
9 oz. pineapple juice
4 tbsp. apple juice concentrate

Place the first seven ingredients in a food processor or blender and blend to an even consistency. This will take several minutes and require stopping occasionally to scrape down the sides. Place the remaining ingredients in a saucepan over medium heat. Pour the blended ingredients in the saucepan. While stirring, let this mixture come to a boil. Reduce heat to simmer and cook for 20 more minutes. Store in airtight, sterilized jars. It will keep for at least 2 months, refrigerated.

SUKIYAKI

Microwave.

1/2 lb. wheat meat
1 (8 oz.) can bamboo shoots
1 (8 oz.) can water chestnuts
1 (16 oz.) can bean sprouts
1/2 lb. fresh mushrooms, sliced

1 med. onion, sliced
3 stalks celery, sliced
3 tbsp. apple juice concentrate
1/3 c. soy sauce
1/2 c. beef bouillon

Slice wheat meat into very thin pieces. Place in 2 quart casserole. Cook on Full power for 4 minutes. Add vegetables to skillet. Combine apple juice concentrate, soy sauce and bouillon. Pour over vegetables. Cook on Full power for 6 minutes.

NORI MAKI SUSHI

1 c. short grain brown rice
2 c. water
4 sheets dried nori

1/2 tsp. Instead of Salt
2-4 tbsp. rice vinegar
2 tsp. honey

FILLING INGREDIENTS

Choose three for each roll:
Grated raw carrot or jicama
Cooked chopped spinach
Toasted sesame seeds
Strips of scallion, bell pepper,
   celery, omelette, lightly
   steamed asparagus, carrot or
   green beans

Pickled umeboshi plum (use just
   a bit)
Avocado
Chopped watercress
Mushrooms

CONDIMENTS:
Shoyu, sweet-and-hot mustard   Pickled ginger

The outside wrapper nori, is made from seaweed. It has best flavor when freshly toasted and eaten soon after.

If you want to include mushrooms, shitakes are traditional, but normal ones work too, sauteed and cut in strips. If you do come upon some dried shitakes, soak several in water, then simmer in 2 teaspoons each shoyu and sherry. Chop fine or cut into strips.

Cook rice uncovered in boiling water for five minutes, then cover and reduce heat to low. Simmer for 45 minutes.

While the rice is cooking, select and prepare your choice of fillings. You'll be making four rolls, it's fun to vary the fillings in each. Combine about three of the suggested ingredients in each.

Unless the nori sheets you have are pre-toasted, wave each one over a flame (a gas burner is ideal), holding it with tongs or fingertips, so that each sheet changes color and texture slightly, becoming light and coarser.

Dissolve Instead of Salt in rice vinegar in a small saucepan and add honey; heat gently to liquify. When the rice is cooked, turn it out onto a large platter or baking dish with sides. Pour the vinegar mixture over it, stirring as you do, and fanning the steam away, a folded newspaper works nicely. When the rice has cooled to room temperature, it is ready.

For rolling the sushi, a traditional bamboo mat is great, but not essential; a big cloth napkin works fine, just a little bigger than the nori sheets. Place the mat or cloth flat in front of you and put the first sheet of nori on it. Moisten your fingers with water or vinegar and spread one-fourth of the seasoned rice on the mat, covering it except for an inch or two at the top, which you'll use to seal the roll.

The rice should be not quite 1/2" thick. Across the middle, parallel to the top, form an indentation and place the filling materials there, forming a thin line from one end to the other. For example: a strip of omelette, a line of chopped watercress, and strips of red bell pepper. Aim for beauty and harmony too.

Grasping the nearest side of the mat, roll it up and away from you toward the top, pressing the whole thing together tightly and pushing the filling ingredients into place if necessary. Dampen the remaining "flap" of nori and seal the roll by pressing the flap along the length of the roll. Place the roll on a cutting board and slice it with a very sharp knife into 1" segments. Arrange cut-side up and serve. Makes about 6 servings.

SWEET AND SOUR SOYBEANS

1 onion, chopped
2 carrots, sliced
1 clove garlic, minced
1 green pepper, chopped
2 tomatoes, sliced
2 1/2 c. cooked soy beans
3/4 c. canned pineapple chunks

1 1/2 tbsp. cornstarch
1 1/2 tbsp. soy sauce
1 1/2 tbsp. sherry
1/2 c. apple juice concentrate
1/2 c. wine vinegar
1/3 c. chicken broth

Saute onion, carrots and garlic. Add green pepper and cook about 1 minute longer. Add pineapple, tomatoes and soy beans and cook for 2 more minutes.

In a bowl, combine cornstarch, soy sauce, sherry, apple juice concentrate, wine vinegar and chicken broth. Pour on top of beans and cook until sauce bubbles and thickens. 6 servings.

SWEET AND SOUR LENTILS WITH BROWN RICE

1/2 c. dry lentils
3 c. water
2 tbsp. vinegar
2 tbsp. honey
1 tbsp. soy sauce
1/2 tsp. grated fresh ginger or 1
   tsp. ground ginger

1/2 c. water
1 tsp. arrowroot or cornstarch
1 sm. onion, sliced
Cooking spray (Pam)
4-5 stalks celery, diagonally
   sliced

To cook lentils, bring water to a boil, then reduce heat and cook about 25 minutes or until tender. Do not overcook. Drain and set aside.

To make sweet and sour sauce, combine next four ingredients and 1/2 cup water in a small saucepan. Bring to a boil. Put arrowroot or cornstarch in a small glass and add a little water. Mix thoroughly and add to boiling water to thicken it. Saute onion in large frying pan lightly sprayed with Pam. When onion is soft, add pieces of celery and cook 5 minutes more over medium heat. Drain cooked lentils and add to frying pan; mix well. Pour sweet and sour sauce into pan and cook for 5 minutes. Serve over a bed of brown rice.

STIR-FRY RECIPE

Fast weight loss.

1/2 c. chicken stock
1/2 sm. onion, chopped
1 clove garlic, minced
4 carrots, sliced or grated
4 celery stalks, chopped
1/2 head cabbage

1/4 green pepper, diced
4 c. bean sprouts
12 lg. mushrooms, chopped
1 bunch scallions, chopped
1 can water chestnuts, sliced

Heat the stock. Add onion and garlic. Stir-fry 1 to 2 minutes. Add the carrots and celery. Stir them quickly to seal in the juices. When these are about half done, add in the cabbage and green pepper. When these veggies are nearly cooked, add in the bean sprouts, mushrooms, scallions and water chestnuts. Stir continuously, until all the veggies are tender-crisp.

SAUCE FOR STIR-FRY VEGETABLES:
1 clove garlic, minced
1 1/2 c. chicken stock
3 tbsp. soy sauce

1/2 tsp. ginger
2 1/2 tbsp. cornstarch

Saute the garlic over low heat. Pour the stock over the garlic and add the soy sauce, sherry and ginger. Turn the heat to medium. Dissolve the cornstarch in a little cold water. Add the cornstarch. Let the sauce boil slowly until it has thickened, stirring almost continuously. Pour this over the stir-fry veggies when they are done and serve over brown rice.

SWEET & SOUR STIR-FRIED VEGETABLES WITH TOFU

1/2 lb. tofu or seitan wheat meat
1 1/2 c. chicken stock
2 cloves garlic, minced

1 tbsp. fresh ginger, finely
    chopped
Fresh vegetables
3 c. of any combination of these
    or other vegetables:

HIGH DENSE:
Carrots
Cauliflower

Green beans
Sweet potato

MEDIUM DENSE:
Snow peas
Broccoli

Red peppers

SLIGHTLY DENSE:
Water
Chestnuts

Bean sprouts

SAUCE:
1/2 c. chicken stock, salt-free &
    defatted
1/4 c. vinegar
1/4 c. apple juice concentrate

1/4 tsp. garlic powder
1/4 tsp. ginger
1 tbsp. cornstarch

Cut tofu into bite sized pieces and marinate at least 1/2 hour in the sauce before the cornstarch is added to it. Prepare vegetables in bite-sized pieces. Preheat wok or large skillet over medium heat. Pour in 1/2 cup stock, add fresh ginger and minced garlic. Saute until stock evaporates and herbs are browned. Deglaze pan by adding 1/3 cup more stock, then turn up fire to high temperature. Start adding vegetables, beginning with the High Dense. Solid, firm vegetables, such as carrots, are the most dense and require the longest cooking time. Cook the most dense vegetables until they are slightly tender (2 minutes), then clear a space in the center of the wok and add the vegetables that are Medium Dense and so on. Repeat until all the vegetables are done, adding stock as needed to keep vegetables from scorching. When they are done, clear a space in the center of the wok and add tofu. Clear space again. Add cornstarch to the sauce mixture and pour sauce into the center of the wok. Cook, stirring continuously until the sauce thickens. Fold the vegetables and tofu into the sauce and serve. Vegetables cooked over a high heat come out best. Overcooked vegetables lose their color, so be careful not to overcook!

SAUCE II FOR STIR-FRY VEGETABLES

1 clove garlic, minced
1 1/2 c. chicken stock
3 tbsp. soy sauce
1/2 tsp. ginger
2 1/2 tbsp. cornstarch
1/2 c. dry sherry

Heat garlic and chicken broth. Add soy sauce, sherry and ginger. Dissolve the cornstarch in a little cold water. Add the cornstarch to broth. Let the sauce boil slowly until it has thickened., stirring continuously. Pour this over the stir-fry veggies and serve over brown rice.

SWEET AND SOUR STIR-FRY: Follow the instructions for basic stir-fry, but include 2 medium ripe tomatoes and 2 cups of diced pineapple, preferably fresh, when you add the bean sprouts, mushrooms, scallions and water chestnuts. For the sauce substitute 1 1/2 cups pineapple juice for the 1 1/2 cups stock and add 1/4 cup white vinegar and 2 tablespoons honey.

SWEET AND SOUR SAUCE III

1 (12 oz.) can vegetable juice
1/2 c. unsweetened pineapple
  juice
1/2 c. unsweetened pineapple
2 tbsp. wine vinegar
1/2 tsp. black pepper
1 tsp. corn flour or 2 tbsp.
  tomato paste
1/2 c. red bell pepper
1/2 c. green bell pepper

Combine all ingredients, stirring frequently and bring to a boil. Boil gently until sauce thickens, garnish with parsley or chives.

SOY LEMON SAUCE

1/3 c. whole wheat flour
1 tbsp. Butter Buds (liquid)
2 1/2 c. water
2 tbsp. lemon juice

2 tbsp. low sodium soy sauce
1/2 tsp. thyme
1 tsp. basil
1/4 tsp. pepper

Toast the flour in a non-stick pan. Add the spices. Then add the liquids gradually while stirring. Simmer 5 to 10 minutes.

SZECHUAN-SPICY NOODLES

3 tbsp. soy sauce
1 tbsp. rice vinegar
1 tsp. minced garlic
2 tbsp. finely chopped scallions
1 tsp. chili powder

1/2 tsp. Szechuan peppercorn
   powder or sauce
1/2 lb. fresh Chinese noodles
2 tbsp. finely chopped roasted
   cashews

In a small bowl combine soy sauce, vinegar, garlic, scallion, chili powder and Szechuan peppercorn powder; set aside.

In a large pot bring 6 to 8 cups of water to a boil over a moderate flame. Drop in noodles and loosen them with chopsticks or a fork. When the noodles and water come to a boil, add 1 cup cold water. Cook noodles until the water comes to a boil again; remove noodles from heat and drain.

Pour the spicy sauce into a large serving bowl and put the cooked noodles on top of the sauce. Mix the noodles and the sauce together, sprinkle chopped cashews on top and serve at once. Serves 4.

EXTRA RECIPES

Main Dishes:
Burgers, Casseroles, Stews, Vegetables

BARBEQUED LENTIL BURGERS

1 c. lentils
3 c. water
1 onion, chopped fine
1 clove garlic, crushed
2 stalks celery, finely chopped

1 carrot, grated
1/2 c. bulgur wheat
3 tbsp. ketchup or tomato sauce
2 tsp. chili powder

Place lentils and water in a medium saucepan and bring to a boil. Add onion, garlic, celery and carrot. Reduce heat, cover and simmer for 30 minutes. Add remaining ingredients. Cook an additional 15 minutes. Remove from heat and let cool. Shape into patties and cook on a non-stick griddle until browned (about 15 minutes). Serve on whole wheat buns with a variety of condiments. Makes 10.

ELEANOR'S OAT BURGERS

In water saute: (approximately 3 minutes)

1 diced onion
1 tsp. garlic powder
2 diced cloves garlic

1 tsp. crushed oregano
1 tsp. sweet basil

Add 4 1/2 cups water and 1/3 cup "green" label Kikkoman Milder Soy sauce. Bring to a boil and add 4 1/2 cups old fashioned "Quaker" oats.

Lower heat and cook 5 minutes. Cover and let set until cooled enough to form patties with wet hands. Bake in 350 degree oven for 15 minutes on each side. Makes 15 medium patties.

KASHA HAMBURGERS

1 c. toasted whole buckwheat
    groats
2 c. water to cook buckwheat
8 tbsp. onion flakes
2/3 c. chopped mushrooms

12 oz. wheat meat
2 tsp. soy sauce
2 tsp. garlic sauce
1/2 tsp. black pepper
6 tbsp. potato flour
3 egg whites

Bring the water to a boil. Add buckwheat, cover and cool on a low heat 10 minutes. DON'T OVERCOOK. At the same time, brown the wheat meat in a skillet. Mix in cooked buckwheat and the rest of the ingredients, mold the mixture into hamburger patties on a cookie sheet. Bake in a 400 degree oven for 20 minutes, or cook individually in the microwave on high for 2 minutes a piece. Delicious served with the tasty sauce below.

SAUCE:

2 (15 oz.) cans tomato sauce
1 (10 oz.) can enchilada sauce

1/4 c. prepared mustard
1/2 tsp. ginger
1/2 tsp. garlic powder
1/2 tsp. onion powder

Combine all sauce ingredients in a saucepan. Heat to blend flavors. Serve hot over Kasha hamburgers or other grain dishes.

MUSHROOM BURGERS

2 onions, chopped
3/4 lb. mushrooms, chopped
3 cloves garlic, crushed
2 lbs. tofu
3 c. rolled oats
1 (10 oz.) pkg. frozen chopped
   spinach (thawed & pressed)

2 tbsp. low sodium soy sauce
4 tbsp. vegetarian Worcestershire
   sauce
1/2 tsp. black pepper
1 tsp. paprika
1 tsp. lemon juice
Whole wheat buns & any garnish
   you wish

Saute onions, mushrooms and garlic in a small amount of water until they are softened and water is absorbed. Mash tofu in a large bowl. Add oats, spinach (make sure all excess water is removed), seasonings and lemon juice. Mix well. Stir in onion-mushroom mixture. Shape into patties and place on non-stick cookie sheet. Bake at 350 degrees for 20 minutes, turn over, then cook an additional 10 minutes. Makes 15 to 18 medium size burgers.

NATURE'S BURGER LOAF OR PATTIES

In large saucepan add:
1 can beef consomme
2 med. finely chopped onions
Lots of chopped parsley

2 c. water
1 tsp. tarragon dry leaves
   (ground to powder form)

Bring to boil and cook 10 minutes. Turn off heat and add:
1 box "Nature's Burger" meatless
   mix (with brown rice as main
   ingredient)

1 c. whole grain flour

Let stand 15 minutes. When cool enough form into patties. Cook in a non-stick skillet about 5 minutes on each side. Variation: Pour into shallow baking dish. Top with 1 can tomato sauce and bake at 350 degrees for 30 minutes.

RED-BEAN PATTIES

4 c. cooked red or pink beans,
drained
4 green onions, sliced thin
1/2 red bell pepper, chopped
1/2 c. chopped fresh parsley

1/4 tsp. cayenne
Tabasco to taste
1/2 tsp. thyme
1/4 tsp. garlic powder
About 1/2 c. apple fiber

In a food processor or blender, combine beans, onions, red pepper, parsley, cayenne, Tabasco, thyme, garlic powder and 1/4 cup of the apple fiber. Process until smooth.

Place remaining apple fiber in a shallow bowl. Dipping your hands in the apple fiber, shape the bean puree into patties about 2 1/2" in diameter and 3/4" thick.

Spray a skillet with Pam or Baker's Joy and heat. Cook patties for 5 minutes on each side. Serve the patties like burgers on whole bread buns with onions, lettuce, tomatoes, ketchup, barbecue sauce or mustard. Makes 12 (2 1/2") patties.

1 patty = 1 serving; 84 calories; .4 grams fat; 0 cholesterol; 100 milligrams sodium.

SUNRISE PATTIES

12 egg whites
8 oz. tofu
1 celery stalk, chopped
1 green onion, chopped
1/2 c. zucchini, shredded

1/8 lb. mushrooms, sliced
1/4 lb. bean sprouts
1 tsp. sherry
1 tsp. soy sauce
Pepper

Crumble tofu into a large bowl, add sherry and soy sauce, let stand 5 minutes. Add the rest of the ingredients.

Heat a griddle or large frying pan over medium heat, spray with Pam. Spoon mixture, about 1/4 cup for each patty onto griddle. From the bowl, spoon about 2 more tablespoons of only the liquid egg over each patty and distribute evenly over vegetables. Cook until egg is set and bottoms of patties are golden brown. Turn and cook other side. 5 servings.

VEGETABLE BURGERS

2 c. shredded carrot
1 c. cooked brown rice
1/2 c. chopped onion
1/2 c. chopped almonds
1/2 c. fine dry bread crumbs
1 tbsp. parsley, chopped

1/2 tsp. ground ginger
1/4 tsp. pepper
1/2 tsp. ground coriander
4 egg whites
2 tbsp. soy sauce
Non stick spray coating

In a large bowl stir together carrot, rice, onion, almonds, bread crumbs, parsley, ginger, coriander and 1/4 teaspoon pepper. Stir together eggs and soy sauce; add to rice mixture and mix well. Cover and chill. Shape rice mixture into 6 patties. Spray a baking sheet with non stick spray coating. Place patties on baking sheet. Broil 3″ to 4″ from heat for 3 to 5 minutes on each side. 6 servings.

WHEAT MEAT VEVESTEAKS

2 1/2 lb. pkg. 100% stone ground
   whole wheat flour
Water

1 lg. onion
2 bay leaves
Soy sauce to taste
Spike seasoning

Pour regular temperature water over the flour and mix until it is like bread dough. Let stand in refrigerator for two hours. Wash it slowly until all starch is out, keep changing the water. Takes about 20 minutes. Will become stretchie like meat. Cut in pieces and flatten out. Have kettle boiling water with soy sauce, onion, bay leaves and spike ready and drop the pieces in and cook until tender. Roll in flour and yeast and brown in non-stick skillet, no oil. Make gravy with broth.

Dale Shinkle

LENTIL SPROUT SLOPPY JOES

3 c. lentil sprouts (1/2 c. dry
   lentils, sprouted for 3 days)
1 c. spaghetti sauce, no oil

1/2 c. sliced onions
10 whole wheat hamburger buns

In processor, grind lentil sprouts with spaghetti sauce, no oil, meatless, sugarless, to make a thin mixture. Heat and serve over warmed, whole wheat hamburger buns. May top with chopped onion if desired.

Mitzi Narramore

ARTICHOKE & PINTO BEAN CASSEROLE

2 (1 lb.) cans pinto or pink beans
1 (1 lb.) can artichoke hearts,
   drained & chopped

1/8 tsp. each cayenne & ground
   cloves
1/2 tsp. ground cumin

Preheat oven to 350 degrees. Empty 1 can of beans and liquid into a 9" square baking pan. Drain and rinse the other can of beans, then roughly chop the beans. Add chopped beans and artichokes to the whole beans. Add spices and chili sauce and mix together well. Set pan in oven, uncovered, and bake for 30 minutes.

Serving Size: 1/4 recipe; 259 calories; 72 grams fat; 0 cholesterol; 80.2 milligrams sodium.

EGGPLANT & PEPPER CAPONATA

Fast weight loss.

1 sm. eggplant
1 red pepper or 1 (4 oz.) jar
  pimiento peppers or roasted
  peppers
1/4 c. salt free tomato paste
2 cloves garlic, minced
1/4 c. onion, finely chopped

1 stalk celery, finely chopped
2 tbsp. sweet basil
1/4 tbsp. red wine vinegar
1/4 tsp. cayenne pepper or
  crushed red pepper
1 tbsp. Butter Buds

With sharp knife, pierce whole eggplant several times and place half whole into baking dish. Cut red pepper in half, discard seeds. Place in pan with eggplant. Place in broiler, several inches away from fire, and broil 10 minutes, or until eggplant and peppers are soft and charred on one side. May also be baked in 450 degree oven. Turn and broil or bake an additional 10 minutes until soft and charred.

In bowl or food processor, place the remaining ingredients, the eggplant and peppers and any liquid from cooking. Process or mash with a fork until ingredients are blended, but still chunky. Chill 1 hour before serving. Serve as a vegetable dip or on bread or crackers. Makes 2 cups (approximately).

CARROT CASSEROLE

1 c. carrot, peeled & shredded
1 c. potato, peeled & shredded
3/4 c. sweet potato, peeled &
  shredded

3 tbsp. chopped onion
1 1/2 c. cooked brown rice
1/3 c. rice milk
1 tbsp. low sodium soy sauce
1 tsp. Mrs. Dash Extra Spicy
  Seasoning

Preheat oven to 350 degrees, then bring 1 cup water to a boil and add vegetables; cook 5 minutes. Add 1/2 cup water to vegetables and add remaining ingredients; mix well. Pour into non-stick casserole dish (use non-stick spray) and bake for 30 minutes. Serves 4 to 6.

CORN ZUCCHINI CASSEROLE

2 (10 oz.) pkgs. kernel corn,
  defrosted
6 sm. zucchini, cut in 1/2" slices
4 ripe tomatoes, cut in 1/4" slices

2 onions, thinly sliced
2 cloves garlic, crushed
1 tsp. red pepper, crushed
Juice of 1/2 lemon
4 low sodium bouillon cubes,
  melted

Place first six ingredients in a covered casserole. Sprinkle with lemon juice and mix together gently. Pour cubes over vegetables. Cover and bake in a preheated oven at 325 degrees for 45 minutes.

RICE CASSEROLE OR STUFFING

2 c. brown rice
2 cloves garlic, minced
1 c. sliced celery
3 tbsp. chopped fresh basil or 1
  tbsp. dried

1/2 c. chopped parsley or 1-2
  tbsp. dried
1 c. chopped onion
5 c. defatted chicken broth
1/2 c. pine nuts

Saute rice in a skillet in a little chicken broth. Add onion and garlic. Saute a little longer. Stir in chicken broth and celery. Bring to a boil. Reduce heat, cover, and simmer 40 minutes or until rice is tender. Toast pine nuts on a cookie sheet in the oven. Watch carefully as they burn easily. For a casserole, add pine nuts, basil and parsley when casserole is about half done. For stuffing, add pine nuts, basil and parsley when rice is done.

CREOLE CASSEROLE

1 med. size eggplant, peeled &
   thickly sliced
2 1/2 c. tomato puree
2 c. water
1 1/2 c. thinly sliced mushrooms
1 1/2 c. coarsely chopped onions

1 c. green chili salsa
1 tsp. Italian seasoning
1/2 tsp. garlic powder
3 c. fresh or frozen okra, cut into
   lg. pieces
1/3 c. whole wheat flour

1. Soak eggplant in cold water to cover for 30 minutes. Meanwhile, combine tomato puree, water, mushrooms, onions, salsa, Italian seasoning and garlic powder in a large saucepan, and bring to a boil. Reduce heat and simmer, uncovered, for 20 minutes. Add okra and cook for another 5 minutes; set aside.

2. Preheat oven to 350 degrees. Pat eggplant slices dry with paper towels. Dredge eggplant slices in flour, place them on a baking sheet and bake for 10 minutes, or until browned. Increase oven temperature to 375 degrees.

3. Line a 9"x11" baking dish with eggplant slices and pour okra mixture over them. Bake for 30 minutes. Makes 8 servings.

GARDEN CASSEROLE

Fast weight loss.

4 potatoes, peeled & sliced
1 zucchini, sliced
1 onion, sliced
2 carrots, sliced
2 tomatoes, cut in chunks

1 c. chicken broth
1/4 tsp. pepper
1 tsp. summer savory
Nutri-Grain wheat flakes

Spread potatoes over the bottom of a 2 quart casserole. Separate the onion into rings and place them over the potatoes. Top these with the zucchini, then the carrots and then the tomatoes. Mix the broth, pepper and savory together. Pour over the casserole; cover and bake at 375 degrees for 1 hour. Sprinkle the wheat flakes over the top. Return to the oven and bake for another 15 minutes. Serves 4.

VEGERONI CASSEROLE

1 1/2 lbs. vegeroni, cooked
2 onions, chopped
2 cloves garlic, minced
1 c. chopped carrot
1 c. chopped celery

1 c. chopped green pepper
1 lb. chopped mushrooms
1/2 tsp. black pepper
5 c. tomato sauce

Pour vegeroni into baking dish sprayed with nonstick. Combine remaining ingredients and pour over noodles. Bake, covered in preheated 300 degree oven for 30 minutes. Bake, uncovered for 10 minutes more. Serves 4 to 6.

VEG-RICE CASSEROLE

1 (20 oz.) bag frozen corn
1 (20 oz.) bag frozen peas
1 (20 oz.) bag frozen broccoli
1 (24 oz.) bag stew vegetables
   (carrots, onions, celery,
   potatoes)

3 c. cooked brown rice
3 c. cream of mushroom soup
   (Hain Natural brand)
2 tsp. garlic powder
2 tbsp. chopped onion (instant)

Place all ingredients in oblong baking dish and bake at 350 degrees for about 1 hour.

SWEET PEA NOODLE CASSEROLE

8 oz. Seitan wheat meat
1 jar sweet peas, drained

1 can kidney beans, drained
1 pkg. whole wheat noodles

Bring 4 cups of water to boil; add noodles. Set aside from heat, let set for 20 minutes. Rinse and drain. In a large mixing bowl combine all ingredients, mix and pour into casserole dish. Bake at 400 degrees for 15 minutes.

LENTIL CASSEROLE

1 c. lentils
2 c. water
1 c. chopped tomatoes
1 green pepper, chopped

1 clove garlic, minced
1 tsp. chili powder
Dash of cayenne pepper

Bring lentils and water to a boil in saucepan. Reduce heat and simmer for 1 to 1 1/2 hours until tender. Add tomatoes, onion, garlic, chili powder and cayenne. Place in a baking dish and bake, covered for 20 minutes at 350 degrees. Serves 4 to 6.

ARMENIAN STEW

1/4 c. dried garbanzo beans
1 1/2 c. dried apricots
5 c. chicken broth

1 c. lentils
3 red onions, sliced
2 tbsp. malt syrup

Soak the garbanzo beans overnight. Soak the dried apricots for 1 hour. In a large pan, bring the soaked apricots and their water to a boil. Add the soaked, drained garbanzo beans and 1 cup chicken broth. Bring to a boil; cook for 30 minutes. Add the lentils, onion and 4 cups chicken broth to the pot. Bring to a boil. Lower heat, cover and cook about 2 hours until garbanzos are tender. Add 2 tablespoons malt syrup and mix well. Serve over brown rice. Serves 8.

BARLEY STEW

1/3 c. each: pinto beans, red beans, lentils, split peas, black eyed peas
6 c. fresh water
1 (24 oz.) can V-8 juice
Garlic powder
Instead of Salt (Health Valley)
1 chopped onion
1/2 c. pearled barley
Any favorite vegetables

Soak beans overnight, covering with 2" of water. Drain off and rinse next morning. Simmer in a large pot soaked beans, water, V-8 juice, garlic powder and Instead of Salt. Simmer, covered over a very low heat for 6 hours, then add onion and barley. Simmer 45 minutes, then add any vegetables. Simmer 30 more minutes. Serves 10.

RAW "BARBECUED" STEW

VEGETABLES:

1 c. fresh corn kernels
1/2 lg. red bell pepper, diced
1/2 lg. green bell pepper, diced
1/4 c. chopped parsley

3 stalks celery, trimmed &
   chopped
1 c. broccoli florets
1 sc. sliced mushrooms
1 c. cubed zucchini

SAUCE:

1/4 med. onion, chopped
6 med. tomatoes, chopped
7 leaves fresh basil
1 sm. clove garlic, pressed

2 tsp. soy sauce or tamari
1/3 c. minced cilantro
2 tbsp. lime juice
1/4 tsp. chili powder

GARNISH:

1 c. mixed salad greens

1 c. peeled & shredded banana
   squash

In a large bowl, combine vegetable ingredients. Set aside. Puree sauce ingredients in a food processor, using a metal "S" blade. Add puree to vegetable mixture and stir to combine. Arrange salad greens on four plates. Top with stew and garnish with banana squash. Serves 4. Per Serving: 167 calories; 9 g protein; 1 g fat; 35 g carbohydrates; 0 cholesterol; 255 mg sodium.

STEW

Fast weight loss.

1 pressure cooker
4 potatoes, peeled & cubed
4 carrots, peeled & sliced
3 celery stalks, sliced

2 zucchini, sliced
6 oz. wheat meat (brand name,
   Seitan)
Dash pepper

Combine all ingredients and 1 1/2 cups fresh water into pressure cooker. Put the lid and regulator on the pressure cooker and once the regulator starts rocking, cook for 10 minutes.

STEW FOR YOU

1 c. garbanzo beans, dry
1 c. kidney beans, dry
1 onion, sliced
1 clove garlic, crushed
1 tsp. curry powder
3 carrots, sliced

2 zucchini, sliced
2 c. whole wheat pasta, cooked
1/2 c. bulgur
1 tbsp. lemon juice
2 c. fresh spinach, chopped

Place beans in a large pot with 2 quarts water. Soak overnight or bring to a boil, cook for 2 minutes, turn off heat and let rest for 1 hour. Then add onion, garlic, and curry powder. Bring to a boil, reduce heat and cook for 2 hours. When beans are almost tender, add carrots and zucchini. Cook for 30 minutes more, then add pasta and bulgur. Cook an additional 15 minutes. Stir in lemon juice and spinach. Cook an additional 5 minutes. Serve immediately. Serves 6.

SUMMER STEW

Fast weight loss.

2 onions, sliced
2 cloves garlic, crushed
6 sm. zucchini, sliced 1/2" thick
4 sm. yellow crookneck squash, sliced 1/2" thick
1 green pepper, coarsely chopped
2 c. snow peas, trimmed & left whole

3 c. tomato chunks
2 c. corn kernels
3 tbsp. low sodium soy sauce
1 tsp. basil
1 1/2 tsp. dill weed
1 1/2 tsp. paprika

Saute onions and garlic in 1/2 cup water in a large saucepan. Cook until soft, about 5 minutes. Add both kinds of summer squash, green pepper, snow peas and tomatoes, plus another 1/2 cup water. Cover and simmer over medium heat for 15 to 20 minutes. Stir occasionally. Add corn and seasonings. Simmer an additional 10 minutes. Mix 1 tablespoon cornstarch or arrowroot in 1/4 cup cold water. Gradually add to stew while stirring. Cook and stir until thickened. Serve hot. Serves 6 to 8.

SUCCOTASH

5 c. peeled, diced potatoes
3 c. low sodium chicken stock, defatted
1 c. coarsely chopped onions
2 1/2 c. frozen corn kernels
2 1/2 c. frozen baby lima beans

2 c. diced fresh tomatoes
1 lg. clove garlic, minced
1 tbsp. low sodium soy sauce
1/2 tsp. dried thyme
1/2 tsp. poultry seasoning

1. Place potatoes, stock and onions in a large pot, bring to a boil, and cook until potatoes are barely tender and almost all of the stock has been absorbed. If potatoes are cooked before all stock is absorbed, puree one third of the vegetables and stock in a food processor or blender and return it to the pot; this will thicken the mixture.

2. Stir in corn, lima beans, tomatoes, garlic, soy sauce, thyme and poultry seasoning and cook for another 10 minutes, or until frozen vegetables are heated through and flavors are well blended. Makes 10 servings.

BROWN GRAVY - NO OIL

7 tbsp. whole wheat flour
2 c. cold water
1/4 tsp. onion powder

1/8 tsp. garlic powder
1 tsp. minced dried onion
1 tbsp. salt reduced tamari

Combine flour and water. Stir until well blended. Cook over low heat until thickened, about 10 minutes. Add remaining ingredients. Continue to cook over low heat for 10 minutes, stirring occasionally. Great over vegetables, rice or casserole dishes or stews. Makes 2 cups.

FAT-FREE GRAVY

6 tbsp. whole wheat flour
2 1/2 c. defatted chicken broth

1/2 tsp. poultry seasoning
Pepper

In a saucepan, whisk flour, stock and poultry seasoning until smooth. Cook, stirring constantly over medium heat, until gravy is thickened, about 10 minutes. Season with pepper. Great on mashed potatoes.

MUSHROOM GRAVY

Fast weight loss.

1/2 c. onion, chopped
1 c. cooked mushroom pieces
1 tbsp. vegetable broth seasoning

1 tbsp. arrowroot
1 c. water
1 tbsp. white wine
1/2 tsp. black pepper
Dash of Tabasco

In a small saucepan, saute onion in small amount of water. Dissolve broth seasoning and arrowroot into cup of water. Add mushrooms to the onions. Cook gently until thickened, then add remaining ingredients. Serves 4. Use on vegetables, casseroles or stews.

AZUKI BEANS AND SQUASH

This makes a nice sweet dish for the autumn.

1 c. azuki beans	1 c. buttercup squash or any
Spring water	winter squash, cubed but not
1 strip Erewhon Kombu, 6" - 8"	peeled
long (seaweed)	Instead of Salt to taste

Wash the beans, cover them with water and soak for 6 to 8 hours. Put the kombu in the bottom of a pot and cover with the squash. Next add the azuki beans. Add water to just cover the squash layer. Do not cover the beans at the beginning. Place the bean mixture over low heat and bring to a boil slowly. Cover after about 10 to 15 minutes. Cook until the beans are 70 to 80 percent done, about 1 hour or more. The water will evaporate as the beans expand, so add cold water occasionally to cover to keep the water level constant and make the beans soft. When the beans are 70 to 80 percent done, add the Instead of Salt and cook until done and most of the liquid has evaporated, another 15 to 30 minutes. Transfer to a serving bowl and serve.

Variation: This dish may also be pressure-cooked. First pressure-cook the kombu and beans for 15 to 20 minutes. Bring down the pressure, uncover and add the squash. Continue to cook without pressure until the beans are 70 to 80 percent done. This makes for a less bitter taste. Then season and continue to cook until done. If you add the squash at the beginning of pressure-cooking, it will melt too much.

BAKED BUTTERNUT SQUASH AND ONIONS

Fast weight loss.

3 c. butternut squash, cut into lg. chunks
1 strip Erewhon Kombu, about 6" long
1-3 tbsp. Kikkoman Lite soy sauce

2 c. spring water
1 c. onions, sliced
2-3 tbsp. Erewhon Kuzu

Put the sliced squash in a baking dish. Add a few drops of water to squash to keep it moist. Cover baking dish and bake in preheated 350 degree oven for about 35 to 40 minutes or until it is almost done. Pour the water into a pot and add the onions and kombu. Bring to a boil. Reduce to simmer for about 15 minutes. Reduce the heat to very low. Remove the kombu from the pot.

BEAN & VEGETABLE LOAF

8 oz. dried white northern beans
4 c. water
1 tbsp. low sodium soy sauce
1 bouquet garni (4 sprigs parsley, 1 tsp. thyme, 1 bay leaf, 1/2 tsp. crushed red pepper)
1/2 c. egg whites (4-5 lg. eggs), slightly beaten

3 cloves garlic, minced
5 lg. Swiss chard leaves, stems removed
1/4 lb. fresh whole string beans
1/4 lb. fresh whole okra
1/4 lb. fresh sm. whole carrots
5 artichoke hearts

Cook beans in water and soy sauce with bouquet garni for 1 1/2 hours. Drain and puree beans in blender. Mix pureed beans with slightly beaten egg whites and garlic. Blanch Swiss chard leaves, string beans and okra for 3 minutes in boiling water and refresh in cold water. Line a nonstick 6 cup loaf pan with overlapping Swiss chard leaves. Spread a 1/4 layer of bean puree, then a layer of vegetables. Continue alternating bean paste and vegetables. The first layer should be okra, then artichokes, then carrots, then string beans, end with beaten paste. Cover with foil and place in a baking pan with 1″ hot water.

Bake in a preheated oven at 350 degrees for 30 to 45 minutes or until mixture is firm. Serve hot with a tomato sauce or cold with a vinaigrette dressing (no oil). Serves 8 to 10.

BELL PEPPERS STUFFED WITH BARLEY

1 c. pearled barley
6 med. green or red bell peppers
1/4 c. chopped onions
1/2 c. raisins

2 tbsp. chopped fresh mint or 2 tsp. dried
3/4 tsp. ground cinnamon
2 tbsp. lemon juice
Pepper

Cook barley in 6 to 8 cups boiling water for 30 minutes; it should be tender but still have some bite to it. Drain and reserve for later.

Preheat oven to 350 degrees.

Cut 1/2″ slice off stem end of each bell pepper. Discard stem but chop up what pepper remains and reserve for later. Empty peppers of seeds and ribs.

Spray a large skillet with Pam or Baker's Joy, add onions and reserved chopped peppers. Stir-fry for a couple of minutes. Add 1/2 cup water to the skillet, cover and simmer over low heat for 10 minutes, or until vegetables are tender.

Add to the skillet the cooked barley, raisins, mint, cinnamon and lemon juice. Stir around for a minute or so and remove from heat. Season to taste with pepper.

Scoop the barley mixture into the hollowed-out pepper cases. Fit the peppers into a baking pan so that the peppers touch and help support each other. Add about an inch of water to the pan, cover and bake for 45 minutes to1 hour or until tender. Makes 6 stuffed peppers.

Serving Size: 1/4 recipe; 193 calories; 77 grams fat; 0 cholesterol; 6 milligrams sodium.

BELL PEPPERS STUFFED WITH RICE ITALIAN STYLE

2 lg. bell peppers
1 1/2 c. tomato sauce
2 c. cooked brown rice
2 tbsp. chopped parsley
1/2 tsp. Italian seasoning

Cut peppers in half lengthwise, remove seeds and membranes. Steam pepper halves until cooked crisp-tender; set aside. Combine 1/2 cup tomato sauce with cooked brown rice, 1 tablespoon chopped parsley and 1/2 teaspoon seasoning. Heat over moderate heat, stirring gently until well blended. Add a little water if need to prevent sticking. Spoon remaining tomato sauce into bottom of a 9" pie pan. Place pepper halves on top of sauce, then fill with rice mixture. Bake at 350 degrees until hot. Sprinkle with chopped parsley and serve. Serves 4.

BELL PEPPERS STUFFED WITH MUSHROOMS

3 lg. green peppers
1 1/2 c. tomatoes
1 c. fresh mushrooms
1 1/2 c. cooked lentils seasoned
  with herbs & drained
1 c. cooked brown rice
1/2 c. diced celery & onion
Dash of garlic powder
Dash of Mrs. Dash

Cut green peppers in half lengthwise, parboil about 4 minutes. Saute 1/2 cup diced celery and 1/3 cup diced onion in Teflon skillet (use Pam spray) until soft. Mix onion and celery with rest of ingredients. Season with a bit of black pepper. Stuff mix in green peppers. Bake 30 to 35 minutes in 350 degree oven or until green pepper is tender. Serve hot. Serves 6.

BLACKEYED PEAS - INDIAN STYLE

1 c. dried black-eyed peas
1 sliced carrot
1 tsp. S & B Sun Bird oriental
curry powder (a combo of
spices)
1 tsp. honey or waffle syrup
1/4 tsp. turmeric

1/4 tsp. cumin
3 c. water
1 chopped onion
2 tbsp. coconut
1/2 tsp. shredded ginger (keep
fresh ginger root in freezer
until ready for use)

Add all ingredients to boiling water and simmer until liquid is absorbed and peas are tender. Makes 4 servings.

BLACK-EYED PEAS SOUTHERN STYLE

1 c. black-eyed peas
1 med. onion, chopped
2 cloves garlic, minced
1 green bell pepper, chopped
1 red bell pepper, chopped
2 c. (1 lg. can) whole tomatoes,
chopped

3 tbsp. Butter Buds
1 tbsp. Worcestershire sauce
1 tbsp. chili powder
1/4 tsp. ground cumin
Pepper to taste

Wash black-eyed peas, cover with water (4 cups) and soak overnight (or bring to boil, boil 3 minutes and let stand 1 hour). Drain and throw away soak water. Cover peas with fresh water and boil gently until tender. Drain. While peas are cooking, saute onion, peppers and garlic in Butter buds for 5 minutes. Add tomatoes and seasonings and simmer 3/4 to 1 hour. Combine with black-eyed peas and reheat.

BLACK-EYED PEA STEW

2 c. black-eyed peas, dry
6 c. water
Salt (opt.)
1/2 c. onions

2 lg. tomatoes
1/4 c. soy sauce
1 tsp. garlic powder
Dash of cinnamon

Soak black-eyed peas overnight. Cook black-eyed peas for 2 hours until tender, soft. Add onions, tomatoes, soy sauce, garlic and cinnamon. Simmer for 15 to 30 minutes to desired tenderness.

CURRIED LENTILS AND BROWN RICE

2 c. lentils, cooked
2 c. brown rice, cooked
2 tsp. curry

1 tsp. garlic powder
1/2 tsp. parsley
Water

Add the ingredients together with enough water to cover. Simmer for about 15 minutes. It's ready to eat.

DELGADO GADO

2 lg. potatoes, boiled & sliced
1 c. carrots, sliced into 1/4"
   pieces
1 c. cauliflower flowerettes
1 c. fresh green beans, sliced into
   1" pieces

1 c. sliced cabbage
1/4 lb. bean sprouts
1 cucumber, sliced

SAUCE:
3/4 c. pecans
3/4 c. almonds
1/4 c. chopped onion
4 garlic cloves, minced
1 1/2 c. coconut milk

2 tsp. crushed red pepper
1 tsp. ground ginger
1/4 tsp. ground cumin
3 tbsp. fresh lemon juice
4 tbsp. soy sauce

Blanch beans, carrots, cabbage and cauliflower separately in water for 3 minutes each. Drain vegetables and arrange on platter. Top with bean sprouts and surround with cucumber and potato slices. Serve from platter, topping each plate with sauce.

To make sauce, place nuts in food processor and mix to paste. In a saucepan, add onion and garlic and saute about 1 minute. Add coconut milk, peppers, ginger, cumin, lemon juice and soy sauce and bring to a boil. Add nuts and cook until sauce is thickened, about 5 minutes.

DAL

1 c. lentils
1 qt. chicken stock (homemade or
   canned, no salt added)
2 tbsp. fresh grated ginger
1/4 tsp. ground turmeric

Pinch cardamom
1/4 tsp. cayenne pepper
1/2 tsp. cumin
2 tbsp. fresh cilantro
Lemon juice

Rinse the lentils and combine them in a medium sized saucepan with the stock. Bring the stock to a boil, then lower the heat and simmer for 1 hour. Add spices, continue to cook briefly and serve with fresh, whole wheat chapati.

MUNG DAL

Mung beans are split yellow mung beans which can be purchased at all Indian grocery stores. If they are not available to you, you may use green split peas or yellow split peas with this same recipe.

1 c. beans	1 tbsp. black mustard seeds
7 c. water	1 green chili, minced
1 c. chopped tomatoes	1/4 tsp. hing
1 med. zucchini, peeled &	1 1/2 tsp. turmeric
chopped in 1" cubes	1 tbsp. salt
Pam spray	Fresh coriander leaves for
1/2 tbsp. minced ginger	garnish
1 1/2 tbsp. cumin seeds	

In 1 gallon saucepan, spray with Pam, add turmeric, hing, and beans. Fry for 30 seconds on medium heat. Add vegetables and fry for 1 more minute. Add water, salt, fresh chili and diced ginger. Bring to a boil over high heat, then cover, lower heat and let dal simmer for 1 hour or until the beans have dissolved into a thick soup. Set aside.

In small skillet spray with Pam. When hot add cumin seeds and black mustard seeds. When the seeds start to crackle pour the mixture into the pot of dal. Garnish with fresh coriander leaves or parsley. Serve hot. Serves 6.

SAFFRON RICE

1/2 tsp. crushed saffron threads	1/4 c. shelled, chopped pistachios
3 tbsp. water	or pine nuts
1 tbsp. Butter Buds	3 c. chicken stock or water
1/3 c. currants or raisins	1 tbsp. Veg-It
	Lg. pinch cinnamon
	1 1/2 c. long grain brown or
	basmati rice

Dissolve the saffron in water. Melt the Butter Buds in a medium-large saucepan and add the currants, nuts and rice. Stir over low heat for several minutes, then add the stock or water and dissolved saffron. Stir once, raise the heat and bring to a boil, then lower heat, cover and simmer for 35 minutes or until steamed. Serves 6 to 8.

FALAFELS

4 c. cooked garbanzos
4 egg whites
1 c. chopped onions
2 tsp. parsley
1/2 tsp. garlic powder

1/4 tsp. basil
1/4 tsp. pepper
3/4 c. matzo meal
1/4 c. potato pancake mix
1/2 c. water

Put garbanzos and water in a blender. Blend until smooth. Mix the garbanzos, egg whites, onions and spices in a large bowl. Add matzo meal and pancake mix. Form into small balls. Bake on a nonstick pan at 350 degrees for 15 to 20 minutes. Serve in pita bread with tomatoes, lettuce, onions, etc.

FRUIT-RICE STUFFING

3/4 c. Butter Buds
1 1/2 c. chopped onion
1 1/2 c. chopped celery
1/2 c. chopped parsley
7 c. cooked brown rice
1 tsp. marjoram
1/2 c. chopped nuts
1/2 tsp. thyme

1/2 tsp. sage
Salt & pepper
3 egg whites, lightly beaten
3/4 c. turkey stock or chicken
   bouillon
6 oz. mixed dried fruit
1/2 c. raisins

Saute onions, celery and parsley in Butter Buds. Remove from heat and combine with rice in large bowl. Stir in marjoram, thyme, and sage. Season to taste with salt and pepper. Add egg whites, stock, fruit and nuts. Mix well. Makes enough stuffing for a 10 to 12 pound turkey or 6 side dishes.

HERBED WHEAT PILAF

1 3/4 c. vegetable stock	2 green onions, sliced
1 sm. carrot	1 bay leaf
1 med. stalk celery	1 c. raw bulgur wheat
1/2 green pepper	1 tsp. vegetable seasoning
1/4 c. chopped mushrooms	

Dice carrot, celery, green pepper and onions. Place small amount of liquid in a heavy pot with a close fitting lid. Add all the vegetables and the bay leaf and stir over medium heat for several minutes. Pour in stock, bring to a boil and simmer for 5 minutes, covered. Add wheat and seasoning and bring to a fast boil again. Cook, covered, over very low heat for 15 minutes. If too moist, uncover and simmer another few minutes until the liquid diminishes. For special occasions, add 1 cup garden peas towards the end of the cooking time. Pilaf can be made with just about any grain. Try millet, cracked wheat, rice or triticale in this dish, or a partial substitution of barley for any of these.

MACARONI NO-CHEESE

3-4 c. butternut squash, peeled & cubed
About 3 c. water
2 tbsp. tahini
2 tbsp. light miso
Pinch salt & white pepper (opt.)
2 c. elbow or spiral noodles
Water for boiling
1 c. or more fresh or frozen green peas, steamed (opt.)
1/3 c. dry bread crumbs
1-2 tsp. no-oil Italian dressing

Place squash in a pot; add water almost to cover. Cover pot and bring to a boil. Lower heat and simmer until squash is very soft, about 15 to 20 minutes. Drain. Place squash in blender or food processor. Add tahini, miso and salt and pepper if desired. Puree until smooth.

Add noodles to a large pot of boiling water and cook until al dente. Drain and rinse. Combine noodles with puree and add peas if desired. Place mixture in an oiled 9" square baking dish.

Preheat oven to 350 degrees. In a small bowl mix bread crumbs with no oil Italian dressing. Sprinkle evenly over macaroni mixture. Bake for 20 minutes. Serve hot. Serves 6. Per serving: 184 calories; 6 g protein; 6 g fat; 29 g carbohydrates; 0 cholesterol; 283 mg. sodium.

LEGUME LOAF

3/4 c. whole grain bread crumbs
1/4 c. oat bran
1 egg white
1/2 c. onion, chopped fine
1/2 - 3/4 c. carrots, grated
1 stalk celery, chopped fine

2 c. garbanzos, cooked & mashed
or chopped in a food processor
or lentils & black-eyed peas,
mashed or chopped or a
combination
1/4 tsp. thyme
1/2 tsp. savory
1 tsp. basil
2 tbsp. fresh parsley or 2 tsp.
dried parsley

Combine the bread crumbs and oat bran. Add the egg white and mix. (If the mixture is not moist, add a little water.) Add the other ingredients. Put the mixture in a loaf pan or casserole dish, non-stick or sprayed with Pam. Bake for 1 hour at 350 degrees. Serve with a tomato sauce or Soy Lemon Sauce.

NUT LOAF

2 c. finely ground mixture of
seeds & nuts, such as
sunflower seed kernels,
almonds, walnuts & cashews
1 onion, chopped
3 cloves garlic, chopped
3 celery stalks, chopped

2 egg whites, lightly beaten
3/4 c. wheat germ
1 c. cooked brown rice
1 tbsp. soy sauce
1/8 tsp. dried rosemary
1/4 tsp. dried sage
1 tsp. caraway seeds

Preheat the oven to 350 degrees. Mix all ingredients together in a large bowl until well blended.

Turn into a 9"x3"x5" pan sprayed with Pam and bake for 40 minutes. Serve like a meatloaf. For leftovers, cold nut loaf can be served with crackers. 6 servings.

VEGETABLE LOAF

1/2 c. Butter Buds
1 c. chopped onion
1 c. minced celery
1 c. grated raw carrots
1 c. finely ground English
   walnuts

1 c. dry whole wheat bread
   crumbs
1 tsp. poultry seasoning
4 egg whites
1 c. chicken broth
1 can tomato sauce

Cook onion in Butter Buds until tender. Add vegetables, nuts, crumbs and seasonings. Saute. Mix egg whites and chicken broth. Combine both mixtures and turn into a loaf pan, sprayed with Pam. Bake at 350 degrees for 40 minutes. Serve with tomato sauce. Serves 4.

VEGELOAF

2 c. canned green beans
1 c. liquid reserved from canned
   beans
1 egg white
3/4 c. brown rice, cooked

1/4 c. spaghetti sauce (no oil, no
   meat)
2 cloves garlic, minced
1/4 c. cooked mushrooms,
   chopped
4 slices whole wheat bread
(crumbs equal 2 c.)

Blend green beans and liquid in blender. Add remaining ingredients except bread crumbs and blend. Pour mixture into a bowl over crumbs and mix well. Pour into a non-stick loaf pan (use non-stick spray). Bake at 300 degrees for 45 minutes. Serves 4.

NICK'S SPICY BROWN RICE & NOODLES

2 c. brown rice
1/4 c. lentils
1/2 c. whole wheat noodles
6 c. chicken broth

1/2 c. Pace Picante Chili Salsa
(med. or mild)
1 clove garlic, minced
Onion powder

Mix all ingredients, except chili salsa and cook in a large covered pan for 40 minutes. Add the chili salsa, cover pan again and let sit for 20 minutes without heat. Ready to eat.

RICE PILAF WITH ALMONDS

1/2 c. Butter Buds
1/4 c. minced onion
1/2 c. chopped blanched almonds

1 c. raw brown rice
2 c. hot chicken broth
Pepper to taste

Heat Butter Buds in saucepan. Add onion and saute until onion is transparent. Do not let it brown. Add almonds and saute for 1 to 2 minutes or until barely golden. Add rice and saute until rice is transparent, stirring constantly. Add hot broth all at once, mixture will sizzle. Cover tightly. Simmer on low heat for 30 to 40 minutes or until rice is tender. Season with pepper. 4 servings.

RED BEANS & RICE, CAJUN STYLE

This is a hearty dish. Serves 8.

1/2 lb. dry red beans (kidney beans)	2 cloves garlic, minced
7 c. vegetable stock	2 bay leaves
1 lg. yellow onion, chopped	1 tbsp. cajun seasoning
1 lg. green pepper, chopped	Salt to taste (opt.)
1 1/2 c. chopped celery	4 c. hot cooked rice
	Freshly ground pepper

Cover beans with cold water and soak overnight. Drain the beans. In a large soup pot, heat vegetable stock. Add the beans, onion, green pepper, celery, garlic, bay leaves and cajun seasoning. Bring to a boil, reduce heat, cover and simmer for 1 hour.

Continue cooking the beans until they become tender. Watch the pot carefully to prevent scorching of beans. Add more water to the pot as needed. When beans are tender, remove bay leaves, salt to taste and serve by ladling a portion of red beans over 1/2 cup hot cooked rice in a large bowl. Pepper to taste. Each Serving: 281 calories.

RATATOUILLE ESPECIAL

2 c. water	1 1/2 c. cooked mushrooms, chopped
2 c. eggplant, diced	2 tbsp. vegetable broth seasoning
1 c. zucchini, diced	4 c. cooked brown rice
1/2 c. green bell pepper, chopped	
1/2 c. onions, cut in chunks	

In large pot combine water and remaining ingredients except rice and cook over medium heat for 30 minutes. Serve over hot cooked brown rice. Serves 4 to 6.

BROWN RICE

2 c. chicken stock   1 c. brown rice

Bring stock to a boil. Stir in rice and bring back to boil. Turn flame low, cover pot tightly and cook for 40 minutes without lifting the lid. Add rice to vegetables, beans or soup.

QUICK BROWN RICE

Microwave.

1 1/4 c. chicken broth   1/2 c. green bell pepper, diced
1 c. brown rice   1/2 c. chopped green onions

Place chicken broth in a 2 quart microwave dish. Cover tightly. Microwave on high for 4 minutes. Stir in rice, bell pepper and green onions. Recover. Adjust power level to medium. Microwave 10 to 15 minutes or until rice is tender and water is absorbed. Fluff with a fork. 6 servings.

BROWN RICE MUSHROOM RING

1 c. brown rice, cooked   1 tbsp. grated onion
1/2 lb. mushrooms, sliced   2 tbsp. parsley, chopped

Combine all ingredients, then spoon into a 1 quart ring mold (use non-stick spray) and set in a pan of hot water. Bake in a preheated 350 degree oven for 30 minutes. Turn out into a platter. Serves 4 to 6.

BROWN RICE WITH ZUCCHINI

1/4 c. Butter Buds	1 onion, chopped
2 zucchini, sliced	Pepper to taste
3 c. chicken broth	1/3 c. Molly McButter (opt.)
	(cheese flavor)

Place Butter Buds and zucchini in saucepan and cook over medium heat, about 3 minutes until zucchini begins to soften. Transfer to a bowl.

Place broth and onion in saucepan, cook until tender, about 6 minutes. Add rice and cover, cook until liquid is absorbed, about 40 minutes. Season with pepper. Add zucchini and cheese flavor, and mix well. 2 servings.

CORN AND BROWN RICE STIR-FRY

1 lg. can corn, drained	2 tbsp. soy sauce (low sodium)
1/4 c. water	1/2 c. chopped green onion
4 c. brown rice	

Place corn in skillet sprayed with non-stick coating. Saute for 4 to 5 minutes. Add water, rice and soy sauce. Continue cooking, stirring frequently until liquid has evaporated. Remove from heat and add green onion. Serves 4.

INDIAN SPICE RICE

2 c. cooked brown rice	1 tbsp. onion powder
1 c. chopped onion	1 tsp. curry powder
1 1/2 c. chopped celery	1 c. frozen green peas, thawed &
1/2 c. orange juice	rinsed to separate
2 tbsp. chopped mint leaves	

Saute onion and celery in non-stick pan (use non-stick spray) for about 3 to 5 minutes on low heat. Add orange juice and continue cooking until liquid is almost evaporated. Stir in mint leaves, onion and curry powder and blend to combine flavors. Stir in the rice and peas and heat through. Serves 4 to 5.

CRUNCHY RICE & PEAS

1 c. leftover rice, cooked, chilled
1/2 c. chicken broth

3/4 c. frozen peas
4 oz. can water chestnuts, sliced
Garlic powder & salt

Add peas, water chestnuts and seasonings and stir-fry over high heat with chicken broth. Toss in rice and heat thoroughly. Makes 2 servings. 1 cup serving provides 151 calories, 85% carbohydrates, 14% protein and 1% fat.

RICE AND VEGGIES

4 c. cooked brown rice
1/2 sm. onion, chopped
1/2 lb. fresh mushrooms, chopped
1 lg. green bell pepper, chopped
4 sm. zucchini, diced

2 tbsp. tomato paste
1 c. water
2 tbsp. chili salsa
1 tsp. oregano
2 tbsp. vegetable broth seasoning

Saute onion and next three ingredients in non-stick skillet (use non-stick spray). Add tomato paste and water and stir. Add remaining ingredients and simmer 15 minutes. Stir in rice and heat through. Serves 4 to 6.

RAINBOW RICE

2 c. cooked brown rice
1 onion, chopped
1 green bell pepper, finely chopped
2 c. whole kernel corn
1 (4 oz.) jar pimiento, chopped

1 tsp. oregano
1/2 tsp. paprika
1/2 tsp. soy sauce (low sodium)
1 c. green peas

In a large skillet, saute onion and green pepper (use non-stick spray), until vegetables are crisp-tender. Add next five ingredients, cooking for another 5 minutes, then add green peas and rice and heat through for about 5 minutes until done. Serves 4 to 6.

SPLIT PEA PUDDING

1 lb. green split peas	1 tsp. dried spices or herbs
1 carrot, chopped fine	according to your taste, as
1 onion, chopped fine	marjoram, thyme, mint, dill,
1 celery stalk, chopped fine	and/or parsley
2 egg whites	Pepper

Place peas, carrot, onion and celery in a large pot. Cover with 8 cups water. Bring to a boil, cut back to a simmer, and cook gently, covered, for 45 minutes.

Preheat oven to 350 degrees.

Drain peas through a colander, reserving liquid for another soup if you wish. Puree peas and vegetables in a food processor, blender or food mill and blend in egg whites. Add herbs or spices and pepper according to taste. This dish can be eaten hot or cold. Bake in 6-cup baking pan for 45 minutes.

Serving Size: 1/8 recipe. 77 calories; 3 grams fat; 0 cholesterol; 21 milligrams sodium.

SPECIAL SANDWICH

1 slice whole wheat toast	2 slices avocado
1 sliced red onion, raw	2 slices tomato

Place onion, avocado and tomato on top of whole wheat toast. Good substitute for a BLT sandwich.

ORANGE SWEET POTATOES

4 med. sweet potatoes, or yams	2 tbsp. apple juice concentrate
1/2 tsp. grated orange rind	1/4 tsp. cinnamon
1/2 c. orange juice	

Steam potatoes and peel. Mash all ingredients together. Bake in casserole dish, covered, for 25 minutes at 350 degrees.

GLAZED SWEET POTATOES

3 lbs. sweet potatoes, cut
   crosswise into 1/2" slices,
   peeled

1/3 c. orange juice concentrate,
   thawed
1 tsp. Butter Buds
1/2 tsp. cinnamon

Preheat oven to 350 degrees. Arrange sweet potatoes in a single layer in two large, shallow baking dishes. Mix orange juice concentrate, Butter Buds and cinnamon and pour over sweet potatoes. Cover dishes tightly with foil and bake until tender, about 30 minutes. Serves 8.

SWEET POTATO STUFFING

3 c. chopped onion
2 c. chopped celery
4 c. mashed sweet potato
8 c. cubed whole wheat bread
2 tsp. dried thyme

1 1/2 tsp. dried marjoram
1/2 tsp. sage
1 tsp. pepper
1/2 c. rice or soy milk
2 egg whites, beaten

Saute onion and celery in small amount of water until onion is done. In a large bowl mix six ingredients together well. Add onion and celery, mix well. In a separate bowl mix milk and egg whites. Beat lightly and pour over rest of ingredients. Toss together. Stuff a 12 pound turkey or 3 chickens. If not for stuffing, bake in a non-stick casserole dish at 350 degrees for 30 to 35 minutes. Serves 8.

WHOLE WHEAT ALMOND NOODLES

Cook and drain 1 pound whole wheat noodles. Stir in 3/4 cup sliced, toasted blanched almonds. Put in serving dish and top with 1/4 cup toasted, whole wheat bread crumbs and an additional 1/4 cup sliced toasted blanched almonds. 4 servings.

ZUCCHINI AND WHEAT MEAT DELIGHT

Microwave.

1 c. wheat meat
4 c. zucchini, sliced
1 onion, sliced
1 clove garlic, minced
2 tbsp. whole wheat flour

2 tsp. instant chicken bouillon
1/4 tsp. thyme
2 tomatoes, cut in wedges
1 c. seasoned salad croutons

Cut wheat meat into bite sized pieces. Place in 2 quart casserole. Add zucchini, onion, garlic, flour, bouillon and thyme. Mix well. Cook at Full power for 8 minutes. Add tomatoes. Cook on Full power for 2 minutes. Garnish with croutons. 4 servings.

BAKED BEANS

1 c. finely chopped celery
2 c. cooked pinto beans
1/2 c. spaghetti sauce (no oil or
  salt)

1/4 c. water
1 med. chopped onion
1 tbsp. unfiltered apple juice
1 tbsp. honey

Mix all ingredients in a 2 quart casserole, cover and bake 45 minutes at 350 degrees. Serves 8 to 10.

GARBANZO MEDLEY

1/2 c. uncooked brown rice
1 (15 oz.) can garbanzo beans
1 green pepper, chopped
2 onions, sliced
1 eggplant, chopped

3 (15 oz.) cans tomatoes
4 stalks celery, topped
2 carrots, diced
Pepper to taste
3 tbsp. Italian seasoning

Combine all ingredients in pot and bring to a boil. Cover and simmer until rice is tender, about 1 hour. Makes 6 cups.

KIDNEY BEANS

1 c. kidney beans
Spring water
1 strip Erewhon Kombu, 6" - 8"
 long

1 1/2 tsp. Erewhon Miso per c. of
 beans, preferably barley miso

Wash and soak the beans for 6 to 8 hours. Put the kombu in the bottom of a heavy pot. Set the beans on top of the kombu and add water to just cover the beans. Bring to a boil. Reduce the heat to medium-low and cover. Simmer until the beans are about 80 percent done, or about 1 hour. Add cold water following the basic shocking method as needed. When the beans are 80% done, add the pureed miso. (Barley miso is best to use with this dish.) Just add the miso on top of the beans and do not mix in. The miso will filter down into the beans as they continue to cook. Continue to cook until the beans are soft and creamy, another 20 to 30 minutes. Transfer to a serving bowl and serve. Variation: Pressure-cook the beans for 45 minutes. Then add the pureed miso and cook, not under pressure, about 20 to 30 minutes longer.

PINTO BEANS

4-5 c. dry pinto beans
Water to cover beans

1-2 tbsp. vinegar

In a large pot, combine above ingredients and boil for 5 minutes. Drain the water and refill with fresh water and more vinegar. Let beans soak on stove for about 1 hour (no heat). After beans have soaked and expanded, drain beans again and refill with fresh water.

Add to beans:

1 onion, chopped
1 clove garlic, minced
2 tbsp. onion powder

1 tbsp. garlic powder
1/4 c. chili salsa
1 chunk fresh ginger

Cook beans, adding water when needed, for about 4 to 5 hours.

CORN BREAD STUFFING

3 c. crumbled cornbread
1 c. whole wheat bread crumbs
2 c. chicken broth, defatted
4 stalks celery, finely chopped

1 onion, chopped
2 egg whites
1/2 tsp. poultry seasoning
Ground pepper to taste

Combine all ingredients in a large bowl and mix well. May be baked at 350 degrees for 40 minutes in a non-stick baking dish.

BREADED EGGPLANT

1 green bell pepper, chopped
1 onion, chopped
2 tbsp. tomato paste
2 egg whites
2 tsp. oregano

2 tsp. basil
4 slices whole grain bread,
   crumbled
8 (1/4" thick) slices eggplant
2 tomatoes, sliced thin

In blender, blend first six ingredients. Pour this mixture over bread crumbs in a large bowl. Mix thoroughly, then arrange eggplant slices on a non-stick cookie sheet (use non-stick spray). Top with bread mixture. Bake at 350 degrees for 30 minutes. Top with fresh tomato slices before serving. Serves 2.

BROCCOLI IN CURRY SAUCE

Fast weight loss.
1 bunch fresh broccoli, sliced
   lengthwise
1 c. chicken broth, defatted
1/3 tsp. curry powder

1/8 tsp. dry mustard
2 tsp. unsweetened apple juice
1 tbsp. cornstarch

Cook broccoli until tender. Bring broth to a boil and add cornstarch (dissolve in small amount of water before adding to broth), stir constantly until mixture thickens and clears. Add remaining ingredients and cook for one minute; pour over broccoli and serve. Serves 4.

CABBAGE PLATE

Fast weight loss.

3 c. coarsely chopped cabbage
2 c. sliced carrots
1 c. chopped celery

1/2 c. apple juice (unsweetened)
1/4 c. hot water
2 tsp. lemon pepper (or Instead
    of Salt)

Combine vegetables. Add apple juice, lemon pepper, and water. Cook in covered pot until just tender, 10 to 15 minutes. Makes 8 servings.

CABBAGE ROLLS

1 med. head cabbage
1/2 c. chopped onion
1/2 c. chopped celery
1/4 c. water
1/2 c. chopped green bell pepper

1 1/2 c. brown rice, cooked
1 c. tomato sauce
1/4 tsp. sage
1/4 tsp. garlic powder

Steam cabbage until leaves can be removed. Simmer vegetables in water until nearly tender. Mix cooked rice, seasonings and vegetables. Place 1/2 cup mix in cabbage leaf and roll. Place in baking dish with tomato sauce and water mixed, pour over rolls. Bake at 350 degrees for 45 minutes, covered until last few minutes. Serves 4.

STUFFED CABBAGE

12 lg. cabbage leaves, prepared
  for stuffing

FILLING:

2 c. cooked brown rice	1/4 tsp. cayenne
3/4 c. mushrooms	1/4 c. almonds, sliced
2 egg whites	2 green onions, chopped

SAUCE:

2 c. tomato juice	1 stalk celery, sliced
4 slices onion	1/2 c. green pepper strips

To prepare filling, mix rice, egg whites and seasonings until evenly blended. Place a small mound of filling, about 3 tablespoons, on each cabbage leaf and roll into bundles.

To prepare sauce, combine broth, onion, celery and green pepper in a 15" skillet. Bring to a boil. Place cabbage rolls in sauce, cover and with heat very low, simmer for 30 minutes. Spoon sauce over cabbage once or twice during cooking. Makes 12 rolls.

To prepare cabbage leaves for stuffing, boil in water until soft.

SWEET-SOUR CABBAGE ROLLS

1 lg. cabbage, cored

SAUCE:
2 onions, chopped	1/4 c. frozen apple juice
1 (28 oz.) can tomatoes	concentrate
1 (8 oz.) can tomato juice	1 tbsp. soy sauce
1/2 c. lemon juice	1/4 tsp. cayenne pepper
	1/2 c. raisins

FILLING:
1/2 c. cooked brown rice	2 c. peeled potatoes, diced med.
1 tbsp. soy sauce	fine
1 tbsp. ground coriander	1 1/2 c. chopped onion
1 tsp. dillweed	1 1/2 c. chopped celery
1/4 tsp. fennel seed, ground in	1/2 c. chopped green bell pepper
blender	2 egg whites, fork beaten

Set the cabbage cored side down in a steamer over boiling water, covered, for about 10 minutes or until leaves are soft. Let cool and separate leaves. Prepare sauce by sauteeing the onions in 1/2 cup boiling water in a large skillet. Cook, stirring frequently, until the water has evaporated and the onions are slightly browned. Stir in the other ingredients, bring to a boil, reduce heat and simmer, covered for about 10 minutes.

Prepare filling by spreading rice in a baking pan and place in a 400 degree oven for about 10 minutes to toast, stirring occasionally so the rice browns evenly. Bring 2 1/2 cups water to a boil in a saucepan. Stir in soy sauce, spices and rice. Return to a boil; then reduce heat to low, cover tightly and cook for 40 to 45 minutes. Keep covered for an additional 10 minutes to allow rice to fluff from steam. Combine the rice, potatoes, vegetables and egg whites, mixing well. Fill the rolls and bake in a covered dish for an hour and 15 minutes at 350 degrees. Makes 12 rolls.

HERBED CABBAGE

Fast weight loss.

1 med. onion, thinly sliced
1 c. cabbage, shredded
1 c. carrots, shredded

1/2 tsp. oregano, crushed
1/2 tsp. dill weed
1 tsp. water

In a non-stick skillet, saute onion in water for 5 minutes. Stir in cabbage and carrots. Cover and cook over medium heat 8 minutes more. Stir in oregano and dill weed. Serves 4.

SPICED RED CABBAGE

Fast weight loss.

3 1/2 c. shredded red cabbage
1/4 c. cider vinegar
1/2 c. water
1/4 tsp. ground cinnamon

1/4 tsp. ground allspice
1/8 tsp. ground nutmeg
2 tart apples, peeled, cored &
    diced
1/4 tbsp. sugar

In a saucepan combine with all other ingredients, except apples. Cover and cook over moderate heat for 15 minutes, tossing several times so the cabbage will cook evenly. Add apples, then cover and cook five minutes longer. Add sugar. When dish is done, all water should have cooked away. Serves 6.

CARROT SOUFFLE FOR ONE

Fast weight loss.

1 (4 oz.) jar pureed carrots (use
Gerber's brand or other baby
food without salt or sugar
added)

1 egg white
1/4 c. minced onion or shallots
1/2 c. thinly sliced mushrooms

SUGGESTED SPICES:
1/4 tsp. sage
1/4 tsp. nutmeg

1 tbsp. parsley

Saute onions (or shallots) with spices in chicken stock. Saute mushrooms separately and place them in the bottom of a souffle or oven-proof dish. Mix carrot puree into sauteed onion and spices. Whip egg white into soft peaks and fold in the carrot mixture. Pile this mixture on top of the mushrooms. Bake for 20 minutes, or until lightly browned on top, at 350 degrees. Garnish with parsley. NOTE: Mushrooms may be mixed in with the carrot mixture if preferred.

SWEET CARROTS

1 (4 oz.) can frozen apple or
orange juice concentrate
2 oz. water

8 lg. carrots, sliced
1/2 tsp. cinnamon

Place juice and water in a medium saucepan. Heat slowly until defrosted. Add carrots and cinnamon. Cook on medium heat until tender, about 10 to 15 minutes. Serves 8.

INDIAN-STYLE CARROTS

Fast weight loss.

4 med. sized carrots
1 c. chicken stock (homemade or canned, no salt added)
3 tbsp. apple juice concentrate

1 tsp. Butter Buds
1/2 tsp. cumin
1/2 tsp. mint
Dash cayenne pepper
Dash cinnamon

Peel or scrape carrots. Cut in medium sized rounds (1/4"). Heat chicken stock in saucepan to boil. Add carrots, reduce heat to light boil, cook until about 3/4 of the stock is boiled away. Add sweetener and spices. Cook, stirring occasionally until carrots begin to glaze. Remove from heat, serve hot or cold.

CAULIFLOWER CURRY

1 head cauliflower, cut into 1" pieces
2 onions, chopped fine
1/2 c. lentils

1/2 tsp. chili powder
1 tsp. curry powder
Juice of 1 lemon

Saute onion in small amount of water 5 minutes. Add cauliflower, lentils and spices. Add cup of water and cook until cauliflower is tender on low flame. Add lemon juice. Serves 4.

CORN-ON-THE-COB

4 ears of corn
Water

butter Buds
Garlic powder

Remove the husks from corn and place husks in the bottom of a 4 quart pan. Add about 1" of water. Remove silky threads from cobs and rinse. Place cobs in pan. Cover tightly and steam for 15 minutes. Remove from pan and dip in Butter Buds and sprinkle with garlic powder. 4 servings.

GREEN BEANS ALMONDINE

Fast weight loss.

3 c. fresh green beans, chopped
10 mushrooms
1 med. red onion

1 clove garlic
2 tbsp. wine (white)
1 packet Butter Buds
1/2 c. hot water

Dissolve Butter Buds in water and heat in skillet along with wine. Saute onions and garlic until soft. Add green beans and mushrooms and simmer until soft.

DILLED GARDEN BEANS

Fast weight loss.

2 beef bouillon cubes
1 c. water
2 tbsp. chopped onion

1/2 c. chopped green pepper
1/2 tsp. dill seed
1 (20 oz.) pkg. frozen French cut
   green beans

In a saucepan, dissolve bouillon cubes in water over a medium heat. Add next three ingredients and cook several minutes. Add beans and cook, covered 8 to 10 minutes until beans are just tender. Serves 6.

FANCY GREEN BEANS

Fast weight loss.

1 (20 oz.) pkg. French cut green
   beans
2 (5 oz.) cans water chestnuts,
   drained & sliced

1 c. sliced mushrooms

Cook beans according to directions, add water chestnuts and cooked mushrooms. Season with pepper to taste.

GREEN BEANS OREGANO

Fast weight loss.

1 (10 oz.) pkg. French cut green
  beans
1 tomato, diced
1/2 c. celery, diced
1/2 c. green bell pepper, diced

3 tbsp. onion, chopped
1/2 tsp. dried oregano
1/3 c. water
Lemon wedges

Combine all ingredients in saucepan and bring to a boil. Reduce heat and simmer covered for 6 to 8 minutes or until beans are done. Garnish with lemon wedges. Serves 4.

LOUISIANA GREEN BEANS

Fast weight loss.

1 lb. fresh green beans
2 c. tomatoes, diced
1/2 c. chopped celery

1/4 c. chopped green bell pepper
1/2 tsp. onion powder

Cook beans until tender, then add remaining ingredients and cook over medium heat until cooked through, about 15 minutes. Serves 8.

SCANDINAVIAN GREEN BEANS

Fast weight loss.

1 lb. fresh tender green beans
1 tbsp. low sodium Dijon or
  champagne mustard
3 tbsp. rice milk

2 tbsp. fresh dillweed, minced
1 tbsp. red wine vinegar or apple
  cider vinegar
1 tbsp. low sodium vegetable
  seasoning

Prepare green beans, snap off stems and cut if needed. Steam in vegetable steamer until tender. Toss with seasonings and serve.

SPANISH GREEN BEANS

Fast weight loss.

4 c. cooked green beans
1 onion, chopped

1/2 c. tomato puree
Pepper to taste

Brown onion in water until golden. Add rest of ingredients. Mix and heat through. Serves 6 to 8.

HERBED TOMATOES

6 tomatoes
1/2 tsp. pepper
3 tsp. dillweed

2 tsp. grated sap sago cheese
(opt.)

Arrange tomatoes in baking pan making a cross on top of each. Sprinkle insides with remaining ingredients. Place under broiler for 8 to 10 minutes. Do not over cook or tomatoes lose their shape. Serves 6.

TOMATO KALE

1 1/2 bunches kale (1-2 lbs.)
1 sm. onion
1 clove garlic

1 tsp. cumin seeds or ground
  cumin
1/2 c. tomato paste
1 c. tomatoes, chopped
1/2 c. peas
Salt, if needed

Wash kale, strip off stems and chop. You should have 12 cups, more or less. Steam until tender and drain.

Meantime, saute onion (and garlic, if desired) in non-stick pan with water as needed, adding cumin when onion is soft. Continue to cook a moment more until the cumin is fragrant. Add the tomato paste and tomatoes and stir to heat through. Add peas, cooking until tender, then add kale. If you have used canned tomatoes or frozen peas, you may not need to add more salt; check and adjust salt to taste. Makes about 4 cups.

Variation: Instead of peas, add a cup of cubed steamed potato or winter squash.

LIMA BEANS, PEARL ONIONS & CARROTS

1/2 c. Butter Buds liquid
1 clove garlic, crushed
3 carrots, sliced

1 (16 oz.) bag frozen pearl onions
3 (10 oz.) bags frozen lima beans

Saute garlic in Butter Buds. Add carrots and onions. Let simmer a few minutes. Add lima beans and simmer until all vegetables are tender.

BAKED POTATO

Fast weight loss.
Microwave potato, covered by glass pyrex bowl. A plain baked potato can be a delicious snack. As topping use chili salsa, barbecue sauce, catsup (no sugar), or Butter Buds.

MASHED POTATOES

Fast weight loss. Serves 4.
4 med. potatoes, peeled & cut
  into lg. chunks
1 med. onion, chopped
2 cloves garlic, crushed

2 tbsp. parsley flakes
1/2 tsp. basil
1/2 tsp. thyme

Place potatoes, onions, garlic and spices in a large saucepan. Add water to cover. Bring to a boil. Cover and cook over medium heat until done, about 30 minutes. Drain and reserve the cooking liquid. Add one cup hot cooking liquid back to the pot. Beat the cooked vegetables with electric mixer until smooth. Serve with gravy or sauce.

NEW POTATOES & BEANS

1 lb. new potatoes, sliced (1/4"
  slices)
1/4 c. julienne green pepper (1
  1/2" x 1/4" strips)
1/4 c. julienne red pepper (1 1/2"
  x 1/4" strips)
1/4 c. chopped onion

2 tbsp. snipped fresh parsley
2 tbsp. defatted chicken broth
1 lg. clove garlic, minced
1/4 tsp. dried rosemary leaves,
  crushed
1 (16 oz.) can Great Northern
  beans or kidney beans, rinsed
  & drained

In 2 quart casserole, combine all ingredients, except beans. Cover. Microwave at High for 10 to 14 minutes or until potatoes are tender, stirring once. Add beans; mix well. Microwave at High for 1 1/2 to 2 minutes, or until beans are hot. 8 servings.

Per Serving: 107 calories; 4 g protein; 19 g carbohydrates; 2 g fat; 4 mg. sodium; 3 g fiber.

POTATO PANCAKES I

Fast weight loss.

2 lbs. baking potatoes, peeled &
  cut into 1" pieces
1 c. minced onions

2 tbsp. whole wheat flour
2 egg whites
Pepper to taste
Applesauce

Finely chop potatoes in processor until pulpy. Do not puree. Transfer to large bowl. Mix in onions. Let stand until water forms at bottom of bowl, about 10 minutes. Drain potatoes and onions through fine sieve, pressing down to extract all liquid. Stir 2 tablespoons flour and egg whites into potato mixture. Season with pepper.

Form into patties and place in non-stick skillet. Cook until potatoes are brown, 1 to 1 1/2 minutes. Turn and cook until the other side is brown. Serve with applesauce. 12 pancakes.

POTATO PANCAKES II

Fast weight loss.

3 lg. potatoes, such as Idaho
1 med. onion, coarsely grated
1 tbsp. low sodium soy sauce

1 tsp. unsalted Dijon style
   mustard
1/4 tsp. baking powder
3 tbsp. matzo meal
2 egg whites

1. Peel and coarsely grate potatoes. Place them in a large bowl and cover completely with cold water. Refrigerate 12 hours.

2. Drain the potatoes, then press them in a kitchen towel to extract as much moisture as possible. Return them to the empty bowl and mix in grated onion.

3. In a small bowl, combine soy sauce, mustard, baking powder and matzo meal. Slowly mix thoroughly into potato mixture. Beat egg whites until stiff and fold into potato mixture.

4. Heat a non-stick skillet, or a regular skillet coated with a non-stick cooking spray, over medium heat. (Pan is ready when a drop of water dances across its surface.) Drop potato mixture onto the skillet by the tablespoon. Cook until well browned and crisp on both sides. Serve hot. Makes 16 pancakes. Potato pancakes may be served with 1/4 cup unsweetened applesauce per serving.

POTATO AND CABBAGE VEGETABLE

Fast weight loss.

1 cabbage, sliced very thin
3 lg. potatoes, cut in 1/2" cubes
Pam spray
1 sm. jalapeno chili, diced finely
1 tbsp. black mustard seeds

1/4 tsp. turmeric
1 tbsp. coriander powder
1 tsp. salt
1 sm. slice lemon

In pan heat Pam spray, mustard seeds, chili and turmeric. When mustard seeds start to crackle add potatoes. Stir for 8 minutes on medium heat. Add cabbage and cook for 15 more minutes until cabbage and potatoes are both tender. Add salt and coriander powder. Sprinkle with lemon juice. Serve hot. Serves 4.

SCALLOPED POTATOES

5 potatoes, peeled & sliced
1 onion, chopped
1/4 tsp. pepper
1/4 tsp. paprika

1/4 c. whole wheat flour
1/2 c. ground nuts
1 c. water
1/4 tsp. dill weed

Layer the potatoes and onions in a large casserole dish. Sprinkle with paprika, flour, pepper and dill weed. Mix ground nuts and water together. Pour over potatoes and onions. Bake at 375 degrees, covered for 1 hour.

TWICE BAKED POTATOES

Fast weight loss.

4 baking potatoes
2 egg whites
2 tbsp. prepared Butter Buds

1 tbsp. thyme
2 tbsp. finely chopped onion

Bake potatoes 50 minutes at 400 degrees. Slice lengthwise in halves. Scoop out pulp into mixing bowl, beat potato pulp with remaining ingredients. Return mixture to potato shells, top with paprika and bake 15 minutes at 350 degrees. Serves 6 to 8.

SAUTEED BEAN SPROUTS

Fast weight loss.

6 c. bean sprouts
3 carrots, shredded

6 tsp. water
1 c. chopped green onions

Put water in a non-stick skillet and heat. Gently stir in carrots and onions and cook, stirring until carrots are tender but not soft. Mix in bean sprouts and cook uncovered over high heat, stirring until bean sprouts are hot. Serves 5 to 6.

STUFFED ACORN SQUASH

1 sm. acorn squash, trimmed &
   halved
1/2 tsp. Butter Buds
1 tart apple, sliced
1 tbsp. chopped pecans

1 tbsp. raisins
1/3 c. apple juice concentrate
1/2 tsp. cinnamon

Preheat oven to 375 degrees. Place squash halves, cut side down, in a baking pan, add 1/2″ of water, cover pan. Bake 35 minutes or until tender.

Saute apple slices in Butter Buds in a non-stick skillet until soft. Add nuts, saute 1 minute more, add raisins and apple juice concentrate. Simmer until juice thickens, about 3 minutes. Add cinnamon.

Remove seeds and fiber from cooked squash. Scoop out flesh and add to apple mixture. Stir well, place back in squash shells. Return to oven, about 12 to 15 minutes. Serves 2.

STUFFED ARTICHOKES

4 whole fresh artichokes
1/4 c. lemon juice
2 peppercorns
4 whole cloves
2 slices toasted whole wheat
   bread

1 c. chopped mushrooms
1 onion, diced
2 tbsp. chopped parsley
1/2 tsp. garlic powder

Cut stem from artichokes and trim points from leaves. In a skillet roll artichokes in lemon juice then place in a pan upright. Add about an inch of water and place peppercorns and garlic in the water. Crumble toast as fine as possible and add rest of ingredients. With a spoon, sprinkle this mixture among the leaves, use small amounts in each place. Cover and cook over a low heat for 30 minutes or until done. Serves 4.

SPICY ZUCCHINI

Fast weight loss. Serves 6 to 8.
2 med. zucchini, thinly sliced
1 lg. carrot, coarsely grated
1 med. onion, chopped

2 stalks celery, chopped
1/2 med. green pepper, thinly
   sliced
2 med. tomatoes, sliced

SAUCE:
1 c. mild green chili salsa
1/4 tsp. dried basil

1 clove garlic, crushed
2 tsp. prepared mustard

Prepare vegetables as directed and layer in a casserole dish, all except for the tomatoes. Combine ingredients for the sauce and pour over the layered vegetables. Place sliced tomatoes over the top. Cover and bake at 325 degrees for 45 minutes. Remove cover and bake for 15 minutes longer.

MARINATED VEGETABLES

Fast weight loss.

1/4 c. vinegar
1 tbsp. lemon juice
1/2 tsp. coriander seed, crushed
1 clove garlic, minced
1/2 tsp. pepper

1 c. water
1/2 c. sliced zucchini
1/2 c sliced yellow squash
1/2 c. chopped broccoli
1/2 c. green beans

Place first six ingredients in a pot and bring to a boil. Add vegetables and reduce heat. Simmer until vegetables are crisp-tender. Chill and serve cold. Serves 2 to 3.

RATATOUILLE I

Fast weight loss.

1 eggplant, diced (peeled opt.)
1 lg. yellow onion, diced
4 sm. yellow or green zucchini, sliced
1 bell pepper (red is best, green will do), diced
1 sm. peeled & sliced cucumber
1 can salt-free tomatoes, or 4 fresh tomatoes, diced

1/4 c. tomato paste or Progresso crushed tomatoes
1 clove garlic, crushed
1 c. red wine
1 tbsp. apple juice concentrate
2 tbsp. sweet basil
Dash hot red pepper to taste

This dish is simple to make and delicious served with a salad of romaine and fresh crusty bread. Combine all ingredients in a large saucepan. Cook on low heat 30 to 45 minutes until all vegetables are tender. Stir occasionally. Serves 6.

RATATOUILLE II

Fast weight loss.

1 med. eggplant
6 med. zucchini
2 green bell peppers
2 lg. onions, sliced
4 lg. tomatoes, cut into chunks

1 clove garlic, minced
1/2 c. minced parsley
1 tsp. crushed oregano
1 tsp. low sodium soy sauce

1. Cut unpeeled eggplant into 1/2" cubes. Slice zucchini into 1/2" rounds. Remove seeds from green bell peppers and cut into 1/2" squares.
2. Combine all ingredients and mix thoroughly.
3. Place mixture in a 6 quart casserole with a cover. Bake at 350 degrees for 1 1/2 hours, covered, and 1/2 hour, uncovered. During the first hour, baste top occasionally with some of the liquid to ensure even flavoring.
4. Serve hot from oven, or cold. Cool to room temperature before refrigerating. Flavors are enhanced if chilled and then reheated before serving. Makes 8 servings. Each serving contains 75 calories; 8% fat; 33 mg sodium; 0 mg cholesterol.
Variation: Place all ingredients in a 6 quart pot. Add 1/2 cup red wine, 1/2 cup tomato juice. Cook, covered on top of stove for 35 minutes.

VEGETABLE CURRY

1 med. onion, chopped
3 tbsp. whole wheat flour
1 c. chicken broth, defatted
1 1/2 tsp. curry powder
1/2 c. water
1 c. broccoli flowerettes
1 c. cauliflower pieces

2 med. carrots, sliced
4 stalks celery, sliced
1 lg. zucchini, sliced
1 med. red or green pepper,
  chopped
1/2 c. frozen green peas
1 (8 oz.) can water chestnuts
1/2 c. raisins

Saute onion in a little water until soft. Add flour, chicken broth, curry powder and water. Bring to a boil and add broccoli, cauliflower, carrots and celery. Cook until veggies start to get tender (broccoli will be bright green). Add zucchini and bell pepper. Cook for about 3 to 5 minutes. Add peas, water chestnuts and raisins. Heat another 3 minutes. Serve plain for weight loss or serve over brown rice.

STUFFED ZUCCHINI

4 lg. zucchini
1 onion, chopped
1 green pepper, chopped
3/4 c. chopped tomatoes

1 1/4 c. tomato juice
1 tsp. dried oregano
2 slices whole wheat toast

Cut the zucchini in half lengthwise, then scoop out pulp. Save shells for stuffing. Dice scooped out zucchini, then place in non-stick skillet with next four ingredients and 1/3 cup tomato juice and oregano. Cook until vegetables are limp and fill the shells with cooked mixture and place on baking dish. Pour remaining juice around zucchini and sprinkle with crumbled toast. Bake at 350 degrees for 30 minutes. Serves 8.

ZUCCHINI CASSEROLE

Fast weight loss.

4 c. sliced zucchini	1 1/2 tsp. oregano
1 onion, thinly sliced	1 tsp. basil
1 (4 oz.) jar chopped pimiento	1 (15-16 oz.) can tomato sauce

Slice the zucchini about 1/4" thick. Lay in the bottom of a medium sized oblong baking dish. Separate onion into rings and lay over zucchini. Next spoon the pimiento over the top of the onions and zucchini. Sprinkle herbs over this, then pour the tomato sauce over it all. Cover baking dish with foil and bake at 375 degrees for 30 minutes. Serves 6.

ZUCCHINI SQUARES

3 c. shredded zucchini	2 tsp. parsley
3/4 c. whole wheat flour	1 tbsp. low sodium soy sauce
1 tsp. baking soda	Dash of Tabasco
1 pkg. Butter buds	2 cloves garlic, minced
1/2 c. onion, chopped	6 egg whites

Preheat oven to 350 degrees. Mix soy sauce, Tabasco and egg whites. Beat until stiff peaks form. Mix dry ingredients; blend with egg white mixture. Pour into 13"x 9"x 2" pan sprayed with non-stick. Bake 25 to 30 minutes until golden brown. Makes 2 to 3 dozen squares.

ZUCCHINI-STUFFED TOMATOES

Fast weight loss.

1 lb. zucchini, chopped
5 med. tomatoes
1 sm. onion, chopped
1 sm. green pepper, chopped
1 clove garlic, minced
1 tsp. each oregano and basil

1/2 tsp. vegetable seasoning
1/4 tsp. pepper
1/2 c. egg whites
4 tbsp., grated Lite Line cheese
(opt.)

Cut out core of tomato. Set upside down to drain. Saute onion and pepper in small amount of liquid until soft. Stir in zucchini, garlic and spices and seasonings. Cook, stirring often for about 5 minutes. Stir in egg whites and 2 tablespoons of the cheese. Evenly spoon mixture into tomato shells; sprinkle with remaining cheese. Bake at 350 degrees for 15 minutes. Serves 6.

ZUCCHINI COLACHE

Fast weight loss.

1 lb. zucchini, unpeeled & sliced
1 onion, sliced
1/2 c. green bell pepper, diced
1/4 c. water
1 c. diced tomato

2 c. whole kernel corn
1/8 tsp. oregano
1/4 tsp. basil
1/4 tsp. marjoram
Freshly ground pepper to taste

Saute zucchini, onion and pepper in non-stick skillet (use non-stick spray) until vegetables are limp. Add water, tomato and corn. Cover and cook squash until tender, adding more water if necessary. Add pepper to taste and other seasonings. Serves 6.

Soups & Salads

AZTEC SOUP

Baked tortilla pieces
3 tbsp. Butter Buds
2/3 c. pine nuts
3/4 c. walnut halves
1 lg. red onion, chopped
2 cloves garlic, minced
12 c. chicken broth

4 c. diced, peeled butternut or
 acorn squash
2 pkgs. frozen corn
3/4 c. toasted, shelled pumpkin
 seeds
1 lg. avocados

Bake tortillas in oven at 400 degrees until crispy, about 10 minutes.

In a pan over medium heat, melt 1 tablespoon of the Butter Buds. Add pine nuts and walnuts and cook, stirring until golden. Remove nuts and set aside.

Melt the remaining 2 tablespoons Butter Buds in pan and cook onion and garlic until onion is golden. Place onion and garlic in a large pot, add chicken broth and squash and bring to a boil. Reduce heat, cover and simmer until squash is tender. Add corn and cook for 5 more minutes. Sprinkle with pumpkin seeds just before serving. Peel and dice avocado. Place avocado, nuts, and tortilla pieces in bowls and pass as condiments at the table to add to the soup. Serves 19.

BARBECUE BEAN SOUP

1 1/4 c. dried legumes (use as
 many different kinds as
 possible)
1/4 tsp. ginger
1 lg. onion, chopped
1/4 tsp. lemon pepper
1 tbsp. barbecue sauce

1/2 tsp. crushed red pepper
1 sm. clove garlic, chopped
1 (16 oz.) can tomatoes
1/2 tsp. chili powder
2 tsp. ketchup
2 stalks celery, chopped

Soak the beans overnight. The next day, cook the beans for at least 12 hours to eliminate any gas problems. Add the ginger while they are cooking. Add the remaining ingredients and cook for 3 hours.

BEAN SOUP

1/4 cup each: black-eyed peas, large lima beans, pinto beans, black beans, kidney beans, navy beans, split peas, small limas, lentils, pear barley, anasazi and Great Northern beans.

Wash thoroughly. Place in large container and cover with water and 1 tablespoon salt. Let set overnight. Next day drain off water and add 2 quarts fresh water. Then add 1/2 pound ham hocks or you may use cooked turkey or sausage. Bring to a boil and reduce heat to simmer. Simmer for 2 to 2 1/2 hours then add 1 large onion, diced, 2 chopped carrots, 1 stalk of sliced celery, 1 large peeled tomato, and 1 teaspoon chili powder. Salt and pepper to taste and add the juice of 1/2 lemon. Simmer another 30 minutes or until done.

BEET BORSCHT

Fast weight loss.

3 c. water
1/2 c. salt free tomato juice
1 med. onion, finely chopped
1/4 head cabbage, finely shredded, about 1 1/2 c.

1 sm. beet, cooked, peeled & julienned
2 tbsp. fresh lemon juice
1 tbsp. cider vinegar
2 tbsp. apple juice concentrate

In a large saucepan, combine 3 cups water, tomato juice, onion and cabbage. Bring to a boil, reduce heat, and simmer, covered, about 15 minutes, until vegetables are tender. Add remaining ingredients and mix thoroughly. Makes 4 servings. This soup freezes well.

BLACK BEAN SOUP

1 c. black beans
4 c. water
3 bay leaves
4 cloves

2 onions, chopped
2 cloves garlic
1/4 tsp. dry mustard
1 1/2 tsp. chili powder

Add all ingredients to boiling water and simmer until tender. Puree. Serves 4 to 5.

BLACK BEAN SOUP WITH CHILLED SPICED RICE

The distinctive contrast of temperatures and textures make this an especially enjoyable main dish. Serve it with a green salad topped with canned mandarin orange sections and creamy avocado slices with poppy seed dressing. Pass crusty, whole grain rolls to complete the meal.

3 beef bouillon cubes
5 c. hot water
1/4 c. minced dried onion
1 med. green pepper, seeded & chopped (3/4 c.)
3 cloves garlic, minced or pressed
1 1/2 tsp. ground cumin
1 1/2 tsp. dried oregano

2 (15 oz.) can black beans, drained (pinto or red beans can be substituted)
1 (4 oz.) can chopped green chilies
2 tbsp. cider vinegar
Chilled spiced rice

In a three quart saucepan, combine all ingredients. Stir, bring to a boil, cover and simmer for 20 to 30 minutes. Ladle into bowls and top with a generous spoonful of chilled spiced rice.

Chilled Spiced Rice: (The rice is best when made the night before or at least 30 minutes before serving to allow flavors to blend.) Combine 1/2 cup finely chopped green onion, 1/2 teaspoon oregano, 1/4 cup each no oil Italian salad dressing and cider vinegar. Mix with three cups cooked brown or white rice. Chill thoroughly before serving.

Nutrient values per serving: Yields: 6 (1 cup) servings. 113 calories; trace fat; 0 cholesterol; 22 gm carbohydrates; 940 gm sodium; 7 mg. protein

BETH'S BLACK KETTLE SOUP

This Black Bean soup is a savory dish popular in Latin American and Cuba. While it is simmering on the back of your stove, it will fill your home with a seductive, mouth-watering aroma.

1 c. dried black beans (available in specialty stores if not in your market)

3 c. salt free beef or vegetable broth

1 c. mild green chili salsa (check for sodium content)

2 cloves minced garlic

1 tbsp. Bakon seasoning or liquid smoke

2 tbsp. fresh green cilantro or dried coriander, minced

1/2 c. dry red wine or sherry

1 bay leaf (remove before serving)

Sprinkle of green scallion onions, chopped as garnish

This soup makes itself. To shorten cooking time, soak beans in bowl of water overnight. Discard water before using beans. Place all ingredients, except scalllions, in heavy bottomed saucepan or soup kettle (if you have an iron pot, it's best to use). Simmer 2 1/2 hours or until beans are plump and tender. Place in bowl and sprinkle with scallions. Serve more salsa and cilantro on the side. Add a salad for a simple, complete and satisfying meal. Makes 8 to 10 servings. Freeze leftovers for an easy meal later.)

BROCCOLI LEMON SOUP

Fast weight loss.

1 c. broccoli, chopped
2 c. clear homemade chicken
   stock
2 egg whites
1/4 c. lemon juice
1/4 c. cooked brown rice or
   pastini (pasta)

1 tbsp. sweet basil
1 clove garlic
1 carrot, diced
1/4 c. diced onion
1 tbsp. apple juice concentrate

In heavy bottomed saucepan, add all ingredients, except lemon and egg whites. Simmer 1/2 hour. Beat egg whites together with lemon juice. Add to soup. Makes 4 to 6 servings.

CABBAGE-VEGETABLE SOUP

Fast weight loss.

1/2 head cabbage, chopped
3 lg. red potatoes, cubed
4 carrots, sliced
1 (15 oz.) can kidney beans,
   rinsed & drained
1 (15 oz.) can tomato sauce

1/4 c. tomato paste
1 1/4 c. chicken broth, defatted
3 c. water
2 tsp. chili powder
1 1/2 tsp. cumin
Juice from 1/2 of lemon

Combine all ingredients together in large saucepan and simmer on stove, covered for about 2 hours.

CARROT AND PARSNIP SOUP

Fast weight loss.

1 1/2 quarts water
1 lg. onion, chopped
2 bay leaves
1/2 tsp. thyme

2 stalks celery & leaves, chopped
very fine
1 lg. parsnip, grated
2-3 lg. carrots, grated

Simmer onion in 1/4 cup water for 5 minutes. Add remaining water, bay leaves, pepper, and thyme. Bring to a boil slowly. Add vegetables to the stock and simmer gently for 1 hour. Puree 2 cups of this soup for a creamier texture. Garnish with carrot curls or chopped parsley. Serves 4.

CAULIFLOWER SOUP

Fast weight loss.

5 c. water
1 head cauliflower, chopped into
sm. pieces
1 c. corn

1 sm. zucchini, chopped
1 1/2 c. cooked barley
1 1/2 tbsp. vegetable broth
seasoning

In a medium saucepan combine all ingredients in water and bring to a boil. Simmer for 20 minutes.

CHICKEN, TURKEY OR BEEF STOCK

These stocks are the secret to flavorful, salt-free cooking, so be sure to keep lots on hand. Use the soups, to saute and wherever you need a flavor boost. They also are delicious as a hot beverage.

CHICKEN OR TURKEY STOCK:

Use either poultry backs and scraps, if to be discarded, or poultry pieces, to be saved for use in other dishes.

Use at least 2 pounds of poultry for each 1/2 gallon of water:

1 carrot	1 onion, sliced in half
1 bay leaf	1 stalk celery

In large sauce or stockpan, fill 1/2 full with water. Bring to boil and add all ingredients. If using chicken parts to be discarded, you may want to tie all the flavoring agents in a large piece of cheesecloth. The stock can also just be strained after cooking. Allow all the ingredients to simmer at least one hour, the longer, the better. If the poultry parts are to be used, remove after one hour. The stock may have some chicken fat floating on the surface. If so, either chill and remove the hardened fat, or use a Gravy Strain. Store strained stock in refrigerator.

Variation: Beef Stock: Use 2 pounds beef bones. Follow recipe as above.

CHILI BEAN SOUP

1 onion, chopped fine	1 (6 oz.) can tomato paste
1 (28 oz.) can kidney beans	1 tbsp. chili powder
1 (28 oz.) can tomatoes	1/2 tbsp. ground cumin

Slowly saute onion in small amount of water in a 2 quart saucepan. Put the tomatoes in a blender and blend for 30 seconds or until they have a lumpy consistency. Add the beans and tomatoes to the onion. Add tomato paste and mix well. Add chili powder and cumin, mix well, then bring the mixture to a boil. Reduce heat and simmer for 30 minutes. Soup is best when prepared a day ahead, refrigerated overnight and reheated. Serves 4.

CHILLED STRAWBERRY SOUP

2 pints strawberries, halved
1 c. orange juice
1 c. red wine
1/4 c. frozen apple juice
   concentrate
1 tbsp. cornstarch
1 c. rice milk
Mint leaves for garnish

Puree strawberries. Blend cornstarch with 1/4 cup of the orange juice in a 2-quart saucepan. Add remaining orange juice, red wine, apple juice concentrate and pureed strawberries. Heat just to boiling. Cool. Stir in rice milk. Cover and refrigerate 2 to 4 hours. Garnish with chopped fresh mint leaves.

CHINESE HOT AND SOUR SOUP

5 c. chicken stock, defatted, low
   sodium
10 oz. firm tofu, cut into squares
   or wheat meat
3 egg whites, lightly beaten
1/2 c. mushrooms, halved
1 carrot
1 bunch scallions
2 stalks bok choy (use cabbage if
   not available)
2 tbsp. dry sherry (opt.)
1/4 c. (or to taste) hot Szechuan
   chili past, or Sanj Szechuan
   Sauce
2 cloves garlic
1 tsp. ground ginger

Heat stock; add pepper, garlic and ginger. Slice vegetables and add to broth. Dice tofu, add to broth and simmer for 10 minutes. With temperature just under boiling, drip egg whites, stirring lightly. Add vinegar and simmer for 5 more minutes. For a variation, add bean sprouts or diced pepper instead of tofu. Serves 4.

CHINESE TOMATO SOUP

Fast weight loss.

1 green chili, seeded, rinsed & finely chopped
1 c. salt free tomato sauce
15 oz. can salt free tomatoes
3 c. low sodium chicken stock, defatted
1 c. bok choy, cut on the bias
2 celery stalks, thinly sliced
1 med. onion, thinly sliced

2 garlic cloves, minced
1/2 c. chopped scallion
1/4 c. cooked brown rice (opt.)
1 tbsp. low sodium soy sauce
1/2 tsp. curry powder
1 tsp. chili powder
1 c. bean sprouts

In a medium saucepan, cook chili, tomato sauce, tomatoes, chicken stock, bok choy, celery, onion and garlic over medium heat for 15 minutes. Add scallion, rice (if using), soy sauce, curry and chili powders and mix thoroughly. Cook for 5 minutes. Add bean sprouts and cook for 1 minute more. Serve hot. Makes 6 servings.

CHICK-PEA SOUP

12 oz. chick peas (garbanzos)
6 c. water
3 or 4 med. parsnips (1/2 lb.), sliced
4 or 5 med. ribs celery (1/2 lb.), sliced
2 med. onions or leeks (1/2 lb.), chopped

3 or 4 carrots (1/2 lb.), sliced
6 c. additional water
1/4-1/3 c. tamari (soy sauce)
2 tbsp. Vogue's Vege-Base or Mrs. Dash Seasoning
1/4 tsp. nutmeg

Soak chick peas overnight. Next day add the vegetables and additional water. Simmer over low heat 1 1/2 hours or more until chick peas are tender. Remove about half the soup and whiz in blender or food processor a few seconds. Return to pot. Add seasonings. This recipe can easily be cut in half or a smaller group. Serves 10 to 12.

CORN CHOWDER

3 c. fresh or frozen corn kernels
2 c. low sodium chicken stock,
    defatted
1 celery stalk, finely chopped
1 onion, finely chopped
1 carrot, peeled & finely chopped
1 potato, peeled & diced

1 red bell pepper, seeded & finely
    chopped
4 garlic cloves, finely chopped
4 oz. canned green chilies, rinsed
    & chopped
2 tbsp. natural rice vinegar
1/4 tsp. white pepper
4 tbsp. potato starch for salt free
    instant mashed potato flakes

1. In a blender, puree 1 1/2 cups corn kernels and 1 cup chicken stock until smooth. Transfer to a large saucepan and add remaining corn and chicken stock, celery, onion, carrot, potato, pepper and garlic. Bring to a boil cover and simmer for 20 minutes.

2. Add chilies, vinegar and pepper and simmer another 20 minutes.

3. Stir in the potato starch (or instant potato flakes) and cook for a few minutes until the soup is thickened. Makes 8 servings.

CURRIED ZUCCHINI SOUP

Fast weight loss.
3 sm. zucchini, diced
2 lg. onions, sliced
2-3 tomatoes, sliced
1 qt. vegetable stock + 3 tbsp.
1 tsp. whole wheat flour

4 tbsp. water
1 tsp. curry powder
1/8 tsp. ginger
Dash of cayenne pepper
Basil
Garlic powder

Heat 3 tablespoons stock and saute zucchini and onion until onion is soft. Add remaining stock and cook 20 minutes. Saute tomatoes in stock and then add to the other vegetables and bring to a boil. Mix flour, water, curry ginger and cayenne. When blended, add to soup. Simmer 6 minutes. Force the mixture through a strainer or spin in blender. Season to taste with basil and garlic powder. Serves 4.

EGGPLANT BEAN SOUP

Soak overnight 1/2 cup each: black eyed peas, pink beans, white beans, red beans and black beans. Drain water off the next morning.

In a large pot on stove, simmer beans in 6 cups water. Season with garlic and onion powder and Instead of Salt. About 6 hours later add:

1 chopped onion
1 c. brown rice
1/2 diced eggplant
1 sliced zucchini
1 fresh yellow crookneck squash
1 spear fresh broccoli, sliced

Simmer another 45 minutes to cook rice and add fresh chopped parsley last. Ready to serve and enjoy anytime.

FLAVORFUL BEAN SOUP

2 c. cooked great northern beans, about 3/4 c. raw
2 c. cooked kidney or red beans, about 3/4 c. raw
1 med. onion, chopped
2 lg. celery stalks, chopped
1 med. potato, scrubbed & diced

3/4 c. string beans, cut into 1" pieces
4 med. tomatoes
1/4 c. dry red wine
1 tsp. dried summer savory
1 tsp. paprika
1/2 tsp. coriander
1/2 tsp. ground cumin
Ground pepper to taste

Soak the northern and kidney beans overnight and then cook them for several hours until tender. Place the onion, celery, potato and string beans in a large pot with just enough water, including the liquid remaining from the cooked beans, to cover. Bring to a boil, cover, and simmer until vegetables are just tender. Add the cooked beans and all the remaining ingredients, plus 2 more cups of water. Simmer, covered, over low heat for 20 to 25 minute. Taste to be sure that everything is done to your liking.

FRENCH VEGETABLE SOUP

Fast weight loss. Serves 8 to 10.

8 c. water
2 onions, coarsely chopped
1 clove garlic, crushed
2 potatoes, chopped coarsely
2 stalks celery, thickly sliced
1 carrot, thickly sliced
1/2 lb. mushrooms, sliced
4 zucchini, thickly sliced, cut in half
2 leeks, sliced or 1 bunch green onions, sliced

2 c. chopped broccoli pieces
1 c. fresh or frozen peas
1 c. chopped cauliflower pieces
1 c. dry white wine
1 tsp. thyme
1 tsp. dill weed
1 tsp. marjoram
1 tsp. basil
3 tbsp. low sodium soy sauce
Fresh, ground black pepper

Place 8 cups water in a large soup pot. Add onions, potatoes, garlic, celery and carrots. Bring to a boil, reduce heat, cover and simmer for 15 minutes. Add remaining ingredients, cook an additional 30 minutes.

Sprinkle with finely chopped green onions before serving, if desired.

FRENCH ONION SOUP

Fast weight loss.

2 lg. onions, thinly sliced lengthwise
4 c. low sodium chicken stock, defatted

1/2 tsp. low sodium soy sauce
1/4 c. dry sherry

1. In a large skillet, cook onions over a very low heat, covered, until soft. Remove lid, increase heat to high and brown onions, stirring constantly to avoid burning. When completely browned, reduce heat to low and add 1/4 cup chicken stock and mix well.

2. Transfer onion mixture to a larger saucepan. Add remaining chicken stock, soy sauce and sherry and bring to a boil. Reduce heat and simmer, uncovered for 30 minutes. Makes 4 servings.

Variation: French Onion Soup with Croutons. Add 1/3 cup whole wheat bread croutons to each cup of soup.

GARLIC SOUP

Fast weight loss.

1 1/2 quarts water
4 potatoes
1 carrot
2 stalks celery

1 onion
2 lg. bulbs garlic
1/2 tsp. thyme
Dash of cayenne pepper

Bring water to a boil. Cut potatoes, celery and onion into 1/2" pieces and place in boiling water. Break garlic bulbs and peel individual cloves. Place in soup together with spices. Cook over medium heat for 20 to 30 minutes. When soup is ready, it can be served in either of 2 ways: (1) strain and serve as a clear broth or (2) puree in blender and serve as a "cream of garlic" soup. Serves 6 to 8.

COLD TOMATO HERB SOUP

Fast weight loss.

2 beef bouillon cubes
1 c. boiling water
3 c. tomato juice
1 sm. onion, grated
1 c. celery, chopped
1 green pepper, minced

1 clove garlic
3 tbsp. lemon juice
Dash Tabasco sauce
2 tbsp. dried basil
1 cucumber, diced
2 ripe tomatoes, peeled & diced

Dissolve the cubes in water. Cool slightly, then add the next four ingredients. Cut the garlic in half and stick a toothpick through both halves. Add to the mixture. Mix and refrigerate for several hours. Just before serving, remove the garlic and add remaining ingredients. Serve cold. Serves 6.

GAZPACHO SOUP I

Fast weight loss.

2 1/2 c. chopped tomatoes
1 c. chopped zucchini
1 c. peeled & chopped cucumber
3/4 c. chopped celery
1/2 c. chopped green onion

1/4 c. chopped green pepper
4 c. tomato juice
1 c. canned green chili salsa
1/4 tsp. Tabasco sauce

Puree 1/3 of the tomato, zucchini and celery, with some of the tomato juice. Mix in the rest of the ingredients. Chill. This Spanish soup, which should be served icy cold, is really a salad in the guise of a soup. Makes almost 2 quarts.

GAZPACHO II

Gazpacho is a soup from Spain. There are as many recipes for this soup as there are cities and villages. Some are hot, some cold, some tomato based and some with no tomatoes! One thing they all have in common is bread or croutons as garnish, an ingredients often left out in Americanized versions. Gazpacho literally means "soaked bread"! This version is wonderful chilled and poured from a pitcher into chilled bowls on a hot summer day.

2 lg. cucumbers, peeled & seeded (if hothouse Belgium type, no need to seed)
4-5 ripe red Big Boy type tomatoes, peeled if you have the time (to peel, pierce skin & place in pan of boiling water 1 minute or microwave until the skin easily slips off)
1 bell pepper, cut with seeds & pith discarded
1/3-1/2 c. chopped green scallions
2 cloves garlic

1/3 c. red wine vinegar or herbed vinegar, such as tarragon, oregano or raspberry
1 c. chicken stock, salt free
1 c. low sodium V-8 juice
Few drops of Tabasco, to your taste
3 tbsp. fresh basil, or 1 tbsp. dried, minced lemon wedges
Whole wheat bread, rubbed with garlic, toasted until dry & crusty & cut into cubes for croutons (may use sourdough bread or check your market for an unseasoned crouton)

This is another soup that makes itself in minutes, despite the long list of ingredients. Place all ingredients in a food processor, process with an on-off motion, until chunky and partially pureed. If using a blender, use same on-off motion, but process in smaller batches. Refrigerate 1 hour before serving. Add lemon if desired. Serve with crouton garnish. Serves 8 to 10.

HOT OR COLD TOMATO LEEK SOUP

Fast weight loss.

2 lbs. ripe tomatoes
1/2 c. firmly packed parsley
   (fresh)
1 lg. leek
2 cloves garlic, minced
1 (6 oz.) can tomato paste

2 tbsp. dry red wine
1 tbsp. minced fresh dill
1 1/2 tsp. paprika
1/2 tsp. dried marjoram
1/4 tsp. dried thyme
Ground pepper to taste

Cut 1 1/2 pounds of the tomatoes into quarters and place them in the blender. Add the parsley and process until well pureed. Dice the remaining tomatoes and set aside. Slice the white part of the leek into 1/4" slices. Chop the tender, light green parts of the leaves. Reserve 2 or 3 of the tough green leaves, wash them, cut in half and discard the rest of the green leaves. Separate the leek slices into rings by poking them in the center. Wash carefully, removing all grit and put them in a large pot along with the reserved green leaves and garlic. Cover with 3 cups of water or vegetable stock, bring to a boil, then reduce heat and simmer for 5 minutes. Add the pureed and diced tomatoes and all remaining ingredients and continue to simmer on low heat for 20 to 25 minutes or until the leek rings are tender. Chill, or let stand for 30 minutes if you are serving this hot, then heat through before serving. Remove green leaves before serving. Serves 4 to 6.

ITALIAN SOUP

1/2 lb. zucchini, sliced
1 (15 oz.) can garbanzo beans
1 1/2 c. dry white wine
1 tsp. minced basil leaves
Pepper, if desired

2 onions, sliced
1 (16 oz.) can tomatoes, chopped
2 tsp. minced garlic
1 bay leaf

Combine zucchini, onions, beans, tomatoes with liquid, wine, garlic, basil and bay leaf in baking dish. Cover and bake at 400 degrees for 1 hour, stirring once after 30 minutes. Season to taste with pepper or other seasoning if desired. This may also be cooked on top of stove. For a variation, place two skinned chicken breasts on top of the soup while cooking. The chicken breasts may then be deboned, cubed and added to the soup for additional flavor.

KALE-POTATO SOUP

1 lg. onion
1 clove garlic
2 big potatoes
1 lg. bunch kale

5 c. hot water or stock
1/2 tsp. salt, to taste
Black pepper

An utterly satisfying soup. How many winter nights does this seem to be the only possible choice? A classic, a favorite, a stand-by. With fresh young kale, it is, perhaps, even a world-class soup.

Saute onion in butter and non-stick pan with water, cooking and stirring until clear and slightly golden. About halfway, add the garlic; when the onion is done, crush the garlic with a fork.

Add the potatoes and 2 cups of water. Simmer, covered until potatoes start to soften around the edges. Meantime, wash the kale, remove stems, chop and steam. (Don't try to cook it with the potatoes; the flavor will be too strong.)

When the potatoes are very well done, puree half of them with remaining water and the salt and pepper. Combine all and heat gently, correcting the consistency if necessary by adding hot water or milk. Makes about 6 cups and serves 4 if no extra water is added.

LEEK SHIITAKE SOUP

Fast weight loss.

5 shiitake mushrooms
2 lg. leeks
6 c. water
1 (7") piece wakame
1 celery stalk with leaves, chopped

2 sm. carrots, sliced, cut in half
2 scallions, chopped (opt.)
The chopped shiitake mushrooms
Chopped wakame
1 tbsp. tamari

Pour a cup of boiling water over shiitake mushrooms. Let soak 20 minutes, remove mushrooms and chop. Chop bottom ends off the leeks. Wash ends, boil 10 minutes for stock with 6 cups water and wakame. Remove and discard ends, remove and chop wakame. Clean rest of leeks carefully, slice white and green parts, keeping separate.

Heat a non-stick pan or use Pam cooking spray and fry briefly the sliced white part of leeks and the chopped green leek tops.

Use a non-stick pan to saute the celery, and carrots for 3 minutes; then add scallions and shiitake mushrooms. Add to kettle with wakame and tamari. Simmer for 10 minutes. Taste and add a little more tamari if desired. Top each bowl with whole wheat croutons and minced parsley. Yield: 6 servings. Per Serving: 35 calories; 1 gm protein; 3 gm carbohydrates and 2 gm fat.

LEMON GRASS SOUP - THAI FOOD

5 c. thin coconut milk
3 c. broccoli, cut into bite sized
   pieces
3 tbsp. dried lemon grass

3 green onions, finely chopped
2 tbsp. coriander leaves, chopped
4 fresh Serrano chilies
Juice of 2 limes

To make coconut milk, boil a piece of coconut in 5 cups water, or, if you cannot obtain fresh coconut, you may substitute shredded, packaged coconut (1 cup) and boil it in water. Strain off the coconut and the resulting liquid is coconut milk.

Lemon grass is available in oriental markets.

In a saucepan, bring the coconut milk to a boil. Add the broccoli pieces and lemon grass. Reduce heat and simmer until the broccoli is tender, about 15 minutes. Do not cover. When the broccoli is tender, add the green onions, coriander leaves and chilies. Bring the heat up just below boiling. Remove the pan from heat and stir in the lime juice. Serves. Makes 6 servings.

LENTIL AND BROWN RICE SOUP

1/2 c. raw lentils, washed
1/3 c. raw brown rice
2 cloves garlic, minced
2 tbsp. soy sauce
1 bay leaves
1 sm. onion, thinly sliced
2 med. carrots, thinly sliced
1 lg. celery stalk, finely chopped
Handful of celery leaves

1 (14 oz.) can imported plum
   tomatoes with liquid, chopped
1/2 c. tomato sauce or tomato
   juice
1/4 c. dry red wine
1 tsp. dried basil
1 tsp. paprika
1/2 tsp. dried marjoram
1/2 tsp. dried thyme

Place the first five ingredients in a large pot and cover with 3 cups of water. Bring to a boil, cover and simmer for 7 to 8 minutes over low heat. Add 2 additional cups of water along with all remaining ingredients. Cover and simmer over low heat for 25 to 30 minutes or until vegetables, rice and lentils are done to your liking. Serves 6.

LENTIL SOUP

1 lb. lentils
1 onion, chopped
2 1/2 c. tomato sauce
2 lg. tomatoes, chopped
2 carrots, sliced

2 lg. red potatoes, diced
2 garlic cloves, minced
1/2 tsp. black pepper
1 tsp. basil
Dash of onion powder
Dash of cinnamon

Cook lentils in about six cups of water until tender, about 1/2 hour. Add rest of ingredients, simmer for an hour or two or until vegetables are tender.

LIMA BEAN CHOWDER

2 1/2 c. dried baby lima beans
8 c. water
2 onions, finely chopped
2 carrots, finely chopped
2 stalks celery, chopped
2 cloves garlic, pressed
1 tbsp. parsley flakes

2 tsp. caraway seeds
1 tsp. dill weed
1/4 tsp. crushed red pepper
1 (10 oz.) pkg. frozen lima beans, thawed
1 c. rice, soy or nut milk

Place dried lima beans and water in a large pot. Bring to boil, boil 1 minute, remove from heat, cover and let rest 1 hour. Return to heat, add onion, carrots, celery, garlic and seasonings. Bring to boil, reduce heat, cover and cook over medium-low heat for 1 hour. Add thawed lima beans and acceptable milk. Cook an additional 15 minutes. Serves 6 to 8.

LIMA LEEK SOUP

1 leek, white part only, finely
   chopped
2 c. cooked dried lima beans
1 c. chopped watercress

2 c. defatted chicken broth
2 tbsp. lemon juice (to taste)

Saute leek in chicken broth or a little water. Add balance of chicken broth and lima beans. Cover and simmer 1/2 hour. Let the mixture cool to room temperature. Puree in a blender of food processor. Mix in lemon juice and pepper to taste.

MEDITERRANEAN BROCCOLI AND MUSHROOM SOUP

Fast weight loss.

1 med. onion, chopped
1/2 c. raw barley
2 bay leaves
2 cloves garlic, minced
2 1/2 - 3 c. chopped broccoli
1/2 lb. chopped mushrooms
1 sm. turnip, peeled & chopped
1 (8 oz.) can imported plum
   tomatoes, with liquid, chopped

3 tbsp. minced fresh parsley
1/4 c. dry red wine
1 tsp. paprika
1 tsp. dried marjoram
1/2 tsp. basil
1/4 tsp. dried rosemary
Freshly ground pepper to taste

Place first four ingredients in a large pot and cover with 2 cups water or vegetable stock. Bring to a boil, cover and simmer over low heat for 10 minutes. Add the remaining ingredients to the pot along with an additional 2 1/2 cups of water or stock. Cover and simmer over low heat for about 35 minutes or until the vegetables and barley are tender. Ideally this soup should stand an hour before serving. Serves 6 to 8.

MINESTRONE SOUP

1 onion, chopped
1 clove garlic, minced
2 tbsp. chopped parsley
1/2 tsp. thyme
1/2 tsp. oregano
3 tbsp. tomato paste
1 lg. can (28 oz.) pureed tomatoes

3 stalks celery, chopped
2 carrots, diced
2 c. shredded cabbage
2 zucchini, diced
1 c. uncooked brown rice
3 c. cooked dried beans
1 1/2 quarts chicken broth, defatted

Put all ingredients except rice and beans into soup pot; bring to a boil, add rice, then simmer covered for 1 hour. Now add the beans. Stir, heat and serve.

BASIC MISO SOUP

Fast weight loss.
1 (3″) piece dried Erewhon Wakame
1 c. thinly sliced onions
1 qt. spring water

1 1/3 - 1 1/2 tbsp. Erewhon Miso
Chopped scallions, parsley, ginger or watercress for garnish

Rinse the wakame in cold water for 3 to 5 minutes and slice it into 1/2″ pieces. Put wakame and onions in a pot and add the water. Bring to a boil, lower the heat and simmer for 10 to 20 minutes, or until tender. Reduce the heat to very low but not boiling or bubbling. Put the miso in a bowl or suribachi. Add 1/4 cup of the broth from the pot and puree until miso is completely dissolved in the liquid. Add pureed miso to the soup. Simmer for 3 to 5 minutes and serve. Garnish with scallions, parsley, ginger or watercress.

MUSHROOM SOUP

Fast weight loss.

1 1/2 lbs. mushrooms, sliced
1 onion, thinly sliced
1 lg. clove garlic, crushed
2 bay leaves
3/4 c. white wine (or apple juice)
4 c. water
1 c. chicken stock

3-4 tbsp. low sodium soy sauce
1 1/2 tsp. basil
2 tsp. dill weed
1 tsp. paprika
Fresh ground black pepper

Combine all ingredients in large saucepan. Bring to a boil, reduce heat, cover and simmer for about 30 minutes. Serves 6.

MUSHROOM, BARLEY AND NAVY BEAN SOUP

1 c. dry navy or pea beans, soaked
   or 2 c. canned beans, drained &
   rinsed
1/2 c. pearled barley
1 lb. mushrooms, sliced thin

2 tsp. garlic powder
1 (8 oz.) can no-salt-added
   tomato sauce
2 quarts fat free chicken broth or
   water
Tabasco

Place all ingredients, except Tabasco, in a large 8-quart pot. Slowly bring to a boil, and simmer, covered, for 2 hours, if you are using soaked dried beans, or for 1 hour if you are using canned beans. If the level of liquid goes down, replace it with water or the soup will end up being too thick. Season to taste with Tabasco. This soup keeps on improving with each reheating.

Serving Size: 1 cup; 126 calories; 1 gram fat; 0 cholesterol; 13 milligrams sodium.

NAVY BEAN SOUP

8 c. low sodium chicken stock,
   defatted
1 1/4 c. dry navy beans
2 bay leaves
1 clove garlic, peeled & crushed
10 oz. pkg. frozen cut green beans
3/4 c. chopped celery
3/4 c. chopped onion

3/4 c. diced fresh tomato
1/2 c. peeled, diced potato
1/4 c. sliced leek
1/4 tsp. dried basil
1/4 tsp. dried dill
1/4 tsp. dried thyme
1/4 tsp. garlic powder
1/4 tsp. onion powder
1/4 tsp. dry mustard

1. In a large pot combine stock, beans, and bay leaf. Bring to a boil over medium-high heat, then reduce heat, cover pan and simmer for 1 hour, or until beans are just tender.

2. Remove and discard bay leaves. Transfer 1/3 of the beans to a food processor or blender, add garlic, and process until pureed; return puree to pot.

3. Add green beans, celery, onion, tomato, potato and leek; cover pot and simmer for about 40 minutes.

4. Stir in basil, dill, thyme, garlic and onion powders and mustard. Simmer, covered for another 10 minutes, adding more stock if soup is too thick. Makes 10 servings.

ONION LEEK SOUP

Fast weight loss.

2 onions, sliced into rings
2 leeks, sliced (white & light
    green)
12 green onions, sliced
1/4 c. minced shallots
2 cloves garlic, crushed
2 tsp. grated fresh ginger root
1/16 tsp. cayenne pepper

2 tsp. whole wheat flour
7 c. water
1 c. white wine or use water
1/4 c. low sodium soy sauce
2 tsp. lemon juice
Fresh ground pepper
Fresh chives, snipped

Saute onions in 1/2 cup water for 5 minutes. Add leeks, green onions and shallots with another 1/2 cup water. Saute a few minutes to soften. Add garlic, ginger and cayenne. Stir a few times, then add flour and stir for a couple of minutes. Slowly mix in water, wine and soy sauce. Bring to boil, reduce heat, cover and simmer for 45 minutes.

Add lemon juice and several twists of ground pepper. Mix. Ladle into bowls and garnish with snipped chives. Serves 6 to 8.

ORIENTAL EGG DROP SOUP

Fast weight loss.

1 oz. dried shiitake mushrooms
3 c. chicken broth
2 tsp. soy sauce, low sodium
1/8 tsp. ground ginger
2 tbsp. cornstarch

2 tbsp. water
2 egg whites
3 tbsp. thinly sliced green onions,
    including top
White pepper

Place mushrooms in a bowl, pour in warm water to cover and let soak for about 30 minutes. Then drain mushrooms.

In a 2 quart saucepan, combine chicken broth, soy sauce, ginger and mushrooms. Stir together cornstarch and water and add to soup. Bring to a boil, over high heat, stirring constantly. Drop egg whites into boiling soup. Remove from heat and continue stirring until egg separates into shreds. Sprinkle with onions and season to taste with pepper. Serve immediately. 5 servings.

POTATO CELERY CHOWDER

Fast weight loss.

1 lg. onion, coarsely chopped
4 stalks celery, sliced
1 green pepper, chopped
2 carrots, sliced
2 cloves garlic, crushed
6 1/2 c. water
4 lg. potatoes, cubed

2 tbsp. low sodium soy sauce
1 tsp. basil
1/2 tsp. paprika
1/4 tsp. pepper
1 (28 oz.) can chopped tomatoes
 in their juice

Place onion, celery, green pepper, carrots and garlic in a large soup pot with 1/2 cup water. Saute for 5 minutes, until vegetables are crisp-tender. Add potatoes, soy sauce, basil, paprika, pepper and remaining water. Bring to a boil, reduce heat, cover and cook over medium low heat for 30 minutes. Add tomatoes, cover and cook an additional 15 minutes. Serves 10.

QUICKIE CORN CHOWDER

1/2 c. water
2 c. frozen corn
1 1/2 c. rice milk
2 tsp. dried onion flakes

1/4 tsp. garlic powder
1/2 tsp. chili salsa
2 tsp. lemon juice

Bring water to a boil. Add corn and cook according to directions. Drain corn and put into blender with remaining ingredients. Blend about 10 seconds. Pour soup into saucepan and simmer on low about 2 to 3 minutes or until heated through. Stir constantly. Serves 2.

RED PEPPER SOUP

Fast weight loss.

1 sm. cauliflower, coarsely
  chopped
2 sm. red peppers, sliced
1 onion, chopped
1 sm. can tomatoes, chopped

2" piece of cucumber, peeled &
  chopped
3 3/4 c. vegetable stock
Pinch dry mustard
Bean sprouts to garnish
Seasoning to taste

Combine all ingredients in a large saucepan and bring to a boil. Cover pan and simmer 15 to 20 minutes or until everything is cooked but still crisp. Soup can be pureed to make a smooth soup. Adjust seasoning and garnish with a sprinkling of bean sprouts. Serves 2.

SAVORY SOUP

1/2 c. uncooked lentils
1/3 c. uncooked brown rice
2 cloves garlic, minced
2 bay leaves
1 sm. onion, chopped
2 tbsp. soy sauce
2 med. carrots, sliced
1 celery stalk, chopped

4 lg. tomatoes, chopped
1/2 c. tomato juice
1/4 c. dry red wine
1 tsp. paprika
1/2 tsp. marjoram
1 tsp. basil
1/2 tsp. thyme
Ground pepper to taste

Place the first 6 ingredients in a large pot and cover with 3 cups of water. Bring to a boil, cover and simmer over low heat for 7 to 8 minutes. Add two additional cups of water along with all the remaining ingredients. Cover and simmer over low heat for 25 to 30 minutes, or until the vegetables, rice and lentils are done to your liking. Makes 6 servings.

SPICY POTATO CABBAGE SOUP

Fast weight loss.

6 c. defatted chicken broth
2 lg. potatoes, peeled & cubed
6-8 stalks celery, cut into 1/2"
  slices
10 fresh mushrooms, sliced

1/2 c. kernel corn, drained
1/2 head cabbage, shredded
3-4 tsp. Mrs. Dash Extra Spicy
  Seasoning
3-4 tsp. garlic powder

Combine all ingredients in a large pot. Cook on low to medium heat 15 to 25 minutes or until potatoes are tender. Seasoning can be adjusted to taste as it is very spicy.

SPICY SOUP

6 c. water
1 1/2 c. Picante sauce
3 cloves garlic, crushed
2 onions, cut into wedges
5 carrots, sliced 1/2" thick
4 med. potatoes, cut into lg.
  chunks
1/2 c. long grain brown rice

1 green pepper, cut into 1/2"
  pieces
1 rib celery, cut into 1/2" slices
1/2 sm. cabbage, shredded
2 c. corn kernels
2 tomatoes, cut into wedges
Fresh chopped coriander

Place 6 cups water in a large soup pot. Add picante sauce (either mild, medium or hot depending on your taste buds). Add garlic, onions, carrots, potatoes and rice. Cook over medium heat for 30 minutes. Add green pepper, celery, cabbage and corn. Cook 20 minutes longer. Add tomatoes and coriander (if desired), heat through. Serve in large bowls. Garnish with lemon wedges, if desired. Pass more hot picante sauce to spoon on at the table. Serves 8.

SPINACH NOODLE SOUP

4 c. chicken broth, defatted
2 cloves garlic, crushed

10 oz. spinach, chopped
1 c. whole wheat pasta shells,
 cooked

Heat broth and add garlic. Stir in spinach and cover until cooked; add pasta and heat through. Serves 4.

SPINACH SPAGHETTI SOUP

8 c. water
2 oz. spinach spaghetti
1/2 onion, chopped
1/2 green bell pepper, chopped
 fine
1/2 head broccoli, chopped into
 1" pieces

1 c. cooked barley
1 c. garbanzo beans (canned)
3 tbsp. vegetable broth seasoning
1/4 c. spaghetti sauce

Bring water to a boil in a large pot and add first six ingredients. Let simmer for 20 minutes, then add remaining ingredients and cook 10 to 15 minutes longer. Serves 4.

SPLIT PEA CHOWDER

4 c. water
1 med. onion, sliced
1 potato, diced
1 c. dry split peas

1 med. carrot, grated
1/2 tsp. sweet basil
1 c. brown rice, cooked or whole
 grain toast

Bring water to a boil and add next three ingredients. Cook until tender. Add grated carrot and basil. Serve over brown rice or whole wheat toast. Serves 2 to 4.

SPLIT PEA SOUP

5 c. chicken stock, salt free
1 c. split peas
1/2 c. diced celery
1 carrot, diced
1/4 c. diced onion
1 clove garlic

2 tbsp. vegetable seasoning (salt free)
1 bay leaf
1 tsp. Bakon seasoning or liquid smoke
1/4 tsp. Tabasco sauce
1/2 c. dry sherry (opt.)

In large pan, heat chicken stock. Add all ingredients except sherry. Simmer, stirring occasionally for 45 minutes, loosely covered. Add more liquid if needed. Before serving, stir in sherry.

TAPIOCA SOUP

3 tbsp. instant tapioca
2 1/2 c. water
1 (6 oz.) can frozen orange juice

6 c. fresh fruit (bananas, strawberries, grapes, blueberries, cantaloupe, etc.)

Combine tapioca and 1 cup of water. Bring to a boil and simmer 2 to 3 minutes. Add orange juice and mix until well blended. Add remaining water. Cover and refrigerate until chilled. Cut fruit into bite sized pieces. Add to chilled soup and serve in chilled parfait glasses. Makes 10 servings.

TARRAGON SOUP

Fast weight loss.

6 c. water
3 leeks, white part only, cleaned
   & cut into lg. pieces
2 carrots, sliced
2 celery stalks, sliced
1 onion, quartered

4 sm. potatoes, quartered
4 cloves garlic, peeled
1 bay leaf
6 whole peppercorns
Ground black pepper to taste
2 tbsp. tarragon, chopped (fresh)

Combine all ingredients except tarragon and pepper in a large pot and bring to a boil. Reduce heat and simmer, uncovered for 30 minutes to an hour. Drain and discard vegetables. Return broth to pot. Heat broth and add pepper and tarragon. Serve at once. Serves 4 to 6.

THAI RICE SOUP

4 c. chicken broth
1 stalk broccoli
1 c. cooked rice
2 tbsp. fish sauce
1 tbsp. ginger, minced

1 tbsp. dried onion flakes
1 tbsp. cilantro, chopped
3 green onions, chopped
1 tsp. dried red chili flakes

Heat chicken broth in a saucepan. Add the broccoli and bring to a boil. Reduce heat to simmer. Add the rice and cook for 2 minutes. Season with fish sauce. Sprinkle ginger, onion flakes, cilantro, onions and chili flakes on soup. 4 servings.

TOFU AND SNOW PEA SOUP

4 c. defatted chicken broth
1 (4 oz.) cake tofu, cubed
1/2 c. mushrooms, sliced
1/2 c. minced green onions
1/2 c. chopped carrots

1 clove garlic, minced
1 tsp. fresh ginger, grated
1 tsp. soy sauce (low sodium)
1 c. fresh snow peas

Place all ingredients except snow peas in a saucepan. Bring to a boil, lower heat and simmer, covered for 20 minutes or until vegetables are tender. Add snow peas and cook briefly until just tender. Serves 4.

TOMATO BOUILLON

Fast weight loss.
4 c. tomato juice
1/2 bay leaf
2 cloves garlic, minced
1/4 tsp. oregano
1/4 tsp. basil

1/4 tsp. marjoram
1/4 tsp. dill weed
2 tbsp. fresh chopped parsley
Freshly ground pepper to taste

Place all herbs except parsley in tomato juice and allow to stand for one hour to allow flavors to blend. Heat to boiling and remove from heat and strain. Garnish with parsley. Serves 4.

TOMATO-CORN CHOWDER SOUP

2 c. frozen Latino Mexicali
  Vegetable Mix or corn kernels
  with kidney beans & red
  pepper
2 c. chicken stock
1 c. diced tomatoes
1/2 c. mild green chili salsa

2 tbsp. minced fresh cilantro or
  coriander
2 tsp. cumin
2 tbsp. salt free chili powder
1 tsp. garlic powder
1/8 c. cornstarch

Bring chicken stock to boil. Add all ingredients except cornstarch and simmer 1/2 hour. In small cup, dissolve cornstarch into water. Add to soup and stir until soup thickens slightly.

TOMATO-EGGPLANT SOUP

1 1/2 lb. eggplant, unpeeled,
   diced
1 lg. (28 oz.) can whole tomatoes
1 c. water

4 tbsp. sesame tahini
2 tbsp. tamari (soy sauce)
2 tbsp. Vogue's Vege-Base or
   Mrs. Dash Seasoning

Cook eggplant and tomatoes (chopped up a little) in water for about 20 minutes or until eggplant is done. Add tahini, tamari and Vege-Base, if using. Puree in blender of food processor for a few seconds. If soup is too thick, add 1/4 to 1/2 cup additional water. Reheat and serve. Serves 6 to 7.

TOMATO-MUSHROOM SOUP

Fast weight loss.

1/2 c. Butter Buds
3 celery stalks, chopped
1 leek (white part only), chopped
1 garlic clove, chopped
1/2 lb. mushrooms, chopped
5 c. peeled, seeded & chopped
   tomatoes

3 c. chicken broth
3/4 c. dry vermouth
2 tsp. tomato paste
1/4 tsp. apple juice concentrate
1 bay leaf
1/4 tsp. oregano
Pepper to taste

Saute celery, leek and garlic in Butter Buds until softened, about 8 minutes. Increase heat to high. Add chopped mushrooms and saute until lightly browned, about 5 minutes. Add tomatoes, broth, vermouth, tomato paste, apple juice concentrate, oregano and bay leaf. Season with pepper. Bring to a boil. Reduce heat, cover and simmer until vegetables are tender, about 30 minutes. 6 servings.

TOMATO SOUP

Fast weight loss.

3 c. canned tomatoes
2 c. water
1 sm. onion, chopped
1 stalk celery, chopped
1 sm. carrot, chopped
1/2 tbsp. parsley flakes

1 tsp. basil
3/4 tsp. oregano
1/8 tsp. marjoram
Dash or two of Tabasco

Combine all ingredients in a soup pot. Bring to a boil. Cover and simmer over low heat for 30 to 45 minutes, until vegetables are tender. Place in the blender and process until smooth for a delicious, familiar texture tomato soup. Serves 6..

TOMATO VEGETABLE SOUP

Fast weight loss.

1 lg. onion, chopped
2 c. chopped cauliflower
1 c. chopped broccoli
1 c. chopped carrots
1 c. chopped celery
2 c. chopped spinach
2 (28 oz.) cans tomatoes, blended
1 c. water

2 tbsp. parsley
2 tbsp. low sodium soy sauce
1/4 tsp. each: cumin, celery seed,
    basil, rosemary, curry
    powder, dill weed, paprika,
    cayenne pepper
Dash of ground ginger
Dash of black pepper

Place all ingredients in a large soup pot. Bring to a boil, reduce heat cover and cook over medium heat until vegetables are tender. Serves 5.

TOMATO VERMICELLI SOUP

1 (28 oz.) can tomatoes
1 onion, minced
4 garlic cloves (more to taste),
   minced or put through a press

Freshly ground pepper
1/2 tsp. dried marjoram (more to
   taste)
1/2 c. vermicelli

Drain the tomatoes and retain the liquid. Return the liquid to the can and add enough water to fill the can. Put the tomatoes through the medium disk of a food mill into a bowl or puree and put through a sieve; set aside.

Heat water in a heavy bottomed soup pot and saute the onion with 2 cloves of the garlic until the onion is tender. Add the tomato puree and cook 10 minutes, stirring. Add the remaining garlic and the liquid from the tomatoes. Add salt and pepper to taste and the marjoram. Bring to a simmer and add the vermicelli. Cook until the pasta is al dente. Taste again, add more garlic if desired, correct seasonings and serve, not too hot. The soup will keep up to 3 days in the refrigerator and can also be frozen, in either case, add the vermicelli just before serving.

TORTILLA SOUP

8 corn tortillas
1 med. onion, chopped
2 cloves garlic, minced
2 lbs. fresh tomatoes, peeled or 1
(28 oz.) can solid pack
tomatoes

4 c. chicken stock or canned broth
1 c. fresh cilantro, coarsely
chopped
Black pepper, red pepper & lime
juice to taste

Preheat oven to 350 degrees.

Cut tortillas in half then cut crosswise into strips 1/4" wide.

Spread tortilla strips on a large ungreased cookie sheet. Heat in 350 degree oven for 10 to 20 minutes, tossing strips every 5 minutes. Remove strips from oven when they are crisp but not brown. Set aside.

Heat water in a large pot and add onion and garlic. Saute over medium heat just until onion is transparent, about 5 minutes.

Puree tomatoes in blender or food processor. Add puree and chicken broth to onions. Bring mixture to a boil.

Reduce heat and simmer for 5 minutes. If soup is prepared in advance, stop at this point. Add fresh cilantro and adjust seasonings at time of serving. Season to taste with black and red pepper and lime juice.

Serve immediately, putting a handful of tortilla strips in each soup bowl. Ladle soup over chips. Serves 8.

VEGETABLE WHEAT MEAT SOUP

2 c. fresh green beans
2 tbsp. lemon juice
1 (2 lb.) can tomatoes
1 onion, chopped
6 carrots, peeled & chopped
3 stalks celery, chopped

1/2 tsp. pepper
1/2 head cabbage, shredded
6 oz. Seitan vegetarian wheat
meat
1 c. brown rice, cooked
2 tbsp. fresh parsley
4 c. chicken broth, defatted

Cut beans diagonally into thirds; toss with lemon juice and steam until tender. Combine next five ingredients with chicken broth in large pot; bring to a boil, reduce heat and simmer 1 to 2 hours or until vegetables are tender. Add beans and cabbage, simmer 15 minutes. Add wheat meat and rice and heat through. Sprinkle with parsley. Serves 4 to 6.

VEGETABLE BROTH

Fast weight loss.

6 c. water
2 med. onions, peeled & chopped
4 lg. carrots, peeled & chopped

6-8 celery stalks, chopped
1 bunch fresh dill or parsley
Pepper to taste

Bring water to a boil, add onions and carrots. Add celery leaves and stalks to pot, simmer 45 minutes. Strain; then add dill and parsley. Serves 4.

VEGETABLE BEAN SOUP

2 c. kidney beans
3 quarts stewed tomatoes
6 quarts water

4 c. celery, chopped
3 lg. onions, peeled & chopped

Optional Ingredients: choose one or more:
12 c. cooked whole wheat noodles
2 lg. carrots, diced

4 sm. zucchini, diced
4 c. fresh corn

Soak beans overnight; drain off water. Add fresh water; bring water to a boil and simmer for 1 1/2 hours. Add remaining ingredients, simmer for one hour more and adjust seasoning to taste. Serves 25 to 30.

VEGGIE HARVEST SOUP

Fast weight loss.
10 c. water
1 lg. onion, finely chopped
2 cloves garlic, minced
4 stalks celery, chopped
1 sm. cauliflower, cored & cut
   into 1" florets
4 carrots, chopped
4 white potatoes, cubed & peeled

1 sm. cabbage, shredded
3 med. zucchini, sliced
2 c. banana squash, cubed
1/2 tsp. thyme
1/2 tsp. basil
2 cubes vegetable bouillon
2 tbsp. fresh lemon juice
Pepper to taste

In a large soup kettle, bring water to a boil and add all ingredients, except lemon juice. Return to boil and simmer for 30 minutes, stirring frequently to break up squash. Stir in lemon juice when ready to serve. Serves 8 to 10.

WILD RICE SOUP

2 onions, sliced
4 stalks celery, sliced
3 carrots, sliced
1 c. sliced green onions
2 oz. chopped pimiento
2 tbsp. dillweed
2 bay leaves
1/2 tsp. turmeric
1/2 tsp. ground cumin
1/4 tsp. garlic powder

Fresh ground pepper (several
   twists)
1/8 tsp. horseradish powder
1/2 tsp. poultry seasoning
12 1/2 c. water
3 tbsp. low sodium soy sauce
3/4 c. wild rice
1/2 c. brown rice
1 lb. fresh mushrooms, sliced

Saute onions, celery, carrots, green onions and pimiento in 1/2 cup water for 5 minutes. Stir in spices and mix well. Add remaining water, the soy sauce, and both kinds of rice. Bring to a boil, reduce heat, cover and simmer for 1 hour. Add sliced mushrooms; cook an additional 10 minutes. Serve hot. Serves 8 to 10.

WINTER VEGETABLE SOUP

1/2 c. each: black eyed peas, red
   beans, pink beans, white beans
6 c. fresh water
1 chopped onion

2 sliced carrots
1 c. chopped celery
2 spears broccoli, sliced
1 (14 1/2 oz.) can S&W Ready
   Cut peeled tomatoes

Soak beans overnight. Drain off water, rinse next morning. Simmer in a large pot beans and water; sprinkle with favorite spices. Simmer, covered over lowest heat for 6 hours. Add remaining ingredients. Simmer one more hour. Serve with hot whole grain bread. Serves 10.

ALFALFA SPROUT SALAD

Fast weight loss.

3 stalks celery, diagonally sliced
1 cucumber, peeled & sliced
6 shallots, cut diagonally
10 button mushrooms, thinly
   sliced

1 red apple, cored & cut into
   strips
2 tomatoes, chopped
1 c. alfalfa sprouts
1 tbsp. parsley
1 tbsp. chives

Combine all ingredients and squeeze lemon juice over them. Toss lightly and serve in lettuce cups or on a bed of shredded lettuce. Serves 2.

ARTICHOKE PASTA SALAD

4 oz. Vegeroni
1 (6 oz.) jar marinated artichoke
   hearts
1/2 c. pitted olives
1/4 lb. mushrooms, sliced

1 c. cherry tomatoes, halved
1 tbsp. parsley, chopped
1/2 tsp. dry basil leaves
Pepper

Cook Vegeroni according to directions. Turn into a large bowl. Add artichokes, mushrooms, tomatoes, olives, parsley and basil; toss gently. Cover and refrigerate for 4 hours. Season with pepper. 6 servings.

3 BEAN SALAD

1 c. cooked garbanzo beans, salt free
1 c. cooked kidney beans, salt free

1/2 c. fresh string beans, steamed lightly & cut into bite sized pieces
Red bermuda onion, a few thin slices (or dice)

MARINADE:
1/4 c. red wine vinegar
1/4 c. fresh orange juice
1 clove garlic, crushed & minced

2 tsp. dill weed, dried or 1 tbsp. fresh, minced
1 tsp. low sodium dijon mustard

Combine all ingredients in a small bowl. Refrigerate and marinate several hours, or overnight, before serving.

BROCCO-BEAN SALAD

1 bunch broccoli
1 can red kidney beans, rinsed
4 green onions, chopped

A dash of Mrs. Dash
A dash of Salad Herbs
3 tbsp. Mrs. Pickford's (no oil) vinaigrette dressing

Steam broccoli (cut up) for 8 minutes; cool slightly. Combine all ingredients and refrigerate 1/2 hour (or more) before serving.

BROCCOLI AND ONION SALAD

Fast weight loss.
2 lbs. broccoli, cut into 1" pieces
1 sm. red onion, sliced
2 tbsp. lemon juice
1/2 c. no oil Italian dressing

1/4 tsp. dry mustard
1/2 tsp. dried tarragon leaves
Ground pepper to taste

Steam broccoli for 1 minute. Cool and toss with onion. Mix together rest of ingredients and pour over broccoli and onion. Marinate in refrigerator for 6 to 8 hours. Serves 4 to 6.

BROWN RICE DELIGHT

2 c. cold cooked brown rice
1 1/2 c. corn kernels

1 c. celery, sliced
1 c. grated carrot
2 onions, chopped

Combine all ingredients and toss with a dressing of your choice. Serves 2.

BULGUR WHEAT AND CHICK PEA SALAD

1/2 c. uncooked bulgur wheat
1 c. boiling water
1/4 c. fresh lemon juice
1/2 c. sliced green onion

1 c. cooked chick peas, drained
1/2 c. chopped parsley
1/2 c. chopped carrots
1 c. sliced mushrooms

Put bulgur in a large heatproof bowl. Pour boiling water over the bulgur, mix to moisten evenly. Allow to stand for 1 hour, bulgur will expand. Pour lemon juice over the bulgur and mix with a fork. Place mixture in a bowl with a snug cover. Layer each vegetable on top of the mixture in this order: green onions, mushrooms, chick peas, parsley and carrots. Cover and refrigerate. Toss before serving. Garnish with tomato wedges. Serves 4 to 6.

CABBAGE SALAD WITH DILL

Fast weight loss.

1/4 head cabbage, cut into thin
  strips
1 sm. cucumber, peeled & sliced
8 spring onions, sliced

1 tbsp. white wine vinegar
2 tbsp. lemon juice
2 tbsp. chopped dill
Black pepper to taste

Mix cabbage, cucumber and onions in large bowl. Stir in vinegar and lemon juice and sprinkle in dill and black pepper. Cover with plastic wrap and chill for several hours. Serves 2.

CARROT SALAD

1/4 c. walnut pieces
1 tbsp. shredded coconut
2 c. grated carrot
1 apple, cored & grated
Zest & juice of 1/2 lemon

1/2 c. orange juice
1/2 c. currants
Mrs. Dash or Instead of Salt
1 1/2 tsp. grated fresh ginger

Toast walnut pieces and coconut in a low 300 degree oven. The walnuts will take about 10 minutes and the coconut 5. Chill. Combine grated carrots, apple, lemon zest, orange and lemon juices, currants, Instead of Salt, and ginger. Add walnuts and coconut and serve. Makes 3 cups, to serve 4.

CARROT AND FRUIT SALAD

3 med. carrots
2/3 c. dates, finely chopped
3/4 c. seedless grapes
1 lg. dessert apple

1-2 tbsp. lemon juice
1 bunch watercress
1/3 c. roasted sunflower seeds

Grate carrots then mix dates with grapes. Coarsely chop the apple and stir into the other ingredients. Add lemon juice at once and toss lightly. Make a nest of the watercress and spoon the carrot mixture into the center. Sprinkle with the sunflower seeds. Serve at once. Serves 2 to 3.

CUCUMBER MARINADE

Fast weight loss.
5 cucumbers, thinly sliced
1 onion, thinly sliced
1 c. red wine vinegar

1-2 tbsp. honey
3 tsp. dill weed
Black pepper (opt.)

Place vinegar and honey in a saucepan and heat until warm. Place cucumbers, onion, dill weed and optional pepper into a large container. Pour heated vinegar mixture over the cucumbers and onions; mix well. Cover and refrigerate at least 2 hours. Tastes even better if eaten the following day. Serves 6 to 8.

CAULIFLOWER MARINADE SALAD

Fast weight loss.

Break a head of cauliflower into small pieces and drop into a kettle of boiling water with:

1/2 tsp. sea salt   The juice of 1/2 lemon (to keep
                                                the white color)

Cook a few minutes, drain and cool. Combine in a salad bowl:

Drained cauliflower   1 red or green pepper, cut in
4 green onions, chopped   matchsticks
2 carrots, cut in matchsticks   1/2 c. celery, sliced thinly

Toss to moisten with 1/4 cup Lemon Vinaigrette Dressing (no oil). Per Serving: 89 calories; 3 gm protein; 8 gm carbohydrates; 1 gm. fat. Yield: 6 servings.

CAULIFLOWER WITH HERB VINEGAR

Fast weight loss.

Flowers of 1/2 head cauliflower   1/4 c. mint, chopped
1 slice lemon   2 c. herb or tarragon vinegar

Lightly steam cauliflower in boiling water with slice of lemon, remove from boiling water and plunge into icy water. Lightly towel dry. Sprinkle with 1/4 cup mint and toss in herb vinegar. Chill for at least 2 to 4 hours, tossing cauliflower through vinegar frequently. Drain and serve. Serves 2.

CHICK PEA AND PASTA SALAD

2 c. whole wheat pasta shells
1 (16 oz.) can chick peas, drained
   & rinsed
3 tomatoes, chopped fine
1/2 bunch fresh broccoli,
   chopped into 1" pieces

1 c. NO OIL Italian dressing
   (Cook's choice or Kraft)
1/2 tsp. fresh ground black
   pepper
1 tsp. dried oregano
1/2 tsp. garlic powder

Mix pasta, chick peas and vegetables together. Mix remaining ingredients in small bowl then pour over pasta and toss gently. Chill for 3 to 4 hours before serving. Serves 6 to 8.

CHINESE CHICKEN SALAD

2 chicken breasts, boned &
   skinned or try 2 oz. firm tofu
   or wheat meat (for a
   vegetarian alternative)
1/4 yellow onion, sliced thin
2 c. fresh bean sprouts

1/2 c. bok choy or napa cabbage,
   shredded
1 lg. carrot, sliced in thin
   matchsticks
1/2 red pepper, sliced in thin
   strips
Sesame seeds, water chestnuts or
   cashews (as garnish)

DRESSING:
1/3 c. rice vinegar
1/3 c. pineapple juice

1/4 tsp. powdered ginger, or
   freshly grated onion
1 tbsp. chinese parsley (cilantro)

Cut chicken into bite sized pieces, stir-fry or boil until tender. Prepare vegetables, toss in bowl with chicken and dressing. Marinate 1/2 hour before serving. Makes 4 servings.

CHINESE HOT SALAD

Fast weight loss.

1 onion, sliced
1 tbsp. grated fresh ginger
3 cloves garlic, pressed
2 tbsp. low sodium tamari
2 stalks celery, thickly sliced
1 green pepper, cut into strips

2 c. bean sprouts
1 c. Chinese pea pods
1/2 cucumber, peeled & cut into
   strips
6 lettuce leaves, coarsely chopped
1 tbsp. lemon juice

In a wok or large pan, saute onion, ginger and garlic in 2 tablespoons water for 1 minute. Add 1 tablespoon tamari and next four ingredients. Cook over medium heat, stirring for 6 minutes. Add the remaining tamari, cucumber and lettuce. Continue to cook 3 minutes longer. Sprinkle with lemon juice. Mix well. Serve hot. Serves 6.

COLESLAW

2 c. shredded green cabbage
2 c. shredded red cabbage
1/2 c. diced carrot
1/2 c. diced celery
1/2 c. diced green pepper
1/2 c. chopped apple
1/2 c. diced, peeled cucumber
1/4 c. finely chopped green
   onions

1/4 c. chopped parsley
3 tbsp. cider vinegar
1 tbsp. Dijon mustard
1 tbsp. lemon juice
1/2 tsp. low sodium soy sauce
1 tsp. honey
1/4 tsp. caraway seeds
1/4 tsp. celery seed

Mix vegetables together in a large bowl. Mix vinegar, mustard, soy sauce and honey together. Pour over vegetables. Sprinkle seeds on top. Toss to mix well. Chill for about 2 hours to blend flavors. Serves 6.

Helpful Hints: If you have a food processor this can be prepared quite quickly.

CRUNCHY BEST SLAW

Fast weight loss.

3 med. beets, peeled & grated
1 med. carrot, grated
1/3 jicama, diced

1/2 tsp. Dijon mustard
2 tbsp. orange juice
2 tbsp. lemon juice
Peel of 1 orange, finely grated

In a salad bowl, combine beets with grated carrot and jicama. In another bowl, stir together orange peel, mustard and juices. Dress slaw and chill briefly before serving. Serves 4.

CRUNCHY PEA SALAD

2 c. fresh peas, steamed & chilled
1 (7 oz.) can water chestnuts,
   drained & sliced
4 stalks celery, thinly sliced
1 c. shredded carrots
4 green onions, thinly sliced
2 tbsp. tomato juice

2 tbsp. red wine vinegar
1 tbsp. low sodium soy sauce
1 tsp. Dijon mustard
1 clove garlic, minced
1 tsp. paprika
1 tsp. frozen apple juice
   concentrate

Combine first five ingredients. To make marinade, mix the remaining ingredients and beat well. Pour over salad, blend well. Cover and chill for about an hour. Drain excess marinade before serving. Serves 8.

FINOCCHIO SALAD

1 1/2 c. raw whole wheat
  macaroni
1/2 c. sliced Florence fennel*
1/4 c. chopped Italian parsley
1/4 c. diced bell pepper
1 c. sliced raw mushrooms

2 tbsp. chopped chives
1/3 c. sliced black olives
2-3 tbsp. lemon juice
2 tbsp. no oil Italian dressing
1/2 tsp. Instead of Salt
Freshly ground black pepper

A mouth-watering pasta salad. Cook macaroni until tender in salted boiling water. Cool and combine with fennel, parsley, bell pepper, mushrooms, chives and olives. Mix 2 tablespoons lemon juice, salt and pepper. Toss salad in dressing, taste and add remaining tablespoon of lemon juice if desired. Makes 5 1/2 cups.

*No fennel in sight? Substitute raw celery or blanched green beans or crisp-tender broccoli.

GARDEN SALAD

Fast weight loss.

2 heads leaf lettuce
1/2 head shredded cabbage
6 Swiss chard leaves, chopped
3 Chinese cabbage leaves,
  shredded
1 head cauliflower, broken into
  florets
3 stalks broccoli, chopped

1 zucchini, diced
5 lg. spinach leaves, chopped
3 carrots, diced
1 red pepper, diced
4 scallion tops, diced
1 beet, diced or grated

Tear lettuce into bite size pieces and cut greens. Combine all ingredients in a large bowl adding no oil Italian dressing (see Dressings). Toss, chill and serve. Serves 10.

GARDEN VEGETABLE SALAD

Fast weight loss.
The success of this salad depends on FRESH ingredients!

1 stalk broccoli (about 1 1/2 c.)	Wedge of cabbage (purple or green)
1 carrot	Thin slice of onion, minced
2-3 button mushrooms	Vinaigrette dressing or Italian no-oil dressing
1 red pepper, sliced	

Bring saucepan of water to boil. While broccoli is still whole, dip the flower head in the boiling water, briefly, about 20 seconds. Slice the pepper. Cut the broccoli into bite sized bits. Peel or scrape the carrot, slice thinly. Cut mushroom caps in half. Cut cabbage into bite sized wedges. Mince onion. Place in salad bowl and serve with vinaigrette dressing. Serves 4.

GREEN SALAD

Fast weight loss.

1 c. torn romaine lettuce	1 tsp. toasted sesame seeds
1 c. torn red leaf lettuce	4 red bell pepper rings
1 c. torn spinach leaves	1/2 c. alfalfa sprouts
1 c. chopped watercress	1/3 c. grated raw beets
1/4 c. chopped parsley	

Toss together first eight ingredients. Divide into 4 salad bowls and top with red pepper rings. Fill rings with alfalfa sprouts and top with beets. Serves 4.

KIDNEY BEAN SALAD

2 c. kidney beans, canned	1 c. carrots, diced
1 red onion, sliced	1 c. parsley, chopped
3 stalks celery, diced	1 head red leaf lettuce, torn
2 c. whole kernel corn, canned	

Combine all ingredients. Chill and toss with no oil dressing of choice.

MACARONI SALAD

2 c. whole wheat macaroni
4 hard cooked egg whites, chopped
2 tbsp. green onions, chopped fine
2 tbsp. minced dill pickle
2 c. canned baby green peas

1/4 c. chopped pimiento
4 tbsp. vinegar
2 tsp. mustard
3 tsp. vegetable broth seasoning

Cook macaroni according to package directions. Drain and rinse in cold water. Add remaining ingredients in order given, tossing with vinegar, mustard and seasoning. Serve on bed of lettuce. Serves 4.

MEDITERRANEAN RICE SALAD

3 tbsp. lemon juice
Dash of cinnamon
Sprinkling of Cilantro
Pepper to taste
1 1/2 c. brown rice
3 c. chicken broth

1 tbsp. Butter Buds (dry)
3/4 c. chopped pistachio nuts
1/2 c. raisins
1/2 c. sliced mushrooms
1/4 c. finely chopped mint leaves

Combine lemon juice, cinnamon, cilantro and pepper; set aside.

In a medium saucepan with a lid, cover rice with chicken broth; add Butter Buds. Bring to a boil, then cover and simmer over low heat for 40 minutes. While hot, toss rice with dressing. Add remaining ingredients. Serves 6.

MEDITERRANEAN SALAD

1 lg. firm red tomato
1 cucumber
1 sm. red bermuda onion

3/4 c. garbanzo beans (or sm. can, well rinsed)

MARINADE:
1/2 c. red wine vinegar
1 clove garlic, crushed
1 tbsp. fresh sweet basil or 1/2 tbsp. dried

1 tbsp. fresh oregano, or 1/2 tbsp. dried
1 tbsp. apple juice concentrate

Cut tomato into wedges. Peel cucumber, slice in half lengthwise, scoop out seeds and cut into slices. Slice onion. Place vegetables into a small bowl. Add garbanzos. Press garlic and add vinegar, herbs and sweetener. Allow to marinate at least one hour, refrigerated, before serving. Serves 3 to 4.

MUSHROOM AND WALNUT SALAD

4 c. bite size pieces of romaine & butter lettuce
10 cherry tomatoes, halved
1/2 lb. mushrooms, sliced
2/3 c. walnut pieces

2 green onion (tops included), sliced
5 tsp. white wine vinegar
2 tsp. Dijon mustard
1/8 tsp. pepper
1/8 tsp. paprika
2 tsp. dry basil leaves

In a salad bowl, combine basil, pepper, paprika, mustard and vinegar. Beat with a fork until blended. Mix in mushrooms and green onions. Let stand at room temperature for at least 30 minutes. Add walnut pieces, lettuce and cherry tomatoes and toss lightly. Serves 4.

NUTTY RICE SALAD

Have ready:

2 c. cooked brown rice   **1/2 c. cooked wheat berries**

Bring a quart of water to boiling, drop in:

1 c. green string beans, slivered   **1 carrot, cut in matchsticks**

Boil for 1 1/2 minutes, drain and run cold water over to set color. Combine with cooked grains and add:

1/4 c. parsley, minced   **1/4 c. green onions, chopped**
1/4 c. chopped toasted walnuts

Serve on a bed of greens with Poppy Seed Dressing. Yield: 6 servings. Per Serving: 112 calories; 3 gm protein; 18 gm carbohydrates; 3 gm fat.

ORANGE ALMOND SPINACH SALAD

1 bunch spinach   **3 oranges, peeled & chopped**
1/2 c. sliced almonds

DRESSING:
1/4 c. red wine vinegar   **1/2 tsp. black pepper**
1/2 c. orange juice

Toss all ingredients together and chill for 1/2 hour.

ORANGE COLESLAW

Fast weight loss.

1/2 head cabbage
2 oranges, peeled & segmented
1/2 c. green pepper, thinly sliced

1/2 c. red pepper, thinly sliced
1/2 tsp. grated lemon rind
2 tsp. lemon or orange rind

Combine all ingredients and let stand for 1 hour. Toss lightly and chill for 2 hours before serving. Serves 2.

DRESSING:

2 tbsp. orange juice
2 tbsp. lemon juice

1 tbsp. vinegar
Black pepper to taste

Combine all ingredients well and toss over cole slaw before serving. Serves 2.

POLYNESIAN FRUIT SALAD

1 lg. pineapple
1 c. peeled, seeded, diced papaya
1 mango, peeled, pitted & diced

1 banana, sliced
1 c. strawberries, sliced
1/2 c. canned lychees
1/2 c. shredded coconut

Halve pineapple lengthwise through crown. Cut out fruit, leaving a 1/4" shell. Remove core, dice fruit and place in large bowl. To pineapple, add other ingredients. Mix lightly. Spoon fruit into pineapple shells. Sprinkle with coconut. 4 servings.

POTATO SALAD

Fast weight loss.

3 cooked potatoes, peeled & diced
1 celery stalk, chopped
1/2 onion, peeled & chopped
1 red bell pepper, seeded & chopped
1 tsp. garlic powder

1 tsp. celery seed
1/4 tsp. dried dill
1 tsp. mustard powder
2 tsp. fresh lemon juice
1 tbsp. apple juice concentrate
1/2 c. red wine vinegar

1. In a medium bowl, combine potatoes, celery, onion and pepper. Mix thoroughly
2. In a small bowl, combine remaining ingredients. Pour over vegetables and mix thoroughly. Chill well before serving.. Makes 8 servings.

QUICK ARTICHOKE PASTA SALAD

4 oz. (1 c.) whole wheat macaroni
1 (6 oz.) jar marinated artichoke hearts, water packed
1/4 lb. mushrooms, quartered

1 c. cherry tomatoes, halved
1 tbsp. parsley, chopped
1/2 tsp. dry basil leaves
Pepper to taste

Cook macaroni according to package directions. Drain, rinse with cold water and drain again. Place into large bowl. Add artichokes and their liquid, mushrooms, tomatoes, parsley and basil; toss gently. Cover and refrigerate for at least 4 hours. Before serving season with pepper to taste. Serves 6.

RAISIN SALAD

6 shredded raw carrots
1 c. raisins

1 can crushed pineapple in its own juice
Section 3 oranges

Mix together in large bowl. Include pineapple juice and squeeze the juice from the orange after sectioning. Refrigerate and serve cold. No mayonnaise or salad dressing necessary.

RICE SALAD

1 1/2 c. cooked brown rice
1 lg. celery stalk, thinly sliced
1/4 c. raisins

1/4 of an onion, chopped
2 tbsp. mango chutney
5 tbsp. Italian no oil dressing
1 tbsp. curry

Combine rice, celery, raisins, onion and chutney. Add curry, dressing and toss to blend. Chill before serving.

SCANDINAVIAN HOT POTATO SALAD

Fast weight loss.
4 med. sized new potatoes

1/2 c. chopped red onion
1/2 c. chopped celery

DRESSING:
1/3 c. cider or balsalmic vinegar
2 tbsp. apple juice concentrate
1 tbsp. Veg-It seasoning
1 tbsp. fresh dill weed or 1 tsp.
   dried dill weed

1 tbsp. "Bakon" seasoning or dash
   liquid smoke
1 tbsp. low sodium Dijon
   mustard

Boil or steam new potatoes until tender, 15 to 20 minutes. Slice thin and place in bowl along with chopped onion and celery. In saucepan, heat together and briefly boil the dressing ingredients. Pour dressing over contents of bowl, gently stir. Cover and serve warm.

SNOW PEA AND RICE SALAD

4 c. brown rice, cold (cooked)
1 c. fresh snow peas, coarsely cut

1/2 c. chopped green onions
1/4 c. chopped parsley
1/4 c. diced red bell pepper

DRESSING:
1/4 c. orange juice
2 tbsp. rice vinegar

1 tbsp. pectin
2 tsp. low sodium soy sauce

Combine the rice and vegetables, then mix well. In a separate container, mix the dressing ingredients thoroughly. Pour dressing over vegetables mixing well. Serve chilled. Serves 4 to 6.

SPINACH PASTA SALAD

8 oz. spinach pasta rotelle
1 c. frozen corn
1/2 c. frozen green beans
1 jar pimientos

1 can water pack artichoke hearts
1/4 c. toasted sesame seeds
Fresh, chopped parsley
Garlic powder to taste
No oil Italian dressing

Boil water, add rotelle pasta and cook 11 to 12 minutes. Drain and rinse with cold water. Defrost and lightly cook corn and green beans. Drain and cool. Add remaining ingredients, draining can of artichoke hearts. Refrigerate and serve chilled.

SPINACH SALAD WITH RASPBERRY VINAIGRETTE

2 bunches fresh spinach
2 hard boiled eggs (no yolk),
    sliced
1 peeled, sliced orange

Cucumber, thinly sliced
Few slivers of red onion
Sesame seeds, slivered almonds
    or toasted pine nuts (as
    garnish)

VINAIGRETTE:
1/4 c. raspberry vinegar (Silver
    Palate or other brand)

1 tbsp. garlic, crushed & pressed

Combine all vinaigrette ingredients in shaker jar, shake and let blend. Cut off spinach leaves at stem, float in large tub of water to clean. Dry in salad spinner or towel, tear and place in salad bowl and add remaining ingredients. Toss with dressing and serve with garnish.

For a variation, warm salad dressing in small saucepan and serve warm on salad. Makes 4 to 5 servings.

SPROUT SALAD

Fast weight loss.

SALAD:

2 c. mixed sprouts (lentils, pea, aduki, etc.)
3-4 green onions, sliced
1 stalk celery, sliced

2.2 oz. jar chopped pimientos
1 c. sliced mushrooms
3-4 tbsp. chopped fresh coriander or parsley

DRESSING:

2 tsp. dijon mustard
1 tbsp. water
2 tbsp. white wine vinegar

1 tsp. Worcestershire sauce
1 tbsp. low sodium soy sauce
1/4 tsp. black pepper

Mix salad ingredients in a large bowl.

Place the mustard and the water in a small bowl and mix well. Add remaining ingredients and mix, then pour over the sprout salad. Toss to coat. Refrigerate before serving.

STEAMED VEGETABLE SALAD

Fast weight loss.

1 c. zucchini, sliced
1 c. carrots, sliced
1 1/2 c. broccoli flowerets
3 med. tomatoes

1 red pepper
3 tbsp. salad dressing (no oil Italian or vinaigrette)
Juice of 1/4-1/2 lemon
Pinch of mint

Steam the carrots 5 minutes or until tender. Steam the broccoli and zucchini 2 to 3 minutes. Let the vegetables cool. Cut the tomatoes in wedges and the red pepper in narrow strips. Combine all the vegetables and toss with the dressing, lemon and mint.

SUMI SALAD

Shred 1 head cabbage. Lightly brown 1/4 cup slivered almond and 1/4 cup sesame seeds. Chop 8 green onions. Munch up 2 packages Ramen noodles (uncooked, without flavor packet). Add snow peas. Combine above ingredients. Add dressing and toss.

DRESSING:

2 tbsp. rice vinegar
Juice of 1 lemon
1/4 tsp. salt
Pepper
1 tsp. Dijon mustard

1 clove garlic, minced
2 green onions, finely chopped

Mix well and toss with salad.

SUMMER SHREDDED SALAD

1 c. bulgur wheat
4 firm, fresh zucchini
2 lg. carrots
1 sm. yellow onion
1 sm. red bell pepper
1 1/2 c. hot chicken stock (salt free, of course)
1 ripe, red tomato

1 bunch (about 1/4 c.) green scallion (spring onion)
1/4 c. fresh parsley
Juice of 3 lemons or 1/3 c. (no salt, no oil) Italian dressing
2 tbsp. fresh mint leaves or 1 tbsp. dried
Dash hot cayenne pepper

Bring 2 cups of water to a boil and add bulgur, cook for 40 minutes until soft. Place bulgur in small bowl. Cover with hot chicken stock and toss. Allow to sit 15 minutes. Mix in all ingredients. Add seasonings, toss again. Garnish with tomato wedges. This is best made ahead and refrigerated a few hours before serving. Serve in pita bread or on romaine lettuce leaves. Serves 4.

SUMMER FRUIT SALAD

Fast weight loss.

1/4 watermelon
1/2 cantaloupe
1/2 honeydew melon
1 lb. seedless grapes

1 pt. strawberries
1 pt. raspberries
1 pt. cherries
1 pt. blueberries

Remove rind from melons. Slice melons into wedges. Stem grapes. Hull strawberries. Pile strawberries in the center of a large basket or tray; surround with melon wedges, raspberries and cherries. Garnish with grapes and blueberries. Serves 8 to 10.

SWEET POTATO-BANANA SALAD

4 baked sweet potatoes, peeled &
    cut in chunks
4 bananas, sliced

2 apples, chopped
1/2 c. raisins
1/2 tsp. nutmeg

Mix the first 4 ingredients together. Sprinkle the nutmeg over the top. Serves 4 to 6.

TABOULI

1 c. bulgur
8 scallions, chopped
1/4 c. finely chopped parsley
1/4 c. chopped fresh mint

3 ripe tomatoes, chopped
1/4 c. lemon juice
1/4 tsp. black pepper

Bring two cups of water to a boil; add bulgur, cook for 45 minutes. Place bulgur in a bowl with water to cover. Allow to soak 15 minutes, then drain and squeeze dry. Mix all ingredients and serve on lettuce leaves or with crackers.

TOMANGO (TOMATO-MANGO) SALAD

Fast weight loss.

4 lg. mangos, peeled & chopped
Juice from 1/2 lemon

2 tsp. basil
5 med. tomatoes, chopped

Combine mangos, lemon juice and basil. Let chill in refrigerator for about 1/2 hour. Stir in tomatoes and chill until serving time.

CUCUMBER DRESSING

3 lg. cucumbers, peeled & cut
4 tbsp. apple juice concentrate
(frozen)
4 tbsp. orange juice concentrate
(frozen)

8 tbsp. lemon juice
1 tsp. dill weed
2 cloves garlic, minced
1 tsp. onion powder

Blend all ingredients in blender until very smooth. Serves 2 to 4.

DRESSING

Fast weight loss.

1/2 c. tomato juice
2 tsp. onion, finely chopped
Dash oregano or dry mustard

1 tsp. parsley
1 tbsp. lemon juice

Combine all ingredients in a jar with tight fitting lid. Shake well and refrigerate. Yield: 3/4 cup.

FRENCH DRESSING I

1/2 c. water
2 tbsp. orange juice
3 tbsp. concentrated apple juice
4 tbsp. lemon juice
1 1/2 tbsp. tomato puree

1/4 tsp. dill weed
1 tsp. onion powder
1 tsp. garlic powder
1/2 tsp. paprika
1 1/2 tsp. cornstarch

Mix all ingredients except cornstarch. Mix cornstarch with 1/2 tablespoon water and add to mix. Bring to a boil and chill. Serves 2.

FRENCH SALAD DRESSING II

2 c. V-8 juice
2 c. vinegar
1 c. tomato sauce
1/2 c. lemon juice
3 1/2 tbsp. apple juice
   concentrate
1/4 c. tomato paste

1 onion
1/4 green pepper
1 tsp. celery seed
1 tsp. dill weed
1/2 tsp. paprika
1/4 tsp. cayenne pepper
1 tbsp. arrowroot

Combine all ingredients in a saucepan. Heat to a boil and simmer 5 minutes. Cool. Chill thoroughly before serving.

FRUITY DRESSING

1 c. orange juice
1/2 c. lemon vinegar
1 cucumber, peeled & seeded
2 cloves garlic

1 tbsp. lemon rind, grated
1 tbsp. orange rind, grated
2 tbsp. chopped fresh herbs
   (parsley, basil, chives, thyme)

Combine all ingredients except lemon and orange rind and fresh herbs. Blend in a food processor for 1 minute. Add other ingredients but do not blend. Shake well and store in sealed jars in refrigerator. Yield: about 2 cups.

GARLIC DRESSING

Fast weight loss.

1 c. vinegar
1/2 c. water
Juice of 1 lemon

1/2 cucumber, peeled & seeded
2-3 cloves garlic
Black pepper to taste

Combine all ingredients in food processor and blend for 1 minute. Place in sealed jars and store in refrigerator. Yield: about 2 cups.

HERBED SALAD DRESSING I

Fast weight loss.

1 tbsp. powdered fruit pectin
1 tsp. apple juice concentrate
1/8 tsp. dry mustard
1/8 tsp. dried basil, crushed
1/8 tsp. paprika

1/8 tsp. pepper
1/4 c. water
1 tbsp. vinegar
1 sm. clove garlic, minced

Combine the pectin, apple juice concentrate, mustard, basil, paprika and pepper. Stir in water, vinegar and garlic. Cover and chill for 1 hour.

HERB DRESSING II

1 c. herb vinegar
1 c. apple juice
Juice of 1 lemon

1/2 cucumber, peeled & seeded
2 tbsp. mixed herbs (parsley, chives, thyme, dill)

Combine the first four ingredients in a food processor and blend for 1 minute. Add herbs but do not blend. Place in sealed jars and store in refrigerator. Yield: about 2 cups.

ITALIAN NO OIL DRESSING

Fast weight loss.

1/4 c. lemon juice
1/4 c. cider vinegar
1/4 c. apple juice
1/2 tsp. oregano
1/2 tsp. dry mustard

1/2 tsp. onion powder
1/2 tsp. garlic powder
1/2 tsp. paprika
1/8 tsp. thyme
1/8 tsp. rosemary

Combine all ingredients in blender and blend well. Refrigerate overnight or longer to allow flavors to mix. Yield: 3/4 cup.

SPICY DRESSING

Fast weight loss.

1 1/2 c. unsweetened apple juice
1 c. cider vinegar
4 1/2 tsp. garlic powder
4 1/2 tsp. cornstarch
3 tsp. crushed oregano

1 tsp. onion powder
1 1/2 tsp. mustard powder
1 1/2 tsp. paprika
1/2 tsp. black pepper

Combine all ingredients in saucepan and bring to a boil. Cook, stirring until thickened. Chill, covered until ready to use. Shake well before using. Yield: about 2 1/2 cups.

SWEET SOUR VINAIGRETTE DRESSING

3/4 c. water
1/4 c. frozen apple juice
  concentrate
3 tbsp. rice vinegar
1 tbsp. cider vinegar
1 tbsp. lemon juice
2 tsp. soy sauce
2 cloves garlic, crushed

1 tbsp. pectin
1 1/2 tsp. arrowroot
1 tsp. oregano
1 tsp. onion powder
1/2 tsp. each garlic powder,
  savory, paprika, dry mustard
Dash cayenne pepper

In a small saucepan, combine all ingredients and stir to blend well. Bring to a boil; then reduce heat and simmer, stirring constantly until thickened, about 4 to 5 minutes. Serve chilled or warmed. Yield: 1 1/2 cups.

TOFU-GARLIC SALAD DRESSING

Blend together the following ingredients:

3/4 c. V-8 juice
2/3 c. lemon juice
2 tbsp. tamari, Quick-Sip, or soy
  sauce
1 lb. tofu

1 tsp. garlic powder or 2-3 garlic
  buds
1 c. sesame seeds
1/4 of an onion
3/4 c. water

This dressing is also very good served over baked potatoes, steamed veggies and grains such as brown rice and millet.

TOMATO SALAD DRESSING

Fast weight loss.

1 c. tomato juice
1 1/2 tbsp. frozen apple juice
concentrate
1 1/2 tbsp. lemon juice

1 tbsp. chopped celery leaves
1 tbsp. chopped parsley
2 tsp. garlic powder
1/4 tsp. basil
1/4 tsp. oregano

Place all ingredients in a blender and blend at high speed. Chill before serving.

TOMATO JUICE DRESSING

Fast weight loss.

1 c. tomato juice
1/4 c. tarragon vinegar
1 c. grated onion

1/2 tsp. dry mustard
1 clove garlic, minced
2 tsp. parsley

Combine all ingredients in blender and mix well. Chill in refrigerator. Before serving shake well. Yield: 2 cups.

Side Orders:

Lean Meat,
Lowfat Dairy

ALMOND CHICKEN

1 chicken, cut up
Pepper to taste
3/4 c. Butter Buds
Minced parsley to taste
1/4 tsp. powdered bay leaf

4 tbsp. minced green onions
4 tbsp. whole wheat flour
2 c. chicken broth
1/2 c. toasted almonds
1/3 c. dry white wine

Season chicken with pepper. In a large skillet, heat 1/2 cup Butter Buds. Over low heat, brown chicken in Butter Buds 30 minutes, turning. Mix parsley, bay leaf and green onion with chicken.

In a small saucepan, blend remaining Butter Buds and flour. Gradually add chicken broth, stirring constantly. Sauce will be fairly thick. Add sauce to chicken mixture. Cook 30 minutes or until chicken is completely tender. Stir in nuts and wine. Serve over brown rice, stir-fried vegetables or whole wheat noodles. Serves 4.

ALL DAY CHICKEN CASSOULET

1/2 c. navy beans
1 1/2 lbs. chicken, skin & fat
  removed, cubed
3/4 c. sodium reduced tomato
  juice
1/2 c. chopped celery
1/2 c. sliced carrot
1/2 c. chopped onion

1 clove garlic, minced
1 bay leaf
1 tsp. instant beef bouillon
  granules
1/2 tsp. dried basil, crushed
1/2 tsp. dried oregano, crushed
1/2 tsp. dried sage, crushed
1/4 tsp. paprika

Rinse beans. In a medium saucepan, combine beans and 2 cups water. Bring to boiling. Boil, uncovered for 10 minutes. Drain, then add 2 cups more water. Return to boiling; reduce heat. Cover and simmer about 1 1/2 hours until beans are tender. Drain, cover and chill. In an electric slow cooker; combine beans, chicken, tomato juice, celery, carrot, onion, bouillon and spices. Cover and cook on low setting for 8 to 10 hours. Remove and discard bay leaf. Serves 4.

ARROZ CON POLLO

2 1/2 lbs. boneless, skinless
   chicken pieces
2 1/2 tbsp. Butter Buds
2 cloves garlic, minced
1/4 tsp. pepper
1/4 tsp. paprika
1/4 c. chopped onion
1/4 c. chopped green pepper

1 c. uncooked brown rice
2 1/2 c. boiling chicken broth
1/2 c. tomatoes, chopped
1/4 tsp. oregano
Pinch of saffron

In a small bowl, combine Butter Buds, 1 clove garlic, pepper and paprika. Brush on chicken; set aside.

In a skillet, add the onion and green pepper and cook until the vegetables are tender.

Add the rice and cook, stirring frequently, for 2 minutes. Add the hot chicken broth, the tomatoes, saffron and oregano. Stir. Cover the skillet and bake at 350 degrees for 20 minutes. Add the chicken pieces and continue to bake another 30 minutes. 6 servings.

GREEN MOLE CHICKEN

3 tbsp. pumpkin seeds
1/2 c. sesame seeds
3 tbsp. slivered almonds
1 1/2" piece thin cinnamon stick, chopped
1/2 tsp. crushed black peppercorns
1/2 sm. onion, diced
1 tsp. garlic, minced

1 lb. tomatillos, husked & quartered
1 romaine lettuce leaf
2 tsp. fresh cilantro leaves
1 fresh serrano chili
1 (3 1/2 lb.) chicken, cut up
1/2 whole wheat bread slice, toasted
1/3 c. chicken broth

Sprinkle nuts and seeds in skillet and stir-fry over medium heat until toasted, about 5 minutes. Grind coarsely in food processor. Stir cinnamon and peppercorns in skillet until aromatic, about 2 minutes. Add to nuts and process to fine powder. Cook onion and garlic in skillet until tender. Add to nut mixture. Add bread to processor and finely grind mixture. Add tomatillos, lettuce, cilantro and chili. Puree.

Preheat oven to 425 degrees. Place chicken in dish and bake for 20 minutes. Add broth and puree and cover. Cook for 25 more minutes. 4 servings.

CHICKEN ENCHILADAS

4 chicken breasts, poached,
   skinned & boned
1/4 c. enchilada sauce

1/4 c. green chili salsa
8 corn tortillas
4 oz. Liteline cheese, grated

SAUCE:
1 1/2 c. chicken stock
4 tbsp. whole wheat flour

4 tbsp. chili powder (mild or hot,
   your preference)

In iron skillet or heavy saucepan, add flour and brown over medium heat a few minutes, stirring constantly to avoid burning. Remove from heat source. Whisk in the chicken stock and chili powder. Return to fire, cook over low heat until sauce begins to thicken. Remove from heat and set aside.

Shred chicken into thin bite sized strips. mix 1/4 cup of sauce and the green chili salsa with the chicken. Dip the corn tortillas into the sauce. Place some filling in each tortilla and roll. Place in baking dish, seam side down. Repeat with each tortilla. Pour enchilada sauce over the tortillas. Sprinkle with grated cheese. Bake 10 to 15 minutes at 350 degrees or until the cheese is melted and tortillas are heated throughout.

CHICKEN PITA SANDWICHES

Microwave.
1/4 c. non-fat yogurt, plain
1/2 c. shredded carrot
1/4 c. chopped celery
1/4 c. chopped green onions
1 1/2 c. chopped, cooked chicken

1/4 tsp. garlic powder
2 whole wheat pita bread rounds,
   halved
1 c. torn spinach leaves
1/3 c. grated Dormans low fat,
   low cholesterol cheese

In a 1 quart microwave safe dish, combine yogurt, carrot, celery, green onions, chicken and garlic powder. Microwave on medium for 50 seconds. Line each pita half with 1/4 of spinach leaves. Spoon 1/4 of filling into each pita half. Sprinkle with cheese. 4 servings.

CHICKEN KABOBS

4 chicken breasts or thighs,
   cubed in lg. pieces (3-4 cubes
   per chicken pieces)
12 cherry tomatoes

12 pieces onion or pearl onions
1 bell pepper, cut into 12 pieces
1 sm. can juice packed cubed
   pineapple

MARINADE:
Juice from pineapple (about 1/3
   c.)
1/2 c. fresh orange juice
1/4 c. mild vinegar

1 tsp. ginger powder
1 tsp. garlic powder (or 1 clove
   garlic, minced)

In large bowl, first combine marinade ingredients. Then add all other ingredients. Allow to marinate several hours or overnight in refrigerator. When ready to cook, alternate ingredients on skewers. Save the remaining marinade to use to baste the kabobs as they cook. Cook over outdoor barbecue, or in broiler 25 minutes at 425 degrees. Turn once to cook evenly. Serves 4 (2 kabobs each).

CHICKEN CREOLE

1 onion, chopped
1 clove garlic, minced
1 c. celery, finely chopped
1 (8 oz.) can tomato sauce
1/2 c. water
1 bay leaf

1/2 tsp. cayenne
1 green bell pepper, finely
   chopped
1 c. chicken, cooked & cubed
1 tsp. fresh parsley
Steamed brown rice

Combine first seven ingredients in a 4 quart saucepan; bring to a boil. Cover, reduce heat and simmer 45 to 60 minutes. Add green pepper and chicken. Cover; simmer 10 to 15 minutes. Sprinkle with parsley. Serve over steamed rice. Serves 2.

CHICKEN AND POTATOES IN MUSHROOM-TOMATO SAUCE

6 potatoes
1/2 c. whole wheat pastry flour
1/2 tsp. paprika
6 sm. boneless chicken breasts
1 1/2 c. defatted chicken stock
1 lg. onion, chopped
1 c. mushrooms, chopped

1/2 c. green bell pepper, chopped
1/2 c. celery, chopped
3 cloves garlic, minced
1 tbsp. soy sauce (low sodium)
1/4 tsp. cayenne pepper
1/2 c. dry white wine
1 (16 oz.) can tomatoes in juice

Place potatoes in pot of boiling water and cook for 25 minutes over moderate heat until partially done. Remove from pot and cool briefly; peel and halve lengthwise. Combine flour and paprika in a shallow bowl, mixing well. Coat breasts with flour mixture, shake off excess and set chicken aside. Bring stock to a boil in a large skillet, then add onion, mushrooms, green pepper, celery and garlic. Cook vegetables over moderate heat for 5 minutes, stirring occasionally. Add soy sauce, pepper and chicken breasts. Cover and simmer for 5 minutes, stirring if needed. Stir in wine and tomatoes. Bring the sauce to a boil; then lower heat. Arrange potatoes around chicken, cover and simmer for 25 minutes or until chicken and potatoes are tender. Stir occasionally, basting chicken with sauce. Serves 6.

CASHEW CHICKEN

2 boneless & skinless chicken
    breasts
1/8 c. Dijon mustard
1/4 c. honey
1/4 c. nonfat yogurt

3 c. cooked brown rice
1 c. crunchy Chinese noodles
1/2 c. cashews
Teriyaki sauce

Combine mustard, honey and yogurt in a bowl. Spread on chicken. Place chicken in oven and broil until tender.

Meanwhile place rice on dish, sprinkle Chinese noodles over rice. Heat cashews in teriyaki sauce just until hot. Sprinkle cashews over rice and noodles. Top with chicken, shredded into bite sized pieces.

CARIBBEAN CHICKEN CUBA

1 frying chicken (3-3 1/2 lbs.) cut up, skin removed
1/4 c. lemon juice
2 cloves garlic, pressed
1 lg. onion, thinly sliced
1 lg. green pepper, seeded & thinly sliced
1/2 c. defatted chicken stock
1 bay leaf

3/4 tsp. oregano leaves & ground cinnamon
1 lg. can (15 oz.) whole tomatoes or fresh tomatoes, peeled & chopped
1/3 c. dry white wine or water
1 tbsp. capers, drained well
4 sm. thin skinned potatoes, scrubbed
1 c. frozen peas, thawed

In a bowl combine chicken, lemon juice, garlic, onion and green pepper. Cover and refrigerate for 1 hour, turning chicken occasionally. Remove chicken form marinade, reserve marinade. In a 5 quart kettle, bring the stock to a boil. Add chicken and cook over medium heat turning until it is opaque, about 10 minutes. Remove from kettle and set side.

Pour in marinade with all the ingredients, and cook, stirring until onion is soft. Add to kettle along with chicken, bay leaf, oregano, cumin, tomatoes, wine and capers. Bring to a boil, then cover, reduce heat and simmer for 20 minutes. Cut potatoes into 1" cubes; add to kettle and continue to simmer until meat near thigh bone is no longer pink when slashed (10 to 15 more minutes). Stir in peas, cook just until heated through. Makes 4 servings.

BARBECUED CHICKEN

Microwave.

1/2 c. onion
1/2 c. green pepper
1 1/2 tbsp. Butter Buds
1 (8 oz.) can tomato sauce with
onions
2 tbsp. soy sauce
1 tbsp. apple juice concentrate

1 tbsp. lemon juice
1 tbsp. vinegar
1 tsp. prepared mustard
1 tsp. Worcestershire sauce
1/8 tsp. pepper
3 lb. broiler-fryer, cut up

Place onion, green pepper and butter in 1 quart casserole. Cook on full power for 2 1/2 minutes. Add remaining ingredients, except chicken. Cook on full power for 1 minute. Arrange chicken in 2 quart utility dish with larger pieces, such as thighs and breasts, at corners, skin side down. Place small pieces such as legs and wings towards center. Pour sauce over chicken. Cook on Full power 18 minutes. Turn chicken pieces over halfway through cooking time. Serve over brown rice.

OVEN-FRIED CHICKEN

4 chicken breasts or thighs
1/4 c. whole cornmeal
1/4 c. flour
1 tbsp. garlic powder
1 tbsp. paprika

2 tbsp. Veg-It low sodium
seasoning
Cayenne pepper
1 egg white
1/4 c. water

Remove skin and fat from the chicken. In bowl beat egg white and water. In another bowl, combine flours and spices. Dip the chicken pieces first in the egg mixture, then dredge in flour. Place on rack on top of baking sheet. Bake in preheated oven at 375 degrees for 45 minutes.

ROSEMARY LEMON CHICKEN

4 chicken breasts, skinned, boned
& cut into several pieces
1/2 c. diced yellow or red
bermuda onion

Season with:
3 tbsp. Parmesan cheese
1/3 c. fresh lemon juice
2 tbsp. Veg-It low sodium
seasoning (or other salt free
vegetable seasoning)

1/2 c. red seedless grapes (green
will do if you can't find red)
1/4 c. pine nuts

1 tbsp. rosemary or 1/2 tsp.
ground rosemary powder
1 tsp. sweet basil
Dash cayenne pepper
Pam spray

Brown onions and chicken in pan lightly sprayed with Pam. Add seasonings and lemon juice. Cook until tender. Toast pine nuts in skillet, shaking to prevent burning. Mix grapes, pine nuts and chicken together. This dish is good served warm with pasta or rice.

ORIENTAL CHICKEN

1/2 c. dry sherry
1 tbsp. soy sauce
3 cloves garlic
2 sm. boneless chicken breast
  halves, skinned & cut in 1"
  cubes
1/2 c. chicken stock
1 1/2 c. sliced mushrooms

1 1/2 c. sliced celery
1 c. coarsely chopped onions
1 lg. green pepper, cut in chunks
2 (8 oz.) cans unsweetened
  pineapple chunks, juice packed
2 tbsp. arrowroot
3/4 c. sliced green onions

Combine the sherry, soy sauce, ginger and garlic in a bowl. Place the chicken cubes in the mixture and marinate in the refrigerator for several hours or overnight. In large skillet, bring the stock to a boil. Add the mushrooms, celery and onion and stir-fry an additional 2 minutes. Stir in the chicken and marinade and cook until the chicken is opaque, about 2 minutes. Drain the pineapple, saving the juice and cut the chunks into thirds, setting them aside. Combine 3/4 cup of the juice with the arrowroot. Stir the mixture into the skillet and cook, stirring constantly until thickened. Fold in the pineapple and 1/2 cup of the green onions. Garnish with the remaining green onions. Serve over hot brown rice. Makes 4 servings.

ORIENTAL CHICKEN AND RICE

2 tbsp. water
1/2 c. green onions, chopped
1 c. celery, chopped
1/2 lb. mushrooms, chopped
1 lb. chicken, cooked, cubed (skin removed)
1 c. unsweetened pineapple chunks (save juice)

1 c. frozen peas, defrosted
1 can water chestnuts, drained & sliced
2 tbsp. cornstarch
1/2 tsp. ground ginger
4 tbsp. soy sauce (low sodium)
1/2 c. chicken stock (defatted)

Heat 2 tablespoons water in non-stick skillet. Add onions and saute. Add celery, mushrooms and chicken; heat over low flame stirring constantly for 5 minutes. Add water chestnuts and pineapple. Separately, combine cornstarch, ginger, soy sauce, pineapple juice (saved from chunks) and chicken stock. Mix well to remove lumps. Add to chicken mixture. Add defrosted peas. Cook until sauce thickens, stirring constantly. Serve over a bed of brown rice. Serves 4 to 6.

SZECHUAN CHICKEN WITH CASHEWS

1/2 chicken breast
2 tsp. cornstarch
2 tsp. soy sauce
1 tbsp. rice wine or sherry
1 egg white
10 dried red peppers
2 tsp. fresh ginger

1 green onion
1/4 c. cashews
2 tsp. cornstarch
2 tsp. rice wine
2 tbsp. soy sauce
1 tsp. vinegar
1 tsp. apple juice concentrate

Mix 2 teaspoons cornstarch with 2 teaspoons soy sauce and 1 tablespoon wine, then add egg white. Place the chicken in the sauce and marinate at least 15 minutes.

In a non-stick frying pan or wok, place a little water and the red peppers. Cook until the peppers turn black. Add the chicken pieces. Reduce heat to medium. Stir-fry until the chicken is white, then add the ginger and green onion. Cook for a few more seconds then add the cashews and cornstarch, wine, soy sauce, vinegar and apple juice concentrate. When the sauce has thickened slightly and is glazelike, it's ready to serve. Serve over brown rice. Serves 2.

THAI CHICKEN

2 whole chicken breasts, skinned,
   halved & boned
4 scallions, minced
1/4 c. water
1 1/2 tsp. powdered ginger

2 tbsp. cornstarch
2 c. chicken broth
3 tbsp. soy sauce
1/4 tsp. dried red pepper flakes
2 tsp. minced fresh ginger

Place chicken between two sheets of waxed paper and pound with a mallet or knife handle until thin; set aside. In a bowl, make a paste of the minced scallions, water and powdered ginger. Spread paste on chicken breasts and wrap each one separately in foil. Steam for 30 minutes.

Mix the cornstarch with 2 tablespoons chicken broth in a saucepan and stir until smooth. Add the rest of the chicken broth and cook over low heat, stirring until thick. Add the soy sauce, pepper flakes and fresh ginger and simmer for 5 minutes. Pour over chicken. Serve chicken over stir-fried green vegetables. Serves 2.

BREADED CHICKEN WITH TOMATO-CHEESE SAUCE

5 sm. boneless chicken breast
   halves
1/3 c. non-fat milk

1 c. fine whole wheat bread
   crumbs

TOMATO SAUCE:
1 onion, chopped
2 cloves garlic, chopped
1/2 tsp. dillweed
1 c. canned tomato sauce
1 c. canned crushed tomatoes in
   puree

3 tbsp. tomato paste
1/4 c. dry white wine
2 tbsp. grated Sap Sago cheese
1 1/2 tsp. basil
1/2 tsp. oregano

Place onion, garlic, dill and tomato sauce in a blender at low speed for about 1 minute. Add the crushed tomatoes, paste and wine. Lightly brown the cheese by placing it in a small aluminum pan and setting in a hot oven for a few minutes. Add the cheese to the blender. Blend the sauce mixture until smooth and transfer to a saucepan. Stir in the basil and oregano and cook over a medium heat for 5 minutes. Spread one cup of the sauce in a baking dish, reserving the rest of the sauce. Dip the chicken breasts in the milk; then roll in bread crumbs, covering well. Place in dish; pour remaining sauce over and cover. Bake at 350 degrees for 1 hour. Serves 5.

CHICKEN CACCIATORE

1 (28 oz.) can tomatoes
1 onion, chopped
3 carrots, thinly sliced
3 stalks celery, thinly sliced
2 tbsp. red wine vinegar

1/2 tsp. pepper
3/4 tsp. sage
2 chicken breasts, halved
3/4 lb. whole wheat macaroni

Combine all ingredients except chicken and pasta in a stew pot or Dutch oven; bring to a boil. Reduce heat; cover and simmer 25 to 30 minutes. Skin and debone chicken; add to sauce and cook 25 to 30 minutes or until tender. Serve over cooked pasta. Serves 2.

CHICKEN TETRAZZINI

16 oz. pkg. whole wheat
   spaghetti, cooked
2 lbs. chicken breasts, cubed
2 onions, chopped fine
3 tbsp. low sodium soy sauce
1/2 tsp. pepper
1/2 lb. mushrooms, sliced

1 tbsp. lemon juice
1/2 c. whole wheat flour
Dash of nutmeg
1/2 tsp. paprika
1 c. nonfat milk

Spread cooked spaghetti in a 13"x9" baking dish (use nonstick spray). Cook chicken, onions and soy sauce in nonstick skillet using just enough water to cover chicken for about 15 to 20 minutes. Remove chicken and onion from pan with slotted spoon. Add 1 cup water, pepper, mushrooms and lemon juice to remaining liquid. Cook for 5 minutes on high; set aside.

Preheat oven to 350 degrees. In a blender place flour, nutmeg, paprika, 2 1/2 cups water and nonfat milk and mix until smooth. Pour into a large saucepan and heat, stirring constantly until sauce thickens. Ad chicken and mushroom mixtures. Cook until heated through. Spoon over spaghetti. Sprinkle with parmesan if desired. Bake for 30 minutes or until top is golden brown. Serves 6 to 8.

SPICY CHICKEN SOUP

1 1/2 lbs. chicken, skinned & cut
   into cubes
2 c. canned tomatoes
1 clove garlic, minced

1/2 c. chopped onion
1/2 c. diced green chilies, canned
2 c. cooked pinto beans

Place chicken pieces in a large saucepan and add enough water to cover. Cook until done, about 25 minutes. Remove chicken from broth and add remaining ingredients. Simmer about 15 minutes. Serves 2 to 3.

COLD AVOCADO CHICKEN SOUP

2 (10 1/2 oz.) cans chicken broth,
   chilled & defatted
1 c. cooked chicken, cubed (no
   skin)

2 ripe avocados, diced
1 oz. sherry
Dill weed
Dash lemon juice

Put chilled broth into blender; add cubed chicken, diced avocados, sherry and lemon juice. Blend well. Sprinkle with dill weed. Serves 4.

PISMO BEACH SOUP

4 c. fresh clam nectar (from jar of
   fresh clams, if not available,
   substitute vegetable or salt
   free chicken broth, defatted)
2 (6 1/2 oz.) cans fresh clams
   (okay if frozen)
1 c. new potatoes, diced
1 stalk celery

2 carrots, diced
1/4 c. onion
1 sm. jar pimientos
1 tsp. curry powder
1/2 c. dry sherry (opt.)
1/2 c. whole wheat flour (to
   thicken soup)
3 tbsp. vegetable seasoning (salt
   free)
3 tbsp. lemon juice
Black pepper & parsley (to
   garnish)

In blender or shaker jar, mix the flour and 1 cup clam nectar or stock until smooth, thin paste is achieved. Set aside. Place remaining ingredients in heavy bottomed saucepan and simmer 20 minutes, or until vegetables are tender and clams are done. Do not overcook. Add flour paste and stir constantly until soup has thickened to a chowder. Serve with cracked black pepper garnish and parsley.

SEVICHE SOUP

1/2 lb. scallops
1/2 c. fresh lime juice
1/3 c. chopped onion
1 1/2 c. tomato juice
2 c. chicken broth, defatted

1 tsp. parsley, chopped
4 tbsp. chopped green chilies
Fresh parsley for garnish
Lime wedges for garnish

Combine scallops, lime juice, onion; marinate overnight in refrigerator. Toss with tomato juice, broth and chilies. Chill several hours. Garnish with parsley and lime wedges. Serves 2.

CORNISH GAME HENS

2 cornish game hens (10 oz.),
    split & cleaned

GLAZE:
1 tbsp. low sodium Dijon
    mustard
2 tbsp. low sugar (Smucker's or
    Welch's Lite) apricot jam
1/4 c. red wine vinegar

1 tsp. poultry seasoning
Black pepper to taste
1 low sodium vegetable bouillon
    cube (available in Salt Free
    section of supermarket or at
    health food stores) or 2 tsp.
    Veg-It

Place halved birds, cut side down in baking dish. Mix together marinate/glaze, brush over birds. If you have time, allow to marinate one hour. If not, it's still good. Just bake one hour in oven, basting occasionally, oven temperature 400 degrees.

ROASTED TURKEY WITH STUFFING

1 c. brown rice, cooked
5 lg. mushrooms
1 sm. cooking apple, chopped
1 stalk celery, chopped
1/2 onion, finely chopped
1 clove garlic, minced

4 tsp. poultry seasoning
Chicken stock as needed
1/3 c. raisins
1/3 c. walnuts
1 lb. turkey breast
3 egg whites

To prepare stuffing, saute the vegetables, apple and 2 teaspoons poultry seasoning in chicken stock. Add the brown rice, walnuts and raisins; set aside.

Coarsely grind the turkey. Beat the egg whites until frothy. Fold turkey and the 2 teaspoons poultry seasoning into the egg whites. Place the turkey on a sheet of wax paper and pat it out into a rectangular shape about 1/2" thick. Spread the stuffing over the turkey, almost to the edge. Roll up, jelly roll fashion. Transfer to a baking dish, and loosely cover dish with aluminum foil.

Bake at 350 degrees for 30 minutes. Baste occasionally. Uncover and continue baking until browned. Serves 4.

TURKEY CHILI

1 sm. turkey breast, skinned
Celery tops
1 onion, sliced
Poultry seasoning to taste
1 c. chopped onions
1/2 c. chopped celery
1/3 c. chopped green pepper
3 cloves garlic, minced
1 1/2 c. broth from cooking
  turkey
1 (28 oz.) can tomato sauce

1 (15 oz.) can tomato sauce
2 tbsp. tomato paste
1 tbsp. onion powder
2 tbsp. chili powder
2 tsp. cumin
1 tsp. garlic powder
1 tsp. oregano
1 tbsp. soy sauce
Dash cayenne pepper
1 1/2 c. cooked pinto beans
1 c. cooked kidney beans

Place the turkey breast in a non-stick baking dish with 1 1/2 cups water. Add the celery tops and sliced onion and sprinkle with poultry seasoning. Cover and bake at 350 degrees until tender, about 1 1/2 hours. Remove the turkey breast. Defat the broth by chilling it in the freezer, then pour the broth through cheesecloth. Or use a cup (available at any supermarket) made especially to defat broth.

Saute the chopped onion, celery, green pepper and garlic in 1/2 cup of the turkey broth. Add the remaining ingredients, except the turkey breast and beans. Simmer the sauce, uncovered for 45 minutes, stirring occasionally.

Meanwhile, dice the turkey breast and grind in a meat grinder, blender or food processor. Add 1 cup of the ground turkey and all the beans to the chili. Cook and stir about 5 minutes more.

TURKEY MEATBALLS

1 lb. turkey, ground
1/4 c. cooked brown rice or whole
   wheat bread crumbs
1 tbsp. poultry seasoning
2 tbsp. minced onion flakes or 1
   tsp. onion powder

1 clove garlic, minced
2 egg whites
Black pepper
3 tbsp. Veg-It low-sodium
   seasonings

This can be cooked either on stove top or broiler. If broiling, preheat oven. Place all ingredients in bowl and mix thoroughly. Form into meatballs. In cooking pan, use nonstick pan or spray. In oven, cook under broiler about 7 minutes, then turn and brown other side. Good with spaghetti, or serve with mushroom sauce. Serves 4 to 6.

TURKEY MEATLOAF

1 lb. ground turkey breast
2 egg whites
1/2 c. oat bran
2 tbsp. ketchup
2 tbsp. Worcestershire sauce
1/2 tsp. Dijon mustard

1/2 sm. onion, chopped fine
1 clove garlic, minced
1/2 tsp. pepper
1/2 tsp. sage
1/2 tsp. marjoram

Combine all ingredients, mix well in a large bowl. Form loaf and place in nonstick loaf pan and bake at 350 degrees for 1 hour or until done. Serves 4.

ORIENTAL TURKEY BURGERS

1 lb. ground turkey breast
1/4 c. oat bran
1 tbsp. low sodium soy sauce

1/2 tsp. ginger
1/2 tsp. coriander

Mix all ingredients together in large bowl. Form into 4 patties and cook in non stick skillet (use non stick spray) until browned. Serves 4.

CIDER TURKEY SOUP

3/4 c. apple cider
1/4 c. water
3 tbsp. sliced green onion
1/2 tsp. grated ginger root
1/4 tsp. dried basil
Dash pepper

1 c. cooked turkey, cubed
1/2 c. shredded zucchini
1/2 c. shredded carrot
1/8 tsp. finely shredded orange
  peel

In a small saucepan, combine cider, water and next four ingredients. Bring to boiling, reduce heat; cover and simmer 5 minutes. Add turkey, zucchini, carrot and orange peel. Return to boiling, reduce heat. Cover and simmer for 3 to 5 minutes more. Serves 1.

LASAGNA

SAUCE:
1 clove garlic, minced
1 sm. onion, chopped
2 c. cooked kidney beans

4 c. tomato puree
1 tsp. oregano
1/2 tsp. dried basil

LASAGNA:
Whole wheat lasagna noodle (for
    weight loss use eggplant
    instead of noodles)

2 c. lowfat cottage cheese
6 oz. Litetime Mozzarella cheese
    (or 3 c. tofu in place of cheese)
1/4 c. grated Parmesan cheese

To prepare sauce, brown garlic in saucepan. Add onion and beans and saute for about 5 minutes until beans are slightly softened and break up easily with a fork. Add tomato puree and seasonings, bring to a boil and simmer for 5 minutes.

Preheat oven to 350 degrees.

To assemble, spread a little sauce in a 9"x 13" pan (or shallow 2 quart) baking dish. Cover with one third of the noodles, half the cottage and Liteline cheese and top with some sauce. Repeat these layers. Top with remaining noodles, sauce and Parmesan cheese.

Cover pan and bake for about 1 hour. Remove cover and bake 15 to 30 minutes longer, until liquid is absorbed and pasta tender. Let sit for 10 minutes before serving.

LASAGNA

SAUCE:

2 c. canned tomatoes with juice
4 (6 oz.) cans tomato paste
2 c. tomato sauce
1 c. fresh parsley, firmly packed

3 cloves garlic, minced
2 lg. onions, chopped
1 1/2 tsp. thyme
1 1/2 tsp. basil
1/2 lb. mushrooms, thinly sliced

Combine all ingredients except mushrooms in a large pot. Bring to a boil, reduce heat; cover and simmer for 45 minutes. Remove from heat and add mushrooms.

FILLING:

1 (8 oz.) pkg. whole wheat pasta lasagna noodles, cooked
4 lg. zucchini
4 egg whites, stiffly beaten

16 oz. dry curd cottage cheese, mashed smooth with buttermilk below
1/2 c. buttermilk (Alpha Beta brand)
3/4 c. Sap Sago cheese, grated

Preheat oven to 350 degrees. Combine all ingredients except noodles and egg whites. Line the bottom of a large, shallow baking dish alternating with noodles, zucchini-cottage cheese mixture and sauce until all ingredients are used up. Be sure to top lasagna with a layer of sauce. Bake 1 hour. Remove from oven and let stand about 8 to 10 minutes before slicing. Serves 8 to 10.

ITALIAN MEATBALLS

1 lb. ground turkey breast
1/4 c. oat bran
1/2 tsp. oregano
1/2 tsp. black pepper

1/4 tsp. thyme
1 clove garlic, minced
1/4 c. onion, finely chopped
1/4 c. green bell pepper, finely
    chopped

Mix dry ingredients together in large bowl, then add remaining ingredients except turkey; mix well. Blend in turkey and form into 12 to 15 meatballs. Cook in nonstick skillet (use nonstick spray) until browned. Serve with whole wheat spaghetti and sauce.

PASTA LA MER
(SEAFOOD AND PASTA)

2 c. cooked whole wheat or
    vegetable shell macaroni
1 c. cooked scallops
1/4 c. chopped celery
1/4 c. chopped green onions
1/4 c. frozen green peas (or fresh)

1/4 c. diced green bell or red bell
    pepper
1 tbsp. vinegar
1 tsp. low sodium Dijon mustard
Juice from 1 lemon
1 c. bean sprouts

Toss all ingredients together in bowl. Chill before serving. Serves 4.

HALIBUT RAGOUT

2 lbs. halibut, fresh or frozen
1/2 c. chopped onion
1 clove garlic, minced
1/2 c. chopped green bell pepper
4 stalks celery, diagonally sliced
4 carrots, chopped

1 (28 oz.) can tomatoes
1 c. water
2 chicken bouillon cubes
1/4 tsp. pepper
1/2 tsp. thyme
1/2 tsp. basil
3 tbsp. chopped parsley

Thaw halibut if frozen. Cut into 1" pieces. Saute onion, garlic, pepper, celery and carrots in pan sprayed with nonstick coating. Add tomatoes, water, cubes and all seasonings, except parsley. Cover and simmer 20 minutes. Add halibut and simmer covered 5 to 10 minutes more or until done. Sprinkle with parsley. Serves 8.

HALIBUT CEVICHE

1 lb. halibut steak
1 onion, sliced very thin

Juice of 4 lemons or green
    oranges
1 or 2 drops Tabasco sauce

Cut halibut into small 1/2" pieces. Place in large mixing bowl. Add sliced onion, mix well. Cover with juice and Tabasco. Let stand, covered, at least 3 to 4 hours, or until fish is firm and very white. The acid in the juice "cooks" the fish. Serve with sliced tomatoes.

BAKED RED SNAPPER IN SAUCE

1 1/2 lbs. snapper fillets, cut into
   6 serving pieces
1/4 c. dry white wine
3 tbsp. orange juice
2 tbsp. lemon juice
1 tsp. low sodium soy sauce

1 tsp. arrowroot
1 tsp. dillweed
2 tsp. onion powder
Dash cayenne pepper
1/2 c. green onion, chopped

Arrange fillets in baking dish; mix together other ingredients, except green onion; pour over fillets. Sprinkle with green onion. Cover dish and bake at 400 degrees for 25 minutes. Serves 6.

CALIFORNIA CIOPPINO

1 onion, chopped
2 cloves garlic, minced
2 tbsp. chopped parsley
1/2 c. tomato juice

5 tomatoes, chopped
1 1/2 lbs. fish, cut into bite size
   pieces
Pepper to taste

Saute onion, garlic and parsley in nonstick pan sprayed with Pam. Cook about 5 minutes. Add tomatoes and juice. Simmer about 15 minutes, then add fish and cook 20 to 30 minutes. Add pepper and serve at once. Serves 6.

CREOLE BAKED FISH

4 white fish fillets (4-5 oz. each)
1 c. chopped tomatoes, fresh
1/4 c. chopped green pepper
1/4 c. lemon juice (fresh) or
   Minute Maid (frozen)
1/4 yellow onion

1 tbsp. dried sweet basil
2 tsp. thyme
1 tbsp. grated lemon peel
1/4 c. dry sherry
2-3 drops Tabasco sauce or dash
   of cayenne pepper
1 clove garlic, minced

Place fillets in lightly oiled or non stick baking dish. Combine remaining ingredients and spoon over fillets. Cover with foil and bake in preheated 400 degree oven for approximately 10 minutes. To serve, spoon juices and vegetables over fillets. Serves 4.

ORANGE ROUGHY WITH SALSA

4 fillets of orange roughy
1 egg white, slightly beaten
3 tbsp. oat bran

3 tbsp. oat bran flakes
1 jar Ortega salsa
Lemon for garnish
1 env. Butter Buds

Wash and pat dry fillets; set aside. Lightly beat egg white. Mix oat bran and oat bran flakes; set aside.

Dip fish into egg white. Cover with oat bran mixture. Heat Butter Buds (as directed). Fry fish 4 minutes per side. Remove. Add heated salsa. Garnish and serve. Serves 4.

RED SNAPPER VERA CRUZ

4 red snapper fillets (4 oz. each)
1 c. mild green chili salsa
1 tbsp. fresh minced cilantro)
   coriander)

1 tsp. chili powder or cumin
Lemon wedges, for garnish

Heat large iron skillet or frying pan over medium flame, lightly coat with olive oil or spray Pam. Add red snapper, fry briefly to sear, then add remaining ingredients, cover and cook 10 minutes or until fish is flaky and tender. Serve with lemon wedge garnish. Serves 4.

NOTE: Serve rice, potato and pasta (starchy) dishes with smaller portions of the fish, chicken and lean meats. Remember to always use the meat as a condiment to add flavor to your meals, rather than as the main dish.

RICE-STUFFED RAINBOW TROUT

4 med. trout, cleaned
1/2 c. cornmeal
2 tsp. chopped parsley
1 tbsp. Veg-It seasoning

1/2 tsp. black pepper
1 c. brown rice seasoned with 2
   tbsp. Veg-It seasoning

Clean fish thoroughly, wipe with damp cloth. Blend cornmeal, Veg-It, pepper and parsley in bowl. Coat trout both inside and out with this mixture. Fill cavity of trout with 1/4 cup of seasoned rice. "Fry" fish on both sides in skillet sprayed with Pam, about 5 minutes on either side, until golden brown.

STUFFED FISH ROLLS

4 fresh fish fillets
1/2 lb. fresh broccoli
4 green onions, halved
  lengthwise
3 tbsp. dry white wine

2 tsp. Butter Buds
2 tbsp. water
1/8 tsp. white pepper
1/2 tsp. chicken bouillon

Cut broccoli stalks into spears. Cook broccoli in boiling water for 5 to 10 minutes, adding onion halves the last 2 minutes.

Sprinkle each fish fillet with Butter Buds. Place 1/4 of the broccoli-onion mixture crosswise in center of each fillet. Roll fillet up around broccoli-onion mixture. Fasten with wooden toothpicks. Place fish rolls, seam side down, in an 8"x8"x2" baking dish. Combine wine, chicken bouillon, water and white pepper. Pour wine mixture over fish rolls. Bake, covered in a 400 degree oven for 15 to 20 minutes or until fish flakes easily. 4 servings.

SZECHUAN SEAFOOD

1/2 c. chopped fresh mushrooms
1/3 c. chopped green onions
1 1/2 clove garlic, minced or
  crushed
1 tsp. grated fresh ginger
1 c. cooked scallops

1/4 tsp. hot dried crushed red
  pepper or Sanj Szechuan sauce
1 1/3 c. chicken stock
1/4 c. dry sherry
1 tsp. soy sauce
1 tbsp. cornstarch

Place a medium skillet over moderate heat and add the mushrooms, onions, garlic and ginger, stir constantly for about 1 minute.

Add the scallops and pepper. Stir in the stock and bring to a boil. Mix the sherry and soy sauce into the cornstarch. Add this to the skillet until thickened, stirring constantly.

FRIED NOODLES

Spring water
1 (8 oz.) pkg. Erewhon Soba or
    Udon noodles
1-2 tbsp. Kikkoman Lite Soy
    Sauce

2 c. shredded cabbage
1/2 c. sliced scallions
1/2 tbsp. dark sesame oil

Cook the noodles according to directions on package. Oil the frying pan and add the cabbage. Put the cooked noodles on top of the cabbage, cover the pan and cook over low heat for 5 to 7 minutes, or until the noodles are warm. Add the soy sauce and mix the noodles and vegetables well. Do not stir the ingredients together until this time; they should be left to cook peacefully until the very end. Cook for several minutes longer and add the scallions at the very end. Serve hot or cold.

Variation: Many combinations of vegetables may be used, including carrots and onions, scallions and mushrooms and cabbage and tofu. Hard root vegetables take longer to cook and they should be sauteed in the oiled frying pan before the noodles are added. Add the soft vegetables just before sprinkling on the soy sauce.

WHOLE WHEAT VEGETARIAN PIZZA

1 pkg. active dry yeast
1 1/2 c. warm water
2 tsp. dry basil
2 tsp. oregano
1/4 c. oat bran
1 1/2 c. whole wheat flour
1 1/2 c. all purpose flour
All purpose flour for kneading
1 lg. red onion
1 (15 oz.) can tomato sauce

1 (6 oz.) can tomato paste
1/2 c. red wine
2 zucchini, thinly sliced
1/2 green or red bell pepper,
  seeded & thinly sliced
4 green onions, including tops,
  thinly sliced
1 can sliced ripe olives
1 (14 oz.) can artichoke hearts,
  drained & quartered

In a large bowl dissolve yeast in water. Add 1 teaspoon basil and 1 teaspoon oregano, oat bran and all purpose flour. Beat until smooth (about 5 minutes, using an electric mixer). Using a wooden spoon, beat in whole wheat flour until dough holds together. Turn out onto a lightly floured board and knead until dough is smooth and elastic, about 5 minutes. Turn over in a greased bowl, cover and let rise in a warm place until dough has doubled in size, about 45 minutes. Meanwhile, prepare tomato sauce.

LUNCH/SANDWICHES

Whole wheat pita bread stuffed with any kind of leftover. Warmed, rolled tortilla filled with one slice Lifetime cheese or Liteline cheese.

Whole wheat bread, mustard, lettuce and tomato sandwich.

Pita bread pizza - pita bread, covered first with spaghetti or tomato sauce and then with garlic powder, oregano, caraway seeds and Lifetime cheese. Warmed in the oven or microwave.

Bread and lifetime cheese.

Bread, turkey, mustard, catsup, lettuce and tomatoes

Bread, tomato, green chili and Lifetime cheese.

SPICY VEGERONI

1 (8 oz.) Vegeroni
1/4 lb. wheat meat
2 (16 oz.) cans tomato sauce
1 can Rosarita enchilada sauce

3 tbsp. raisins
1 onion, chopped
1/2 c. celery, chopped
1 tsp. garlic powder

Cook Vegeroni. Directions on box. Cook ground beef, drain off fat, then add cottage cheese, tomato sauce, enchilada sauce, onion, raisins, garlic powder, Vegeroni and Liteline cheese.

ANGELED EGGS

6 hard boiled eggs, peeled
1 baked or boiled potato, cooled
  (1/2 c. at least)
1 stalk celery, minced
1/4 c. minced onion

1 tbsp. chutney, salt free
1 tsp. curry powder
1-2 tbsp. Nayonnaise (no
  cholesterol, less fat imitation-
  found in Health Food Stores)

Cool and peel hard boiled eggs. Cut in half lengthwise. Remove and discard egg yolks (high cholesterol). In small bowl, mash potatoes, celery, onions, curry powder, chutney and mayonnaise. Add a little more mayonnaise if too dry. With teaspoon, stuff mixture into the center of egg halves. Sprinkle with paprika and chill 1 hour before serving. Yield: 12 egg halves.

HUEVOS RANCHEROS

2 corn tortillas

3 egg whites

SAUCE:
2 lg. onions
1 green bell pepper

1 (14 oz.) can tomatoes
1 (14 oz.) can chicken broth

GARNISH:
Fresh cilantro
Chopped green onion
2 thin slices avocado

2 slices low fat, low cholesterol
    cheese

Place one to two cooked tortillas on a plate. Scramble egg whites and place on top of tortillas. Add 1/2 cup of sauce and garnish with fresh cilantro, chopped green onion, avocado and low fat cheese.

To prepare sauce: In a frying pan, saute onions and green pepper in a little water until soft. Add tomatoes and broth. Boil, uncovered, stirring to prevent sticking, until sauce is reduced to about 2 1/2 cups.

SUPER NACHOS

1 onion, chopped
2 cans vegetarian refried beans
1 (4 oz.) can diced California
    green chilies
1 c. low cholesterol, low fat
    cheese or soy cheese (opt.)

3/4 c. green taco sauce
8 c. tortilla pieces
1/4 c. chopped green onion
1 c. olives, sliced

Spread beans in a shallow 10"x 15" ovenproof dish. Sprinkle chilies over beans, then cheese, then taco sauce. Bake, uncovered at 400 degrees for 20 minutes. Remove from oven and add 1/4 cup chopped green onion and 1 cup pitted sliced olives. Arrange tortilla pieces around edges of bean mixture and serve at once. Serves 10.

CHEESE AND HERB PANCAKES

3/4 c. whole wheat flour
1 1/4 tsp. baking powder
1/2 c. water
3 tbsp. Butter Buds
2 egg whites
1 tbsp. minced fresh basil

1 1/2 tsp. minced fresh thyme
1 1/2 tsp. minced fresh rosemary
1 1/2 tsp. minced fresh sage

Mix all ingredients together. Heat nonstick griddle or skillet. Ladle batter onto griddle. Cook until bottom side is brown, about 2 minutes. Flip over. Makes 1 dozen pancakes.

CHEESE OMELET

8 egg whites or Egg Beaters
3 tbsp. Butter Buds
1/4 c. walnut halves
1 sm. potato, diced
1/4 c. onion, chopped
1/3 c. brown rice, cooked

1/4 c. Dorman or Lifetime low
    fat, low cholesterol, muenster
    cheese, diced
3 tbsp. grated Dorman's low fat,
    low cholesterol cheese
1 tbsp. chopped parsley

Brown walnuts in frying pan with 1 1/2 tablespoons Butter Buds. Remove nuts and set aside. Add potato and onion and cook until soft and lightly browned. Remove and set aside.

Add 1 1/2 tablespoons Butter Buds and egg whites. When top of omelet is almost set, but still moist, sprinkle evenly with potato-onion mixture, diced cheese and parsley. Garnish with grated cheese and walnuts. Cut in wedges and serve from pan. 4 servings.

ELEGANT EGGPLANT

1 eggplant, sliced
1 part low fat mayo & 1 part
  Hain's mild natural mustard

1/2 c. Parmesan cheese
1/3 c. (toasted) wheat germ
1/3 c. Italian bread crumbs

Preheat oven to 400 degrees. Slice eggplant 1/2" thick, spread both sides thinly with mayo/mustard. In a large bowl, mix equal parts of bread crumbs, Parmesan and wheat germ. Dip both sides of eggplant into crumb mixture, coating moistened slices. Then layer on ungreased cookie sheets and bake about 400 degrees for 20 to 25 minutes. No necessary to turn. They will brown on both sides. Delicious and healthy.

ARTICHOKE SOUFFLE

14 oz. marinated artichoke hearts
1 med. sized onion, chopped
10 egg whites
Black pepper to taste

2 tbsp. whole wheat flour
6 oz. Liteline cheese, grated
1 oz. Parmesan cheese, grated

Saute the onions. Thinly slice or quarter artichoke hearts. Beat the eggs with some pepper and the flour until the mixture is perfectly smooth. Stir in the grated cheese. Add the artichoke hearts to the onions and stir them around a little bit and then transfer these to casserole dish. Spoon the egg and cheese mixture over the vegetables, and bake the souffle in a preheated 350 degree oven for 20 to 25 minutes, or until it is completely set, golden brown and slightly crusty on top. Serve 4 to 6.

BAKED ASPARAGUS

3 tbsp. bread crumbs
1/2 c. Butter Buds
1/2 c. chicken broth
Dash of nutmeg

1 lb. asparagus, boiled
1/2 c. low fat, low cholesterol
cheese, grated

In a small saucepan, simmer bread crumbs, Butter Buds, chicken broth and nutmeg for about 5 minutes. Arrange cooked asparagus in a casserole dish. Pour sauce over asparagus and sprinkle with cheese. Bake at 350 degrees for 30 minutes. Serves 3.

BAKED STUFFED POTATOES

Microwave.
4 baking potatoes, scrubbed,
    pierced
1/2 c. nonfat yogurt, plain
1/3 c. chopped green onions

1/2 pkg. Butter Buds, prepared
1/8 tsp. white pepper
1/4 c. shredded Dorman's or
    Lifetime low fat, low
    cholesterol cheese

Place a paper towel in bottom of microwave oven. Arrange potatoes in a circle on paper towel. Microwave on full power 9 to 11 minutes or until potatoes give slightly when squeezed. Cool. Cut in 1/2 lengthwise. Scoop pulp from each potato half, leaving a 1/4" thick shell, into a medium bowl, set shells aside. Mash potato pulp. Stir in yogurt, green onions, Butter Buds and pepper. Spoon potato mixture into shells. Arrange stuffed potatoes on a plate. Microwave on full power 3 minutes. Sprinkle with cheese. 8 servings.

BROCCOLI SOUFFLE

2 c. broken broccoli flowerettes
3/4 c. lowfat ricotta cheese, hoop
   cheese or nonfat cottage cheese

3 tbsp. Parmesan cheese
1/4 tsp. nutmeg
1 tbsp. low sodium vegetable
   seasoning
3 egg whites

Prepare broccoli by cutting flowers from stems, if you wish to use stems, peel away tough outer layer with a sharp knife. Steam in a vegetable steamer until well cooked, about 10 minutes. Place with rest of ingredients in food processor or blender and blend until pureed. Turn out into souffle dish, bake in preheated oven, 325 degrees, for 25 minutes or until done in center. Serve immediately. Makes 4 servings.

GREEN BEAN CASSEROLE

2 (20 oz.) bags frozen green
   beans
4 c. fresh bean sprouts
2 (8 oz.) cans water chestnuts

3 c. cream of mushroom soup -
   Hain Naturals brand
1 onion, chopped
2 tbsp. soy sauce

Place all ingredients in oblong baking dish and bake at 400 degrees for about 30 minutes.

POTATO-CHEESE SOUFFLE

2 c. mashed potatoes, prepared
   with water & Butter Buds
4 egg whites
4 slices Liteline cheese

1/4 tsp. pepper
1/4 tsp. garlic powder
Paprika

Beat the eggs into the mashed potatoes. Add the other ingredients, except paprika, and beat into the mashed potatoes. Turn into a 1 quart casserole dish. Sprinkle with paprika. Bake at 375 degrees for 25 to 30 minutes. Serve at once.

SQUASH CASSEROLE

6-8 med. yellow squash, sliced
1 lg. onion, chopped
3 stalks celery, diced
1/2 green bell pepper, diced
2 tbsp. water
3 egg whites, beaten

1 (13 oz.) can evaporated skim
  milk
1 1/2 c. dry curd cottage cheese,
  crumbled
1/2 c. unsalted matzo crumbs
1/4 tsp. white pepper

Preheat oven to 350 degrees. Boil squash until tender, not mushy, and mash. Saute onion, celery and green pepper in 2 tablespoons water in a nonstick pan; add to squash along with egg whites, milk, cottage cheese, matzo crumbs and white pepper; mix well. Pour into a nonstick pan and sprinkle top with more matzo crumbs. Bake at 350 degrees for about 45 minutes. Serves 6 to 8.

SPINACH PARMESAN

1 lb. spinach, washed & chopped
  or 1 pkg. frozen chopped
  spinach
1/4 c. Butter Buds

1/8 tsp. nutmeg
4 egg whites
3 tbsp. grated Parmesan cheese

Cook spinach in 1 cup water for 5 minutes. Drain. Place in a saucepan with Butter Buds and nutmeg and cook 4 minutes, stirring well. Add egg whites and Parmesan cheese and continue stirring 2 or 3 minutes. Serve immediately. Serves 4.

STUFFED TOMATOES

Microwave.

6 lg. firm, ripe tomatoes
1/2 c. green onion, chopped
1/4 c. celery, chopped
2 tbsp. Butter Buds
2/3 c. cooked brown rice

1/2 c. Dorman low fat, low
   cholesterol muenster cheese
1 (4 oz.) can mushrooms, drained
1/8 tsp. pepper
1/4 tsp. basil
Dash cayenne pepper

Cut 1/4″ slice off top of each tomato. Scoop out pulps, drain and reserve. Place onion, celery and Butter Buds in 1 quart casserole. Heat on full power 2 minutes, or until onion and celery is tender. Add tomato pulp and remaining ingredients to onion and celery. Spoon mixture into tomatoes. Place in casserole dish. Cover with plastic wrap. Bake on full power for 3 minutes.

TOMATO BROCCOLI PIE

In blender, puree:

1 c. lowfat cottage cheese, rinsed
1 c. nonfat yogurt
1/4 c. whole wheat flour
1/4 tsp. baking powder
1/2 tsp. baking soda
Pinch of white pepper & garlic
   powder

3 egg whites
3 tbsp. Parmesan cheese
1 tomato, thinly sliced
1 (10 oz.) pkg. frozen broccoli

In a 9″ nonstick or lightly sprayed with Pam, pie dish, arrange a layer of sliced tomatoes on bottom of dish. Place broccoli on top of tomato. Pour half of mixture over broccoli. Arrange another layer of sliced tomatoes on top. Pour remaining mixture on top. Bake 30 to 35 minutes at 350 degrees or until golden brown. Let stand 10 minutes before cutting pie.

ZUCCHINI LOAF

3 c. shredded zucchini
1 c. cooked brown rice
1 c. oat bran
1 1/4 c. cheese
1 c. chopped walnuts
2 c. sliced, fresh mushrooms

4 green onions, sliced
6 egg whites
1 tsp. oregano
4 garlic cloves, minced
1/2 tsp. thyme
1/2 tsp. sage
Pepper

Preheat oven to 375 degrees. Combine all the ingredients (except 1/4 cup of the cheese) in a large bowl. Mix until well blended. Pour into a 9"x5" loaf pan. Sprinkle top with remaining cheese. Bake for 50 minutes, or until brown. 6 servings.

ZUCCHINI BOATS

Microwave.
2 med. zucchini, cut in half
   lengthwise
1/4 c. chopped green onions
1/2 c. chopped fresh tomatoes

1/2 c. Dormans low fat, low
   cholesterol muenster cheese,
   shredded
1/8 tsp. marjoram
1/4 tsp. pepper
1/4 tsp. basil

Hollow out inside of each zucchini half, leaving a 1/4" thick shell. Chop zucchini pulp. In a medium bowl, mix zucchini pulp, green onions, tomato, 1/4 cup of cheese and spices. Fill zucchini halves with mixture. Place in a shallow dish. Cover tightly. Microwave on high for 5 minutes. Sprinkle with remaining 1/4 cup cheese. 4 servings.

SALAD NICOISE

1 sm. head Bibb lettuce
1 (6 oz.) can low salt tuna, packed
in water
2 sm. red new potatoes, cooked &
cut into lg. chunks

1 ripe red tomato, cut in wedges
or cherry tomatoes
1/4 lb. green beans, steamed
1 hard boiled egg (yolk
discarded), sliced

DRESSING:
Juice of 2 lemons
1 tsp. low sodium Dijon mustard
1 clove garlic, minced

2 green onions (scallions), finely
chopped
1 tbsp. yogurt

Prepare salad dressing and set aside. Wash lettuce well, dry in salad spinner or between paper towels. Tear into large pieces in salad bowl. Drain tuna, arrange in chunks on top of lettuce. Add remaining salad ingredients. Dress with salad dressing. Serve chilled. Serves 4.

BROILED RED PEPPER AND EGGPLANT ANTIPASTA

1 round, sm., firm purple
eggplant or 4-5 Japanese
eggplants
1 lg. red bell pepper (in season
mid-spring to late fall)

1/2 tsp. granulated garlic
2 tbsp. minced sweet basil

With sharp knife, cut eggplant into very thin sheets. Cut into 2″ strips lengthwise, if using round eggplant. Seed and cut red pepper into quarters. Prepare baking sheet by lightly spraying with Pam (or use nonstick cookware). Place eggplant and peppers close together on baking sheet and sprinkle with spices. Place in broiler fairly close to flame. Broil until browned and tender. Eggplant will become moist as broiled. This also is good cooked on a barbecue grill. Serves 4 to 5 as side dish or appetizer.

CHICKEN STIR FRY SALAD

8 c. torn fresh spinach
2 c. wheat meat or chicken
1/2 c. water
1/2 c. tarragon vinegar
1/4 c. sliced green onion
4 tsp. cornstarch
1/2 tsp. dry mustard
1/4 tsp. pepper

1 clove garlic, minced
Nonstick spray coating
2 c. sliced cauliflower florets
1 c. sliced carrots
1 c. cherry tomatoes, halved
1/2 c. sliced celery

Place torn spinach in a large salad bowl; set aside. Cut wheat meat or chicken into bite size pieces. For sauce, combine water, vinegar, onion, cornstarch, mustard, pepper and garlic. Set aside.

Spray a wok or large skillet with nonstick spray. Preheat over a medium high heat. Stir fry cauliflower and carrots for about 5 minutes or until crisp-tender. Spray skillet or wok again and add half the wheat meat to wok and stir fry for 3 to 4 minutes or until done. Remove chicken; add remaining and stir fry another 3 to 4 minutes. Return all chicken to wok. Push chicken from center of wok. Stir sauce, then add to center of wok or skillet. Cook and stir 2 minutes more. Return vegetables to wok. Add tomatoes and celery. Stir ingredients together to coat with sauce. Pour chicken mixture over spinach in bowl. Toss lightly to coat. Serve immediately. Serves 6.

MINNESOTA CRANBERRY SALAD

2 c. whole, raw cranberries
1 lg. apple, diced (red or green)
1 can pineapple, diced or 2 c.
   fresh pineapple

1 orange or tangelo
1 c. raspberries, fresh or frozen
   (no sugar added)

DRESSING:
1 lg. ripe banana
1/2 c. pineapple or orange juice
1/4 c. nonfat plain yogurt

2 tbsp. honey
1 tsp. cinnamon

Wash and pick over cranberries. With steel blade, process in blender or food processor very briefly, until cranberries are "slushy" but not liquified. Add meat grinder will also work, using the coarsest blade. Dice remaining fruit, place in bowl with cranberries. Blend together dressing ingredients, mix into fruit. Chill before serving. Makes 4 to 6 servings.

POTATO SALAD

4 lg. potatoes
1/4 red onion
3/4 c. nonfat yogurt
2 tsp. mustard

1/4 tsp. pepper
1 tsp. garlic powder
1 tsp. basil

Boil the potatoes until they are very tender. Peel and chop them. Add onions, pepper, yogurt, mustard and garlic powder to taste. Chill 1 hour before serving.

CURRIED CREAM OF BROCCOLI SOUP

You needn't worry about the calories in creamed soups when the "cream" is actually rice milk. Preparation Tip: This soup has enough flavor to permit omission of all added salt. It can be frozen before or after pureeing but preferably before the addition of the milk.

1 Butter Buds
1 lg. onion, chopped (1 c.)
2 cloves garlic, chopped (2 tsp.)
3/4 tsp. curry power or more to taste
Freshly ground black pepper, if desired, to taste

1 2/3 c. chicken broth, canned or homemade
1 c. water
1 bunch broccoli (about 1 lb.), cut into flowerets, stems cut into 1/2" slices
1 lg. potato, peeled & cut into 1/2" cubes
1 c. skim milk or rice milk

1. In a large saucepan, melt the butter or margarine and saute the onion and garlic for a few minutes.

2. Add the curry, pepper, broth and water to the pan and bring the soup to a boil.

3. Add the broccoli and potato. When the mixture returns to a boil, reduce the heat, cover the pan and simmer the soup for about 20 minutes or until the vegetables are tender.

4. Puree the soup in batches in a blender or food processor. Return the puree to the pan, stir in the milk and cook the soup over low heat until it is hot, but do not boil it.

SWEET POTATO BREAD

Here's another use for leftover baked or boiled sweet potatoes or yams, when you get tired or putting them in your lunch.

1 c. mashed sweet potato or yam, cooled
3/4 c. canned evaporated skim milk or nonfat milk
1/2 c. frozen apple juice concentrate
1 tsp. soy sauce
1 tbsp. cinnamon
1/4 tsp. nutmeg
1 env. active dry yeast, dissolved in 1/2 c. lukewarm water
4 c. whole wheat pastry flour
1 tbsp. rice milk

Blend potato, evaporated milk, apple juice, soy sauce and spices in food processor or blender. Transfer the mixture to a large bowl and stir in dissolved yeast. Slowly add 3 1/4 cups of flour, stirring to combine well. Knead for 3 to 5 minutes, gradually adding rest of the flour. Shape into a nonstick loaf pan (dough will be sticky), and set the pan in a warm oven. (Preheat the oven to 150 degrees, then turn off heat just before setting pan in it.) Let dough rise for 1 hour. Bake at 425 degrees for 10 minutes; then prick the surface with a fork in several places and brush with the tablespoon of rice milk. Lower heat to 375 degrees and continue baking for 35 to 40 minutes. Cool before slicing. Cover with foil or plastic wrap to keep moist. Makes 1 loaf, about 16 slices.

QUICK YEAST BREAD

STEP A:
2 pkgs. or 2 tbsp. dry yeast
   dissolved in 3/4 c. warm water
1 1/4 c. soured milk (add 1 1/2
   tsp. lemon juice to 1 1/4 c.
   nonfat milk, let stand 5
   minutes)

2 1/2 c. whole wheat flour
1 tbsp. baking powder

STEP B:
1 c. whole wheat flour

In large bowl, mix ingredients for Step A. Blend 1/2 minute on low speed, then 3 minutes at medium speed, scraping bowl all the time. Gradually stir in ingredients for Step B. Dough should remain soft and slightly sticky. Turn dough onto well floured board and sprinkle with flour so it doesn't stick to hands. Knead about 250 turns, adding flour as desired. Shape for placing in loaf pan. Place in 9"x5"x3" loaf pan that has had cornmeal sprinkled on bottom. Let rise in warm place until doubled in size, about 1 hour. Gently slash top of dough with razor blade or sharp knife. Bake in preheated oven on lowest rack position. See instructions below for oven temperatures and baking time. Cool about 5 minutes on cake rack until bread shrinks from sides of pan. Remove from pan and cool on rack.

Bake at 375 degrees for approximately 35 minutes.

Extra Quick Version: After placing dough in baking pan. Bake immediately at 375 degrees for approximately 45 minutes.

MONTIE'S CORNBREAD

1 c. Alpha Beta buttermilk
2 egg whites
1 c. whole grain yellow cornmeal
1/2 c. whole wheat flour

2 1/2 tsp. baking powder
1/8 tsp. baking soda
2 tbsp. apple juice concentrate or
   yinnie syrup (opt.)

Combine all ingredients in a 9"x5" loaf pan and beat a long time. Batter should be thin. Bake at 375 degrees for about 25 minutes. Serves 6.

CAROB MINT MOUSSE

4 env. unflavored gelatin
4 tbsp. carob powder
2 c. frozen apple juice concentrate

2 tbsp. vanilla
6 1/2 c. nonfat milk or rice milk
2/3 c. dry nonfat milk
1/2 tsp. mint flakes

Mix gelatin, carob powder and 1/2 cup apple juice in large bowl. Heat remaining apple juice and vanilla to a boil in saucepan and then reduce heat. Add gelatin mixture and stir constantly over low heat for about 5 minutes. Refrigerate until cool. Place milk (dry and liquid), mint flakes and gelatin mixture in blender, half at a time if necessary and blend. When fluffy, transfer to mixing bowl and chill until cold and thickened, but not frozen. Whip with an electric mixer. Return to freezer, then whip once more before serving. Do not freeze. Garnish with fresh mint sprigs. Serves 8 to 10.

CHEESECAKE I

3 c. lowfat cottage cheese
1/2 c. nonfat buttermilk
2 env. unflavored gelatin
1 (8 oz.) can unsweetened
  crushed pineapple

1/2 c. frozen apple juice
  concentrate
1/2 c. water
1 tsp. vanilla extract
3 egg whites
1 1/2 c. Grape Nuts cereal

FRUIT TOPPING: (Optional)
2 bags frozen strawberries,
  unsweetened or 2 boxes frozen
  blueberries, unsweetened

1/2 c. apple juice concentrate
1/2 c. water
1 tsp. vanilla extract
Cornstarch

Blend cottage cheese and buttermilk in blender to a thick but smooth consistency. In a bowl, moisten the gelatin with the crushed pineapple; mix well. In a saucepan heat the apple juice and water to boil. Pour the boiling liquid over the gelatin pineapple mixture; stir well to dissolve. When cooled, add the cheese mixture and vanilla. Beat the egg whites until stiff peaks form; fold in. Pour the batter into 2 (9") pie pans with a bottom crust of enough Grape Nuts dampened with a little additional apple juice to form a cohesive layer. Refrigerate for several hours.

To Make Topping: Bring to a boil frozen strawberries or blueberries and the apple juice-water combination. Thicken well with cornstarch which has first been blended with a little water. Stir in vanilla. Cool; then spread over the chilled pies. Refrigerate until the topping is set. Each pies serves 6 to 8.

CHEESECAKE II

CRUST:

    1 c. of any of the following alone or in combination:

Homemade granola   Back to nature cereal
Grape Nuts cereal   Chestnut flour
1 tsp. cinnamon
1/4 c. apple juice concentrate

FILLING:

1 c. low fat cottage cheese or   1/2 c. maple syrup or honey
    fresh hoop cheese   1 1/2 tbsp. vanilla
1/4 c. nonfat or low fat yogurt   1 tsp. grated lemon peel
1 env. gelatin dissolved in 1/4 c.   2 egg whites, beaten to soft peaks
    hot water

Crust: Combine cereal and cinnamon in blender or food processor and process until in small crumbs. Place in a pie tin and add juice concentrate. Mix well and press lightly into pie tin. Bake at 350 degrees for 15 minutes. Cool.

Filling: Combine cheese, yogurt, gelatin dissolved in hot water, vanilla and sweetener in a food processor or blender and process until smooth. Place in a bowl and fold in egg whites and lemon peel. Pour into pie crust. Garnish with fruit and chill several hours.

PUMPKIN CHEESE CAKE

CRUST:
1 c. granola cereal
1 tsp. ginger

2 tbsp. (or more) apple butter, to moisten
1 tbsp. apple juice concentrate, to moisten

FILLING:
1 pt. lowfat cottage cheese
1/2 c. nonfat yogurt
1 (15 oz.) can solid pack pumpkin
1/2 c. sweetener (apple juice concentrate)

2 tbsp. pure vanilla extract
1 tbsp. cinnamon
2 tsp. pumpkin pie spice mix
2 egg whites

Blend all crust ingredients in food processor or blender, spread evenly in bottom of pie dish, sprayed with Pam. Blend all filling ingredients in food processor or with hand mixer until light and creamy. Pour into pie shell. Freeze. Serve slightly defrosted. Serves 4 to 6.

pineapple-LEMON MERINGUE PIE

CRUST:

1 1/4 c. whole wheat bread
   crumbs
3 tbsp. frozen apple juice
   concentrate

1 tsp. vanilla extract
1/8 tsp. lemon extract

Place ingredients in a bowl, mixing well. Using a rubber spatula, press the mixture firmly into the nonstick pie pan (bottom and sides) to form an even crust. Bake the crust in a 350 degree oven for 15 minutes until lightly browned. Remove from oven and allow to cool. Fill as directed below.

FILLING:

1 (20 oz.) can unsweetened
   pineapple, juice packed
1 1/3 c. evaporated skim milk or
   rice milk
1/2 c. frozen apple juice
   concentrate
3 tbsp. lemon juice
2 tbsp. frozen orange juice
   concentrate

1 env. plus 2 tsp. unflavored
   gelatin
2 tsp. arrowroot
Dash of turmeric (for color)
1 1/2 tsp. lemon extract
1 1/2 tsp. vanilla extract
3 egg whites

Place the filling ingredients, except for the flavor extracts and egg whites, into a blender and blend at high speed for 5 minutes. Set a large strainer over mixing bowl and pour mixture through strainer, discard residue in strainer (this insures a smooth pie filling). Transfer the filling mixture to a double boiler; cook for about 5 minutes, stirring with a wire whisk, until mixture is very hot. Stir in vanilla and lemon extracts. Let filling cool slightly, then pour into prepared crust. Beat egg whites until stiff peaks form. Swirl the beaten egg whites gently over the filling. Place the pie in the oven on a middle rack under a hot broiler. Watch meringue carefully, brown just lightly; then remove from oven. Chill pie for several hours or overnight until firm. Serves 6 to 8.

DELICIOUS CORNBREAD

1 1/2 c. whole grain cornmeal
1/2 c. Millet
1 tsp. baking soda
1 c. non fat milk or rice milk
1 egg white

1/2 c. unsweetened applesauce or
    creamed corn
3 tbsp. honey or apple juice

In a large bowl combine all ingredients and mix well. Pour into muffin tins sprayed with non stick. Bake at 425 degrees for 15 to 20 minutes. Very good and very healthy.

INDEX

EASY BLUEBERRY SAUCE 34
FRENCH RAISIN TOAST 28
FRENCH TOAST 28
FRUIT SYRUPS 34
GRANOLA I 30
GRANOLA II 30
HUEVOS RANCHEROS 28
OAT BRAN CEREAL 29
OATMEAL PANCAKES 32
OMELET WITH STRAWBERRIES 26
OMELETTE 25
ORANGE APPLE MARMALADE 35
PEACH JAM 35
PEACH OR APRICOT JAM 36
TROPICAL MUESLI 30
VEGETARIAN OMELET 26
WAFFLES 33
WHOLE WHEAT PANCAKES 32
YEAST CREPES 27
ZUCCHINI PANCAKES 33

Breads, Muffins & Desserts

APPLE CORN MUFFINS 43
APPLE CRISP 71
APPLE SPICE CAKE 51
APPLE SPICE COOKIES 47
APPLESAUCE OATMEAL COOKIES 47
APPLESAUCE SOUFFLE 85
APRICOT COBBLER 70
APRICOT MOUSSE 83
APRICOT PIE 60
APRICOT SORBET 80
BAKED APPLE 86
BAKED BANANAS NEW ORLEANS 86

BANANA AMBROSIA 87
BANANA BREAD I 39
BANANA BREAD II 39
BANANA COOKIES 47
BANANA CREAM PIE 61
BANANA MOUSSE 84
BANANA PECAN PIE 61
BANANA RAISIN COOKIES 48
BANANA-PINEAPPLE ICE CREAM 79
BISCUITS 43
BLUEBERRY CAKE 51
BLUEBERRY HONEYDEW ICE 83
BLUEBERRY-APPLE CRISP 72
BRAN MUFFINS 44
BROWN RICE PUDDING 84
BURGER BUNS 44
CAROB BROWNIES 48
CARROT BREAD 40
CARROT CAKE 52
CHAROSES 78
CHERRY COBBLER 70
CHERRY SOUP 91
CHOCOLATE BANANA BROWNIES 73
CHOCOLATE BANANA ICE CREAM 79
COFFEE CAKE 53
CRUMB TOPPED FRUIT PIE 62
CRUNCHY CARROT CAKE 52, 58
DATE CAKE 54, 58
DATE FROSTING 54
DATE NUT BREAD PUDDING 85
FLAMING PINEAPPLE 87
FRENCH APPLE PIE 64
FROZEN CHERRY MOUSSE 84

Main Dishes: Italian

Main Dishes: Mexican

Main Dishes: Oriental

Main Dishes: Burgers, Casseroles, Stews, Veggies

Soups, Salads & Dressings

Side Dishes/Lean Meat & Dairy

PASTA LA MER 289

PISMO BEACH SOUP 281

POTATO SALAD 308

POTATO-CHEESE SOUFFLE 302

PUMPKIN CHEESE CAKE 315

QUICK YEAST BREAD 311

RED SNAPPER VERA CRUZ 293

RICE-STUFFED RAINBOW TROUT 293

ROASTED TURKEY WITH STUFFING 283

ROSEMARY LEMON CHICKEN 275

SALAD NICOISE 306

SEVICHE SOUP 282

SPICY CHICKEN SOUP 280

SPICY VEGERONI 297

SPINACH PARMESAN 303

SQUASH CASSEROLE 303

STUFFED FISH ROLLS 294

STUFFED TOMATOES 304

SUPER NACHOS 298

SWEET POTATO BREAD 310

SZECHUAN CHICKEN WITH CASHEWS 278

SZECHUAN SEAFOOD 294

THAI CHICKEN 278

TOMATO BROCCOLI PIE 304

TURKEY CHILI 284

TURKEY MEATBALLS 285

TURKEY MEATLOAF 285

WHOLE WHEAT VEGETARIAN PIZZA 296

ZUCCHINI BOATS 305

ZUCCHINI LOAF 305